CRAFTING in GLASS

CRAFTING in GLASS

Molding, Fusing, Embellishing, Designing

ANITA and SEYMOUR ISENBERG

CHILTON BOOK COMPANY, Radnor, Pennsylvania

On the cover. Front panel: Glass flowers and cart; design by Kay Kinney, artist Anita Isenberg. Portrait panel; Marie Snell.

From ghoulies and ghosties
And long-legged beasties
And things that go "bump" in the kiln . . .
Good Lord deliver us!

Preface

This book was planned as an encyclopedia of glass techniques. Since glasscrafting depends heavily on devices, we included a complete survey of tools and equipment. So complete was the book that the material outweighed the available pages. A number of chapters already snugged into the overall design had to be omitted; these dealt with such glass modalities as bottle crafting, flameworking, enamel painting, use of solder glass, and glass flowers (a logical extension of the leafmaking chapter). These topics and more will form the basis of a subsequent volume, along with coverage on the new tools and devices that appear in the interim.

Although this book is complete in itself, it is also meant to interlock with the succeeding volume. We have tried to establish a rhythm of didactic and practical material, topped off by informal get-togethers with successful practitioners who share their techniques in these pages. Essentially, this will be the format in the following volume, which will also cover approaches to glasscrafting that could not be included here.

We would like to thank all who contributed to this book: manufacturers, craftspeople, distributors. We would especially like to thank Peter and JoAnne Nervo and the Glass Expo series of trade shows where we met so many nice people and got so many helping hands.

Anita Isenberg
Seymour Isenberg

Contents

**PART I
Materials,
Tools, and Procedures**

PART III

**Sagging and
Molding Glass**

PART IV

**Projects:
Putting It All Together**

Introduction

If you have never worked with glass, you are embarking on what can be a most exciting, rewarding, and even profitable hobby. Today, many of our students are running commercial enterprises based on what was originally a diversion.

This book covers many aspects of working with glass. Whether you hope to start a business or merely to pass some pleasant hours, you will find the guidance in these pages. We have tried to provide not only a guide to glass techniques, including patterns and projects, but also to introduce and describe many of the new machines that are available to help (or hinder) these operations. Machines are fairly new in a field that has long been strictly a handicraft operation. It is not necessary to purchase or even use any of these machines or tools other than the classic "basic" ones to do your glass work. However, if you want to sell many of the things that you make, even if only to provide a small return for labor and materials, you may well find a few of these new labor-saving devices of interest. And, of course, if you are going to go into any sort of mass production, however modest, a number of them may be indispensable.

Since all our books are teaching projects, we felt we could not ignore the phenomenon of what has become an all but overwhelming invasion of the market by machinery. Some of these items are not only imaginative, but redundant. Duplication of devices has brought for many glass workers a sense of confusion that borders on panic. Remember, your own two hands are still the best machines. At the same time, machinery is fun, doesn't tire, and can save time, materials, and prevent boredom, especially if you are duplicating products.

Some of the tools and devices we discuss may give you insights into the craft and stimulate your imagination. And you may find them becoming indispensable. It's a wide open field—and, at the same time, a very personal and individual one. Manufacturers are listed in the back under *Sources of Supply*. What is really needed is a descriptive catalogue for all the items now available for the craft. We try to take a step in that direction in Chapter 3.

We have attempted to make this a practical, down-to-earth handbook including a wide range of glassworking modalities. Stained glass is only a factor in the wide world of glass itself. Many forms of glass are at your disposal, such as window glass and plate glass, mirrored glass and stained glass, opalescent glass and clear glass. There are also slab glass, nonreflective glass, blown glass, and rolled glass. You can sculpt it, paint it, heat it, bond it, bend it, twist it, blow it, cut it, score it, grind it, etch it, and break it—artistically, of course. There are all sorts of paths to which glass can lead. One place we don't want it to lead, though, is to the emergency room.

Safety Factors

Although small children have taboos against stepping on the cracks in sidewalks for fear of breaking some spell, no such impediment seems to exist for them where breaking glass is concerned. Check out any abandoned building. The windows are the first to go. The activity appears to fulfill some primitive need. To paraphrase Hillary Belloc:

> Children of the middle class
> Enjoy the sound of breaking glass.

Most children eventually outgrow this behavior. Those who do not, either come to a bad end or develop into glass artisans. The worker in glass can enjoy all the sensual abandon of breaking glass with the knowledge that something creative will result along the way.

But let's face it—glass cuts. Or, rather, people cut themselves on glass. Yet you need not come to grief if you follow instructions and don't get careless. Carelessness with glass takes two forms: underconfidence and overconfidence. The underconfident student may want to use gloves to handle the glass. We discourage this. Gloves provide a false sense of security and can lead to carelessness. Also, cotton gloves or rubber gloves do not grip glass surfaces securely, certainly never as securely as bare fingers. Rubber gloves have the additional disadvantage of providing no air circulation for the skin; they quickly become uncomfortable, and this discomfort leads to carelessness by encouraging shortcuts. Aesthetically, gloves get in the way as well. By wearing them, you are placing a barrier between yourself and the material you are attempting to associate with.

Most glass crafters, however, don't get into trouble from overcaution. In fact, as time goes by, even the undercautious students, finding glass so much less threatening than they imagined, begin taking the material for granted. All of us do mindless things at times, but it is masochistic to do them around machinery and glass. What other art form offers such possibilities to the latent masochist? The pianist may occasionally stub a finger, the painter may poke his eye with the end of a brush, the ceramist may drop clay on his foot, but the opportunities for self-mutilation to the worker in glass are practically limitless. Even the simplest reflexes are invested with hazard; a normal kitchen reaction—brushing crumbs off the table with one's hand—will, when applied to glass

crumbs, provide you with multiple puncture wounds of a span and variety that can leave you breathless. Just the normal act of bending over can be an artistic, if dismaying, triumph, especially if it is done in front of the glass bin where the corner of a large sheet is peeking forth.

However, such major displays as these are not a normal everyday occurrence. Here are some others that we have culled from a long, choice list. Perhaps you can add your own vaiation.

1. Cut a piece of glass in a perfect square. It looks great. But you can't resist running your finger around the edges to make sure they're smooth. They're not.
2. You can't decide what color or what thickness of glass to use in your new project. Hold several pieces up to the light. They won't do. Place them on the table, one on top of another, regardless of size. Select others. Place them on the same growing pile of rejects. Very shortly you have a nuclear missile that a slight nudge of the table will set in motion.
3. You remove a large sheet of glass from the bin. It presents a long crack that is almost but not quite complete. You know you can get it to your work table before it falls apart. A race against time. Sporting blood.
4. Hidden deep within the scrap glass box is that one particular piece of glass you need to complete this project. You can see only a corner of it. Don't bother to clear away the covering pieces. Time is short. So are your fingers.
5. Although the top bin requires a small stepladder to select from it adequately, your arm can stretch. The glass of your choice rolls out smoothly, but its neighboring piece, unbidden and unseen, comes along with it as an extra attraction.

It's not only glass, of course, that gives pause in the day's occupation. Many practitioners of self-destruction prefer the soldering iron. Grasping it firmly by the hot barrel while looking in another direction is a favorite ploy. Hot solder under a fingernail is another.

Does all of this appear to be farfetched and oversimplified? Actually, glass crafting is one of the safest of all hobbies, and glass itself one of the most benign materials. But you must treat it with respect. Such a piece of advice as, "Always wash your hands after working with chemicals, paints, or metal," sounds obvious. But we have seen many people not bother. Our observation and experience over many years has taught us that "Safety First" is itself an oversimplification. We would change it to, "Use Your Head." If you do this, your hands will take care of themselves. Then you will never have to ask, as one student did years ago in class, "Has anyone here seen my fingers?"

The Nature of Glass

Glass is as old as the earth itself. When the earth was being formed, molten masses of rock and magma occasionally cooled so rapidly that the usual aggregate of crystalline minerals did not have sufficient time to form. In its place, natural glasses such as obsidian were found and used well before the dawn of civilization. The natural glasses (so called) were easily broken into sharp fragments that readily lent themselves to the needs of man, the hunter, as arrowheads, spearheads, and knife blades. Later, natural glass was used for ceremonial purposes, jewelry, and primitive mirrors. Obsidian grew in importance until it actually became an article of commerce during the Bronze Age.

Little is known about the earliest man-made glass, but it is widely suspected that it dates from the first chapter in the history of civilized man. Once man had discovered how to make a fire, a whole new world of discovery was opened to him. Some archaeologists feel that the discovery of glass making came after, and was a consequence of, the development of metallurgy. However, it seems more likely that both metallurgy and glass making were outgrowths of the potter's art.

It is possible that the earliest production of glass was the result of an accidental discovery. The most famous account is given by the redoubtable historian, Pliny the Elder, who lost his life in the eruption of Mt. Vesuvius in A.D. 79. His story goes as follows:

In Syria, there is a region known as Phoenice, adjoining to Judea, and enclosing, between the lower ridges of Mount Carmalus, a marshy district known by the name of Cendebia. In this district, it is supposed, rises the river Belus, which after a course of five miles, empties itself into the sea near the colony of Ptolemais. The tide of this river is sluggish, and the water unwholesome to drink, but held sacred for the observance of certain religious ceremonials. Full of slimy deposits, and very deep, it is only at the reflux of the tide that the river discloses its sands; which, agitated by the waves, separate themselves from their impurities and so become cleansed. It is generally thought that it is the acridity of the sea-water that has this purgative effect upon the sand, and that without this action no use could be made of it. The shore upon which this sand is gathered is not more than half a mile in extent; and yet, for many ages, this was the only spot that afforded the material for making glass.

The story is, that a ship, laden with nitre, being moored upon this spot, the merchants, while preparing their repast upon the seashore, finding no stones at hand for supporting their cauldrons, employed for the purpose some lumps of nitre which they had taken from the vessel. [Nitre, or niter, is either sodium or potassium nitrate in natural deposits, as in Chile Saltpeter.] Upon its being subjected to the action of the fire, in combination with the sand of the sea-shore, they beheld transparent streams flowing forth of a liquid hitherto unknown: this, it is said, was the origin of glass.

The discovery of glass making as described by Pliny is quite possible, but there exist many pieces of man-made glass that predate the Phoenician traders by many hundreds of years. The earliest known glaze is found on stone beads of the Badarian Age in Egypt, about 12,000 B.C. The oldest pure glass is a molded amulet from about 7000 B.C. Fragments of opaque glass appear in the First Dynasty, about 5000 B.C. Most, if not all, of the glass from Egypt before 1500 B.C. was probably imported from Asia, however.

There is some evidence that the first glass manufacturing was done in Mesopotamia in Asia Minor.

Glass is one of the most unique materials in the world, but precise and accurate definitions of it have escaped man until relatively recently. One of the earliest descriptions was supplied by Christopher Mernett in 1662, translating an earlier work, "The Art of Glass" by Antonio Neri:

> Glass is one of the fruits of the fire, which is most true for it is a thing wholly of Art, not of Nature, and not to be produced without strong fires. I have heard a singular Artist merrily to this purpose say that their profession would be the last in the world; for when God should consume with fire the Universe, that then all things therein would Vitrifie and turn to glass. Which would be true upon supposition of a proportionable mixture of fit Salts, and Sand or Stones.
>
> 'Tis much like all sort of mineral or middle mineral. I find Authors differ much about referring Glass to its Species. Agricola maketh it a concrete juice, Belluasensis calls it a stone, Fallopius reckons it amongst the Media mineralia, and the workmen, when it is in a state of fusion, call it metall. But to me, it seems neither of these, which this general Arguement sufficiently evinceth, that all the forementioned are natural concretes, but Glass is a compound made by Art, a product of the fire, and never found in the bowels of the earth, as all the others are. But to shorten this comparison, I shall here set down the proprieties of glass whereby any one may easily difference it from all other bodies.
>
> 1. Tis a concrete of salt and sand or stones.
>
> 2. Tis artificial.
>
> 3. It melts in a strong fire.
>
> 4. When melted tis tenacious and sticks together.
>
> 5. It wastes not nor consumes in the fire.
>
> 6. When melted it cleaves to iron, etc.
>
> 7. Tis ductile whilst red hot, and fashionable into any form, but not malleable, and may be blown into a hollowness.
>
> 8. Breaks being thin without annealing.
>
> 9. Tis friable when cold, which made our proverb, As Brittle as Glass.
>
> 10. Tis diaphanous either hot or cold.
>
> 11. Tis flexible and hath in threeds motum rectitutionis.
>
> 12. Cold and wet disunites and breaks it, especially if the liquors be saltish, and the glass suddenly heated.
>
> 13. It only receives sculpture and cutting from a diamond or Emery stone.
>
> 14. Tis both coloured and made Diaphanous as precious stones.
>
> 15. Aqua fortis, Aqua Regis and Mercury dissolve it not as they do metals.
>
> 16. Acid juices nor any other thing extract either colour, taste or any other quality from it.
>
> 17. It loseth nor weight nor substance with the longest and most frequent use.
>
> 18. It gives fusion to other metals and softens them.
>
> 19. It receives all variety of colors made of metals both externally and internally, and therefore is more fit for Painting than any other thing.
>
> 20. It is the most plyable and fashionable thing in the world and best retains the form given.
>
> 21. It may be melted but twill never be calcined.
>
> 22. An open glass filled with water in the Summer will gather drops of water on the outside, so far as the water reacheth, and a man's breath blown upon it will manifestly moisten it.
>
> 23. Little balls as big as a Nut filled with Mercury, or water, or any liquor and thrown into the fire, as also drops of green glass broken fly asunder with a very loud and most sharp noise.
>
> 24. Wine, Beer nor other liquors will make them musty, nor change their colour nor rust glass.
>
> 25. Glass may be cemented as Stones and Metals.
>
> 26. A drinking Glass filled in part with water (being rubbed on the brim with the finger wetted) yields Musical notes, higher or lower, according as tis more or less full, and makes the liquor frisk and leap.

Needless to say, such a definition tends to frisk and leap itself. But doesn't it stimulate you to want to get to know the stuff better?

The *New Standard Dictionary* of 1932 defines glass as

a fused mixture of silica, usually in the form of natural sand, and two or more alkaline bases such as soda, lime or potash. It is generally transparent or translucent, is brittle and sonorous at ordinary temperatures, and when heated becomes soft and ductile, finally melting. The point of fusion varies with its composition. It breaks with a conchoidal (commonly called citreous) fracture, and is acted on by hydrofluoric acid, but not by ordinary solvents.

However, both definitions are too restrictive as far as composition is concerned. It is possible, for instance, to have pure silica glass without the need for other constituents. Furthermore, there is no actual "point" of fusion. And neither definition brings out the essential continuity from the fluid melt at high temperatures to the rigid glass at lower temperatures.

Probably the best and most widely accepted definition of glass was given by Morey in 1938: "A glass is an inorganic substance in a condition which is continuous with, and analogous to, the liquid state of the substance, but which, as the result of having been cooled from a fused condition, has attained so high a degree of viscosity as to be for all practical purposes rigid."

In 1960, Phillips wrote that "Any material which has cooled from the liquid state to a rigid condition, without crystallizing, is properly called a glass, regardless of its chemical composition." This definition includes both inorganic and organic materials.

As glasses cool from the melting temperature, they tend to become unstable, and crystals form. At the temperature where crystals first begin to appear, and the temperature range just below it, the viscosity of glass is very high and the atoms have difficulty rearranging themselves into the ordered network characteristic of crystals. If, in cooling, this temperature range is passed through rapidly, the forces creating this crystal net-

work continue to increase, but the mobility of the atoms decreases at an even faster rate. In this tug-of-war of atoms versus viscosity, the rapidly increasing viscosity soon wins out, crystallization becomes impossible, and the "supercooled" glassy state has been attained.

Glasses, then, are indeed true liquids. In the technical sense, they are not solids, even though they appear to be absolutely solid. Windowpanes removed from very old houses prove this rather surprising fact. Accurate measurements of the thickness of the windowpanes show that they are slightly thicker on the bottom than on the top. Over hundreds of years, a barely perceptible amount of flow has occurred as a result of gravity. It is this feature of glass, its liquid state, that permits it to be scored and "broken out" by pressure—a hydrostatic pressure similar to that applied to the brakes of a car.

Glass can be made from ordinary silica sand without any other components. Next to "fused silica" or "silica glass," the simplest glasses are the alkali silicates. Adding 25-percent sodium oxide to silica drastically lowers the melting temperature and thus acts as a powerful fluxing agent. Pure silica (sand) melts at 3110 degrees F. The resulting substance is a thick, syrupy compound that is commonly called "water glass" because it is water soluble. Obviously, products made from sodium silicate would not last long because of this idiosyncrasy. The ancient glass makers, either by accident or by trial and error, discovered that the addition of lime (calcium carbonate) to the mixture of silica and soda overcame the problem of water solubility. This further decreased the melting temperature of the mixture. Because the ancient glass makers had primitive furnaces, this was a particularly fortuitous discovery. The durability of these ancient soda-lime-silica glasses was only fair. This lack of durability could have been largely overcome by adding more lime and decreasing the soda content, but this would increase the tendency of the glass to crystallize on cooling. However, the problem could have been corrected by adding other oxides, such as alumina, boric oxide, or magnesia.

The basic raw materials needed for glass

making are abundant. The Second Epistle of Peter in the New Testament reveals that "the heavens shall pass away with a great noise, and the elements shall melt with fervent heat, the earth also and the works that are therein shall be burned up." It has been postulated that if this holocaust came to pass, the earth, oddly enough, could turn into a great sphere of glass.

Such is the nature of this material that we will be working with!

CRAFTING in GLASS

Chapter 1

Working with Sheet Glass

Nature's Sandbox

An understanding of how sheet glass is made today and a comprehension of its flexibility and limits are essential if your projects are to be successful.

Many people think of glassblowing as a forceful art, but it isn't. Only a small amount of breath is required. It is a manipulative, controlled blow rather than a vehement one, a blow controlled from lips and mouth, rather than from the lungs. Thus the blowpipe is central to the glass-making operation. This hollow metal rod, about six feet long and two inches in diameter, is smaller at the end where the breath is applied and wider at the opposite end, where the glass is gathered on it from the furnace. The molten glass that gathers will be fairly heavy, so the glassblower must be prepared to account for this weight. Because of the weight of the end of the pipe, special rests are used to allow the pipe to lean. He gathers the glass by dipping the blowpipe into the molten "batch" in the furnace. Then he begins to turn the pipe, and withdrawing it from the furnace while still turning it, allows the molten glass to cool. As it cools, it adheres to the pipe. He again dips the pipe into the furnace for another "gather" and repeats the process.

After the third dipping, the mass of glass on the end of the pipe will be shaped like a pear, about ten inches in diameter and a foot or so long. While this cools (some workers sprinkle it with water to cool it faster), the glassblower begins to hollow out the glass by blowing through the tube. He also swings the mass back and forth on the end of the rod to elongate it. The glass now assumes a more cylindrical shape, although the lower end is actually hemispherical.

The blower's assistant then puts a hole through his end of the mass with a steel rod, making it into a cylinder.

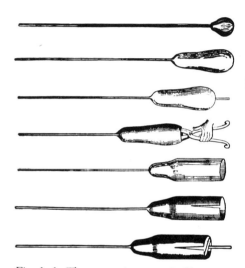

Fig. 1–1. The successive stages in blowing a cylinder of glass before it is made into a sheet.

Once more the glass is returned to the oven to keep it at the proper temperature. Once again the glass is removed from the furnace, and the assistant, using a special pair of large shears, enlarges the hole and pushes it ever further inward until the whole glass cylinder, except where it is attached to the pipe, becomes hollow. Once more the glass is heated. The assistant cuts the cylinder through half its length, beginning at the open end and continuing toward the point where it is attached to the blowpipe.

The next step is to transfer the glass from the blow-pipe to a pontil, a solid iron rod smaller in diameter than the blowpipe. Attached to the end of the pontil is a metal crosspiece. The pontil is thoroughly heated at the end, and a small quantity of molten glass from the furnace is gathered on this crosspiece. This is applied to the open end of the cylinder—the end opposite to the blowpipe—and allowed to cool so that it adheres firmly. The cylinder of glass is supported in front by the blowpipe and at the back by the cylinder rim against the pontil.

The blowpipe is now removed. The simplest way to remove it is to cool the glass with some water at its point of attachment. This will crack it immediately away from the pipe, and the cylinder will fall entirely on the pontil. With the blowpipe out of the way, the cylinder is cut to join with that already made on the other end. This new cut joins with that from the other side, leaving the cylinder divided on one of its sides throughout its length.

At this point, the cylinder is placed with the cut side upward on an iron shovel or table, where it is separated from the pontil. Then it is carried to the annealing oven, where it is gradually heated again to redness. The blower must watch that it doesn't overheat, or it will begin to sag. When it has been heated to the proper degree of flexibility, it is opened up, turned on its rounded surface, and allowed to flatten of its own weight. It is then passed through the lehr (or cooling oven) in the various cooling stages and comes out the other end as a piece of flat glass.

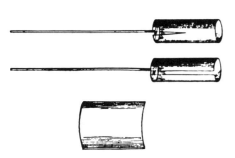

Fig. 1–2. The transformation of a cylinder of glass into a sheet of glass. This is the "antique" method of glass making, or *hand-blown* glass, as opposed to *rolled* glass.

This is the basic, classic method of making *hand-blown* sheet glass, and it has been much improved upon with machines and by the float process of manufacture, a fairly recent invention. In the 1930s, the float process (floating glass on molten tin) even speeded up the continuous-flow method of making flat glass, a process established in 1916.

Not all sheet glass is hand blown: Some stained glass, for example, is rolled. The process, based on characteristic liquidity of glass, is simple, rapid, and efficient.

The molten batch is removed from the furnace with a shovel and placed on an iron table. A special roller "flattens out" this batch once the glass worker has molded (mixed) it properly. The process is similar to wringing out clothes in an old-fashioned press. Once the sheet has been pressed, it is transferred to the lehr and annealed. In the case of stained glass, different colors of glass can be added to form a *streaky*. These colors, heated in separate furnaces, combine metallic oxides in the "batch" to impart the particular hue. The batches are then mixed together on the rolling table just before the sheet is pressed.

Thicknesses of Glass

Single-strength, double-strength, and plate glass are stocked by dealers in various dimensions. Some hardware stores carry pieces up to 36 by 36 inches, although you will not need anything so large for the projects in this book. However, you may want to keep sheets of this size or larger in storage, so you will want to have a sturdy bin in your workshop to hold them.

Since the dealer charges to cut the glass for you, it is cheaper (and more fun) to cut your own. Always purchase a piece larger than a project requires. To store the leftover pieces, you should have a few small bins and one or two large bins. In addition, you should have a scrap box for keeping pieces of glass that still have a workable surface. Almost all scrap glass can be used at some time or another. Never store glass on the floor, and never lean it against anything, even temporarily. Someone will surely walk into it—and it might even be you.

Most of the projects in this book are made with single-strength sheet glass, which measures $\frac{3}{32}$ inch in thickness. One of the advantages of this glass (especially for beginners) is its ease of cutting. Another is the price: Single-strength glass is cheaper than either stained glass or double-strength or plate glass. This doesn't mean that you should limit your explorations to this one type of glass, but it is a good place to begin. Each type of glass has idiosyncracies that you can exploit to bring out particular facets of your creativity.

The thinnest glass, picture glass, is particularly good for glass jewelry or ornaments, where weight is a factor. Although the glass is thin, don't think that factor alone makes it easy to cut. Thin glass is more often than not *hard* glass. This means that it is brittle and therefore rather difficult to cut. However, in applying heat to it, as in fusing or laminating, it has the characteristics of single-strength glass. We like to use single-strength glass for laminating because when the sheets are sandwiched together, they are still not overly heavy.

Double-strength window glass, which is $\frac{1}{8}$ inch thick and sturdier than single-strength, is good for sagging ashtrays and plates, where increased bulk is desired. It is sometimes necessary to laminate double-strength glass (making the thickness about $\frac{1}{4}$ inch) for sturdy objects, especially fairly large ones.

Plate glass is usually $\frac{1}{4}$ inch or more in thickness. It is the most difficult of all the glasses to cut—that is, to break out from a score line—but it is not difficult to use. There are a number of advantages to using plate glass in projects because of its softness. Remember, the thickness of a glass doesn't mean that it is necessarily chemically hard (brittle).

Textured glass can be of any thickness and is categorized according to the ease or difficulty of working it, regardless of its surface characteristic. Many textured glasses are $\frac{1}{8}$ inch and more. Industrial glass is usually a hard, brittle $\frac{1}{8}$-inch-thick glass in various shades of greens and yellows. Some of it can be very difficult to cut because of its brittleness. Crystal, on the other hand, is usually easy to cut, and it also fires well. Obviously each glass has its own peculiarities, and they can be determined only by working with it. In general, colorless edges indicate a hard, brittle glass. Thus in fusing, more heat is necessary regardless of the thickness. Turquoise edges usually mean that the glass will dull or even frost when heated.

Stained Glass, Colored Glass, and Painted Glass

Colored and stained glass are one and the same. The word *stained* (not "stain glass," as many amateurs call it) is a misnomer that has come into general usage. "Stained glass" is colored *after* rather than during production. It is also a particular type of glass technique, a process using silver nitrate stain to achieve a golden color. Such a "stain" is permanent. The brilliancy of hue depends on the type of glass used, the percentage of silver nitrate, the amount of heat employed, and the length of time the object is left in the kiln. Such glass may well be called "stain glass." However, we will use the words *colored* and *stained* to mean the same thing.

Painted glass is something else again. This term involves the surface layering and detailing of glass pigments over clear (or colored) glass. They can also be used for painting on glass, using the glass as a canvas or emphasizing (mostly in colored hand-blown glass) some point of interest in the glass itself. These paints usually must be fired in the kiln after they are applied.

Fig. 1–3. Painting on window glass has all the advantages of a canvas, but it reacts to light, which not only passes through it, but reflects from it. Painting on glass can make a unique and impressive statement.

The Coefficient of Expansion

The most important principle that you must understand if you are going to work with glass *and* heat is the coefficient of expansion of glass. Keep in mind that glass is a "liquid," that it is "frozen" at low temperatures and that it "flows" at higher ones. The coefficient of expansion is the changeover point from the solid to the liquid state; and the temperature range varies widely, depending on the glass. The thing to remember is that within this temperature range the glass changes its physical quality in addition to expanding.

This "thermal expansion" merely means that glass, like many metals, changes its length and breadth as it is heated. It expands when heated, contracts when it cools. The principle can be compared to a thermostat. Two metals of different coefficients of expansion are bonded together, and when heat is applied, one of them expands more than the other. This results in a curvature of the two, and the curvature acts as a switch: Movement is achieved. However, glass is not a metal, and it is a notoriously poor conductor of heat, so when you bond or fuse two different glasses together, the stress of the differing coefficients of expansion may cause them to crack or shatter.

In addition, as it is heated, glass can change in other ways: It can vary its reaction to light and go from transparent to opaque, or to any quality in between, from hazy to cloudy. Often the transparency, or lack of transparency, of heated glass is a function of the quantity of heat as well as the length of time over which the heat is applied. Both factors involve the coefficient of expansion.

Let's take a quick look at some of the different types of sheet glass and see how they react to coefficients of expansion.

Characteristics of Sheet Glasses

Regarding coefficients of expansion, we must take into account brittleness, hardness, fusing temperatures, bonding qualities, cutting qualities, painting and staining qualities, sagging (or slumping) ease, shrinkage tolerances, and, in stained glass, color fastness. Many of these qualities will be inherent in any glass you select, and you can determine them by test-firing.

Picture Glass. This is thin glass, and as such you might think that it would sag and bend at a comparatively low temperature. Not so. Because it is thin, it is made quite hard and has a tendency to be brittle even when cut before any heating is done. You may have to go to fairly high temperatures to get it to react in the kiln. This glass must be cooled very, very slowly. We try not to use it for any complicated bends or sags. Because it is so lightweight, it is probably best to use it for small ornaments. Nonreflective picture-frame glass functions in about the same way as reflective glass.

Single-Strength Window Glass. This is very useful in laminating. In almost all instances, it is the best glass for practicing cutting because it scores easily and tends to follow the score line docilely during the breaking-out procedure. It is also cheap, fits well into lead came, and foils well.

Double-Strength Window Glass. As the name implies, this is about twice the thickness of single-strength glass, and it can be used for larger sagging projects. Laminating two pieces of double-strength glass will provide you with a thickness of about $\frac{1}{4}$ inch. This is ideal for many objects because it is strong enough to sustain the stresses of everyday knocking about, yet it is not so thick as to look clumsy.

Plate Glass. Many people are afraid to work with plate glass because it is difficult to break out a score line. The trick in cutting plate, which is an extremely soft glass, is to use a blunt cutter. This will make a thick score, and it will "run" better than a thin, deeper one. Breaking out the score lines sometimes leaves irregular edges because of the thickness involved, but these can be easily smoothed with a grozzer. Also, more pressure is needed to break out a score line from plate glass than with any other glass. One might think that with so many strikes against it, plate glass would be used only as a last resort. But plate glass is fun to work with, and once you establish your technique and get used to its characteristics, it can involve you in many rewarding projects and experiences. Plate glass generally requires a lower firing temperature in the kiln than other glasses since it is such a soft glass.

Stained Glass. Firing stained glass, as well as cutting it, is a technique all its own. Its idiosyncracies are legendary, for here you are dealing not only with the coefficient of expansion of the glass, but with the modifications that result from the impurities in it. These are the metallic oxides that give the glass its color or colors. But don't let this challenge scare you away. If you do, you will miss out on some of the most beautiful effects that can be achieved in glass crafting.

Stained glass can be fired alone or in combination with other glasses. True, you must be prepared for problems, and you may have to do quite a bit of test-firing, but the results will be worth the effort—as well as the additional knowledge you will acquire about fusing possibilities.

There are different thicknesses of stained glass, just as there are of clear glass. English antique, for instance, is quite thick and irregular, which means that it is difficult to cut *and* to fire. In general, it is not so much the variance in thicknesses that gives problems, but the color. When heated, certain rubies turn orange, some caramels fade almost to a dirty white, and some yellows turn a deep brown. Some stained glasses, in particular many of the opalescents, resent being fired, and they will flake away from the surface in chips or strands, almost like sunburned skin. No matter how cold you allow the kiln to get after firing one of these glasses, you will still hear it sullenly pinging away as pieces break off.

A Few Particulars about Stained Glass

Stained glass can be divided into two categories for firing purposes—opalescent glass and transparent glass. Opalescent has long been used for lampshades, and it has been bent into forms by machine in great quantities. Many of these panels, pressed into a mold, are caramel-brown streaky. Opalescent glass tends to hold up well in the kiln, barely changing hue even when grossly overfired (although this often depends on the manufacturer). In general, it will fire at slightly higher temperatures than will transparent glass. Most opalescents are approximately the thickness of double-strength window glass and will bend over a mold at about 1250 degrees F. Many have a tolerance of approximately fifty degrees either way. The only way to make sure is to open the kiln and have a look. We use a top-loading kiln for this purpose. A lighter brown-hued opalescent may slump at 1175°F for instance, and change color irreversibly at 1200°F. It is precisely these colors that will fool you if you take them for granted. Fortunately, opalescents as a family are fairly thick-skinned so far as color fastness is concerned, and they will remain tolerably good-humored even if you forget to shut off the kiln at precisely the right temperature.

Transparent stained glass can be another matter. Here you must be very watchful that a color change does not occur with heating. Some hues will get lighter, others darker. It may happen that a color that has faded because of overfiring will come back as the glass cools, but you can't depend on this. Reds are particularly touchy, and since red glass is expensive, you don't want to have to buy more because you were careless with the kiln.

Sheet-Glass Fusing Qualities

The technique of fusing—getting glass to adhere to glass through the application of heat—is one of the principal activities of this book. We will consider glass not for its utilitarian value (windows, coffee-table tops, storm doors, picture framing), but for its aesthetic capabilities. In its more mundane uses, glass has built-in provisions for whatever function it is meant to fulfill. Plate glass is thick to withstand pressure. Picture glass is extra thin to avoid weight. The craftsperson can take advantage of these various manufactured qualities of glass and put them to use in specific projects.

What you will want to know is how such glasses will react to stress, how they will react to laminating, bending, and fusing, and what surface problems will be encountered in painting. You will also want to know about each company's product and how to capitalize on any built-in features. The composition of glasses differs, and because of this often unknown quality, our projects will be given an X factor that is impossible to take into account. This factor can lead to disaster if you are unwary (it can lead to many interesting effects as well), but it is this awesome unpredictability of glass that creates both a great deal of frustration and no small measure of excitement about the craft.

A Glass-Working Summary

Now that we've discussed some of the various glasses, you should be able to make a logical choice for a particular project. Some dimensions might help: Picture glass is less than $\frac{1}{16}$ inch thick. Single-strength window glass measures roughly $\frac{1}{16}$ in thickness, as do many machine-rolled stained glasses, both transparent and opalescent. Double-strength window glass and certain opalescents and hand-blown stained glasses measure $\frac{1}{8}$ inch and up. Plate glass, the thickest of all the glasses other than *dalle-de-verre*, goes from $\frac{1}{4}$ inch and up. Dalles measures an inch in thickness.

It isn't only the shape of the end result that you want to keep in mind. In any of the clear glasses, you will want the same transparency to be there at the end as when you began. Many clear glasses have a tendency to *devitrify*—that is, to form a crystallized haze on their surface. This is usually the result of overfiring. While this might be an effect you are anxious to produce, more than likely it will dismay you. So the lesson here is to avoid overfiring. Stained glass can also devitrify but usually not without a fading in color. Both stained and clear glass on overfiring tend to develop rolled margins along their perimeters. If the overfiring continues beyond this point, these glasses will shrink and develop holes. A great deal of accidental art is produced in this manner, although it usually can't be exhibited for very long because of the corresponding brittleness.

What you are really after is the *planned result*, and in glass crafting this comes about through a combination of keeping your eyes open and taking your time. Glass, in particular, doesn't like to be rushed, so working with it requires discipline. At its most fluid, it chugs along. You can't make it do better than that. But when you see the results of this chugging, you will find all the work worthwhile.

How to Budget Your Time, Money, and Materials

No one wants to spend money needlessly. Yet for many people, once they have decided to take up a hobby, they find it hard to resist the temptation to acquire in one fell swoop just about everything available in that hobby. Our advice is not to get everything all at once. It isn't even necessary to buy new items: You can save a lot of money purchasing what you need secondhand. Check local garage sales; inquire of any of your friends who have been doing glass work. They may have accumulated extra tools that they will be happy to sell you—even a kiln that they may want to replace for a more sophisticated one.

Many people are leery about buying secondhand supplies. However, tools for glass crafting usually have no hidden flaws. It isn't like buying a used car, where you might well be buying someone else's troubles. If a tool is defective, you should easily be able to tell right away. Look it over and, if you can, try it out. Even a kiln can be tested easily.

Of course, even secondhand, it is a good idea not to buy what you do not need at the moment. Too often you may find your interest veering toward a facet of the craft that either you aren't ready for or may never get that involved with. To buy an expensive Badger blender on the assumption you are going to do a lot of painting (even if it is a "good deal") and then decide that you really prefer using enamel paint is impractical. Keep your hobby *practical*. As you go along, you will quickly discover which tools and supplies you need and which would only be nice to have. Of course, if funds are no object and you can't resist tools and machinery, you can go ahead and acquire at least one of everything. This will undoubtedly make you the darling of the trade shows, although how much time you will have left for actually working with glass is debatable.

Our last suggestion about buying tools is that you shouldn't buy (at least at first) anything that you can reasonably make yourself, or that you can adapt from a tool you already have. The key word here is *reasonably*.

To spend several hours devising an item that you could buy fairly inexpensively is counterproductive. As for the more complicated machines, however, don't attempt to make your own simplified version. If it could have been made simpler, it would have been. On the other hand, don't try to work without the proper tools, and don't attempt to force tools to do jobs they were not meant for just because you have them on hand. To make electrician's pliers do the work of glass grozzers will probably cost you more in the long run for ruined glass than a standard grozzer would. To use an old, dull glass cutter (with a boxed wheel to boot) will make your cutting many times more difficult, if not completely inaccurate. This will not only waste glass, but it will probably ruin your temper for the day. We have seen workers use needle-nose pliers for breaking pliers, soldering pencils instead of soldering irons, and all sorts of other impetuous improvisations. If you select wisely for your needs at the time, learn to make the most of the tools you do select within their capabilities, and get the feel of how glass reacts to you and how it reacts to your tools, you will never have cause to regret a purchase.

Chapter 2

Kilns: Choosing and Using Yours

It is impossible to fire glass without using a kiln. A regular kitchen oven won't serve the purpose for any sort of craft work. We know some students who fire their paints in their oven, but even low-fire paints will not cure properly at these temperatures. And more important, impurities from any craft chemical will lodge in the oven and possibly contaminate your food.

If you are going to pursue glass crafting, you must use a kiln, and preferably you should own one. Purchasing and using a kiln need not be a traumatic experience. There is one for every pocketbook and every purpose. Besides, kiln work is fun, and it is also far less expensive than you might think.

A kiln is nothing more than an oven made out of a special type of brick that is durable, retains heat, and is lightweight. The actual heating takes place in the kiln chamber, and the size of this chamber determines the cost of the kiln and its operation. Kilns come in all shapes and sizes and with different power sources— from wood burning to gas burning to electric.

Advantages of Owning Your Own Kiln

If you are going to be at all experimental and creative, and if you want any sort of comfort and freedom in your craft, you will want to own your own kiln. In addition to creative freedom, there are practical reasons for owning your own kiln. If you are dependent on a friend's kiln, you will eventually find the traipsing back and forth wearisome. You may even begin to put off projects just because of this inconvenience, and sooner or later it will begin to inconvenience your friend. We have known instances where not only the kiln was lost, but the friendship as well.

It can also be inconvenient to pay for the use of a professional kiln. You also must wait your turn. The charges are based on the size or number of the pieces and the time involved. Added to this are the costs of transportation to deliver the piece and pick it up. Knowing that you have to go to all of this trouble just to fire a piece (and if it misfires, having to repeat the entire procedure) is enough to make you think twice before attempting any sophisticated project. Instead of making the firing of the kiln an experience to be anticipated, it becomes pure drudgery. It is not surprising that many people give up and find a hobby that is less demanding than glass crafting.

So, our first word of advice is to get your own kiln. Then you can use it whenever you wish, and you won't have to worry about experimenting. And you will end up paying less than you would if you rented one. If you can't afford a new kiln, even a small enameling one, try to get one secondhand. There are a number of them around. Garage sales are good for finding all sorts of things, even kilns. You run only minimal risk (or so we've found) in buying a secondhand kiln. There's not all that much that can go wrong, and a test firing before purchasing will give you a good idea of how it works. Inspect the chamber to see if it is in good shape, and look at the elements. Frayed wiring and any broken elements should be immediately replaced. Almost everything in a standard kiln is either in plain view or can be inspected by removing a few screws and covers. In the end, you will have bought yourself a lot of enjoyment for comparatively little money. On the other hand, if you want a new kiln, you should have a good idea of what you want before you buy, since only you can tell which kind will be best for the work you want to do.

Choosing a Kiln

All right, you're sold. Now, how do you choose a kiln? Our advice for a power source is electricity. Electric kilns, almost universally available, work with the least amount of effort and have a low installation cost compared with fuel-fired kilns. An electric kiln is as safe as any other electrical appliance. The heat that it generates is kept within the chamber, so the outside barely gets warm. Of course, your electric kiln should be well designed and have no shock hazards, but this is the case with almost all of them. Naturally you should take the same precautions with this as with any other electrical appliance.

Special wiring may not be necessary for the kiln you buy. Small kilns can be plugged in anywhere. Larger kilns do require a 220-volt line, but this can be brought in easily by any electrician. While the operating cost for an electric kiln is not cheap, it is far from prohibitive.

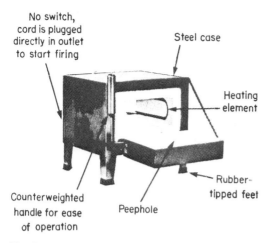

No switch, cord is plugged directly in outlet to start firing

Steel case

Heating element

Rubber-tipped feet

Counterweighted handle for ease of operation

Peephole

Fig. 2–1. Small enameling kiln.

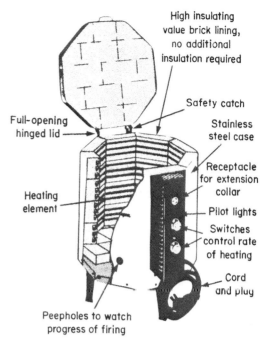

High insulating value brick lining, no additional insulation required

Safety catch

Full-opening hinged lid

Stainless steel case

Receptacle for extension collar

Heating element

Pilot lights

Switches control rate of heating

Cord and plug

Peepholes to watch progress of firing

Fig. 2–3. Deluxe hobby kiln.

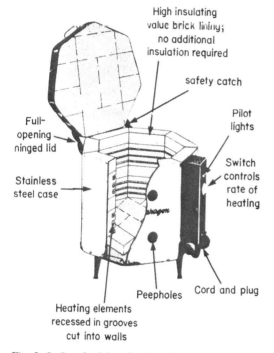

High insulating value brick lining; no additional insulation required

safety catch

Full-opening ninged lid

Pilot lights

Stainless steel case

Switch controls rate of heating

Peepholes

Cord and plug

Heating elements recessed in grooves cut into walls

Fig. 2–2. Standard-duty hobby kiln.

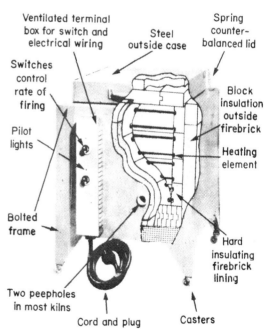

Ventilated terminal box for switch and electrical wiring

Steel outside case

Spring counter-balanced lid

Switches control rate of firing

Block insulation outside firebrick

Pilot lights

Heating element

Bolted frame

Hard insulating firebrick lining

Two peepholes in most kilns

Cord and plug

Casters

Fig. 2–4. Heavy-duty studio or hobby kiln.

13

And, you can cut the cost even further by firing a full load of pieces whenever possible. If you are economical in using your kiln, you can probably operate it for what it would cost you for a custom firing for a single piece. And firing glass, rather than ceramic items, further helps to lower your cost because it is fired at almost a thousand degrees less than ceramics.

While learning to operate a kiln is simple, learning to use a kiln to achieve consistently fine results in glass is an art. Every kiln has different characteristics. The kiln you buy should have a technical procedure about as complicated as an electric toaster. At a recent show, we were asked to look at a kiln that was made "specifically for glass." And it did have several features that appeared to be calculated for the glass artisan. But also, according to the salesperson, it had to be used by an "expert." We couldn't quite figure out why, since it had the same old switches on this highly overpriced unit; it seemed the price was based on snob appeal.

In a large kiln, specific switches control the various element banks. A small kiln is even simpler, usually employing an off/on switch and perhaps an additional switch to raise the temperature at intervals. Many glass workers use pyrometric cones (inexpensive clay pyramids) to tell them when the proper firing temperature has been reached. These cones are placed inside the kiln as it is loaded so that they can be seen through the peephole. When the cone bends, the kiln should be turned off.

We prefer a *pyrometer* rather than cones, and we recommend that you buy a kiln that is equipped with one. In the years that we have been kiln-firing glass, we have come to rely on a number system rather than on the temperature of the cones. We feel this is more scientific, more accurate, and far more secure. It is easy to have a pyrometer put in at the time you buy the kiln, and it is less expensive than having someone journey to home or studio to do it later.

A *kiln sitter* is also nice to have, and it, too, can be added when you buy the kiln. However, it is more of a luxury, and we will discuss it at length under *Kiln Accessories*.

More of a necessity than a luxury is the *input holding control*, which allows you to maintain a constant temperature for a given length of time. This comes in handy when fusing different types of glass, where conflicting coefficients of expansion would otherwise cause trouble. They may cause trouble anyway, but the input holding control at least gives you more of a chance of success.

Before you buy a kiln, you should consider where you will put it. Placement of a gas or wood-burning kiln is necessarily limited. An electric kiln can go just about anywhere in the home or studio. Your convenience is the only determination—and convenience is why you are purchasing the kiln in the first place. It isn't necessary to back up your electric kiln against a stone wall, although many kilns do end up that way, since many workshops are in basements or garages. And if you want to put an electric kiln in your bedroom for insomniac nights, there's no reason why you can't.

The size of the kiln is another concern. But since you will be firing glass, you don't *have* to have a large chamber, which is the case for most ceramic kilns. Still, it should be large enough in case you want to stack shelves so that you can fire a number of painted projects at one time.

Should you buy a top-loading or a front-loading kiln? Each type has advantages. A front-loading kiln takes up the most room, since in placing it you must take into account the full swing of the door. A top loader is a more compact unit. For bending glass on nonrigid mold material especially, we find a top loader just about indispensable. For sagging glass into a fixed, preformed mold, either a front- or top-loading kiln can be used. Some workers find a top loader is easier to work with, since you can look down on your project rather than crouching and looking in at it. Also, if you have a small enameling kiln, it would be a front loader, probably on a table, so you wouldn't have any choice.

Both top- and front-loading kilns can have stacked shelves. The heating efficiency of both types is about the same as for ceramics, but it is quite different for glass. In a top-loading kiln, the elements stretch around the periphery of the chamber. In a front loader, elements surround the chamber on three sides only; the door is strictly firebrick. This leaves a "cold area," which can be critical. Many workers using this type of kiln are careful to keep the glass toward the rear wall of the kiln. Whether or not this actually makes a difference is a constant source of argument; what cannot be argued is that since the elements are not surrounding the space, the heating has to be uneven. For glass, probably the most efficient type of heating would be from above, as in a "flash" kiln. (This is a kiln used mostly by professionals; the area of glass exposed to heat can be very accurately calculated.) But we, and other workers, have achieved fine results for years with a standard ceramic kiln. For the beginner, even a small enameling kiln will give many hours of pleasure. We do most of our bending and sagging in a top loader and our painting and fusing in a front loader, although this is simply a habit that we have established over the years.

The question of shape can also be confusing to the first-time kiln buyer. Students are puzzled by the differences in the square or polygonal-shaped kilns. Theoretically, the polygon offers lower cost per cubic inch of firing space. The square kiln has a slightly higher cost per volume, but you can take advantage of more space. In general, the square kiln is a heavy-duty piece of equipment designed for advanced hobbyists, studios, and institutions. An advantage to the square kiln is that you can more readily fire circles of glass, such as round plates. On the other hand, polygonal-shaped kilns tend to heat faster and cool more quickly.

What about rapidity of firing? We feel that this is not that important. Glass crafting is a series of steps, each definitive and precise, and not the least of which is the firing process. We prefer a kiln that fires slowly but efficiently. Glass doesn't respond well to a sudden burst of heat, and we have had better results with a slow-firing than a fast-firing one for both painting and fusing. Probably the best choice is a kiln that can be fired either fast or slow, since sometimes you will want a faster fire. This type will have several banks of elements, and each bank is controlled by a switch.

Speaking of raising the heat, how do you want your kiln to fire? Most hobby kilns will fire all types of material and will go as high as 2300 degrees F. With such a kiln, you can fire ceramics, porcelain, pottery, china paints, and gold (possibly making your own ingots!). But do you *need* such a high degree of heat? If you want to melt glass, make your own glass globs, and work with certain metals, you do. But if you are not interested in such exotic techniques, you can probably cut down your expense with a low-firing kiln. The top heat you will need is about 1400 degrees F. You can discuss with your dealer how best to limit your kiln to this temperature and how much money you will save by doing it.

As for the outer surface of the kiln, except for your aesthetic sensibility, it doesn't matter whether you have a stainless steel case or a painted one. Both last well and long. Of course, stainless steel looks better, but a painted case is somewhat cheaper, and you might want to put the money saved into the size rather than the surface. The operating cost of either a stainless steel kiln or a painted one is the same, regardless of what you may have heard.

Kiln Accessories

We have already mentioned pyrometers and cones. Remember that pyrometers measure temperature only; cones measure the amount of heat treatment that actually will be received by the material to be fired. You can use a cone in addition to a pyrometer if you want to determine as exactly as possible how much heat a particular piece of glass will get. Such a critical end-point firing is rarely necessary in routine glass work. Always make notes of each firing process when you use any new type of glass. Your notes should include the type of glass (manufacturer), color, thickness, type of kiln, the firing end-point, and the length of cooling time. Usually it is best to start and finish with a cold kiln—but we don't always do this ourselves, and you might find instances where you don't want to. Not all kilns fire the same, and if you want to duplicate a creation, you should do it in the original kiln and follow the first procedure as closely as possible.

The kiln sitter is an electrical switch that is turned on by hand and turned off by the action of a pyrometric cone bending under a rod. When the switch is turned off, the power, and thus the heat, is interrupted. Unfortunately, the kiln sitter may either go too far or not far enough, so you should not depend on it to do the entire job. However, it should keep you from ruining work by overfiring. Since a kiln sitter is a mechanical device, it cannot be considered an absolute guarantee, and you should check on it from time to time. Still, it's nice to know that you can go about other work without having the temperature in your kiln get out of hand. We use a kiln sitter to duplicate projects rather than for a first-time firing, where we cannot be completely certain where the end-point firing will occur. Here you have to watch and wait. It's a good idea to set a timer when you put work into the kiln, and be sure to check the kiln when the timer goes off. Setting the timer at, say, fifteen-minute increments and reducing these as the piece approaches its firing temperature will keep you in mind of the project, but it won't do any good if you don't check and reset the timer. In this case, you will always be too late.

Kiln furniture, such as posts and shelves, is used more for ceramics than glass, but some of it comes in handy for layering out glass pieces for fusing or painting. Especially when fusing, "stacking" the kiln with shelves can change the temperatures of each shelf depending where it is in the stack. This introduces another variable into the fusing process, and it is one you don't need. In stacking shelves, you can modify this variable somewhat by making sure you allow for ample air circulation between shelves. There should be at least a good four inches between the bottom of one shelf and the top of another. Never overload the shelves with glass, and keep the stacking to a minimum. Remember that the smallest expense in firing is the power source. While we don't advise you to fire your kiln when it is only one-third full, you shouldn't panic for space either. If you sandwich in pieces that will come out badly because of crowding (either as a result of the pieces touching or poor heat circulation from excessive shelves), you will waste both time and electricity or fuel. You can't win when you play against yourself.

Kiln wash is a powder used to prevent glass from sticking to the shelf. Various mixes can be purchased from ceramic shops, but we make our own, using a mixture of diatomaceous earth, calcium carbonate and powdered mica in a ratio of 1:2:1. Although kiln wash is not really a kiln accessory, you will use quite a bit in our mold-making projects.

Repairing a Kiln

Not all that much can go wrong with a kiln, and what does go wrong you can usually fix yourself. Most dealers carry a stock of parts, and many also have a repair service. It is usually difficult to get a repairperson when you need one—which is instantly—and the service is not cheap. Don't be afraid to fix your own kiln, or at least to try to see if you can figure out what is wrong. You can call your dealer or manufacturer, describe the problem, and find out what you can do to fix it. The kiln manufacturers we have spoken to are extremely generous with advice and patient with questions. And repairing your own kiln is fun—certainly more fun than parting with the money.

Many manufacturers include illustrated instructions with their kilns, both parts lists and wiring diagrams. A map of the innards of your pride and joy can be more daunting than helpful. In fact, it may convince you that you had best keep hands off and wait for the repairperson. But don't be afraid: It is unlikely that your kiln has gone totally into "self-destruct." In fact, the most frequent (possibly the only) repair job you will ever have with your kiln is replacing the elements. That is the only job we have ever had to do with our kilns in more than fifteen years of steady use. Many kiln manuals will tell you that with normal use and proper care a heating element should last five years. We have not found this to be precisely the case, although they do last for a long time.

Heating elements are attached to the sides of the kiln in several ways. It would appear, logically, that the straight recess-groove type would be best. But this isn't the case, because the elements, which are composed of lengths of nichrome wire, tend to grow in length and to bulge out of the grooves with use. There are devices to hold the elements in place, such as pins and clips, but these can obstruct the heat flow and cause a higher temperature within the wires at the point of contact. The wires will usually break at this point. Thus clips will shorten the life of the elements, so it's a good idea to check how the elements are held in place before buying your kiln. The best kind of groove to keep the elements from protruding into the chamber, and yet not short circuit them, is a dropped recess groove. Dropped recess grooves offer excellent heat transfer. In addition to keeping the elements in place, they allow for easy repair and replacement.

Eventually you will have to replace the elements, so the first rule is to keep an extra set of elements on hand. Wires have a habit of giving out at night, on long holiday weekends, and in the midst of an extremely important job. The very first thing you must do before replacing the elements is to make sure your kiln is unplugged or that the appropriate breaker is off. Do this *yourself*—don't trust anyone to do it for you. If you don't have a replacement wire for the broken element, you can twist the broken ends together to complete the circuit. This can be tricky, though, because the wire will be fragile and may break off in your hands. It is still strong enough to cut your fingers, however. If the elements have snaked out into the heating chamber, try to replace them gently, even if only temporarily.

Some advice on repairing the elements:

1. Make absolutely certain the kiln is unplugged.
2. Take one element out at a time. Often a single element will supply two "banks" in the wall. Label all terminals for each element and follow each wire along separately. Never pull wires at random because you will quickly become confused.
3. Clean all kiln wash from the kiln even though it adds time to the whole procedure. Kiln wash tends to scatter, and you shouldn't inhale it. Piling the wash in the center of the chamber, as we have seen some do, is inefficient. The time you spend fighting it can be better served getting rid of it.
4. If you are changing one element, change them all. This is a great time-saver. If one element has gone, others will go shortly. Then you have the whole job to do over again.
5. Before plugging the kiln in again, double check that all elements are connected to their specific terminals, that all nuts are tight, that you don't have any leftover parts (always a disconcerting surprise), and that your assistant (if you have one) isn't still fiddling with a wire or connection. The assistant may not be quite so willing to help you the next time.
6. Once all the elements are replaced and the kiln is working, test fire to see what your effective tem-

peratures are. Essentially you will be working now with a "new" kiln, and the characteristics of the "old" kiln may have changed.

A Quick Course on Heating Characteristics

The amount of time necessary to achieve proper firing temperature of the kiln depends upon how rapidly it will accept heat. This rate is controlled by one or more switches, which in turn connect various combinations of the heating elements to the power supply. A kiln is easier to heat when the temperature is low. Thus it is best to fire your kiln with only a small amount of power initially. This is usually the "low" switch on a three-stage heating panel. You can switch on additional elements as the temperature increases and as an even rate of heating is obtained. Firing time can be varied by increasing the time between switch changes—from *low*, to *medium*, to *high*. You can switch directly from low to high, but it is always best to start with the low heat rather than the medium, even though it takes more time. Some kilns have only low and high switches.

Remember to keep your kiln vented when starting a fire. This means keeping the door partly ajar. The chamber air can escape as it heats and expands, and it cleans impurities out of the chamber, especially if you are heating any surface chemicals on your glass. Glass requires gradual heating to allow the expansion coefficient to gradually come into play over the entire surface. Some kilns have no switches; they are controlled simply by plugging them into an outlet. On this type of kiln, firing time cannot be regulated, so you should not use this type for critical firings.

How do you tell if a kiln has good heating characteristics? Without having experimented with the kiln, you can make only an educated guess. Part of the education is likely in the brand name. This doesn't mean that an off brand-name kiln will not do a proper job, but reputation should count for something. Of course, you can study the specifications that come with each kiln. This is fine if you are acquainted with various terms and concepts. But the average hobbyist just wants something that will work. The glass is of prime importance, not physics.

Keep in mind that the size of the kiln, the shape, the element spacing, and the insulation all have an effect on the heating characteristics. Hobby kilns, meaning those with single walls, are easy to heat during the early period of the firing. They also require very little power to bring them up to medium temperature, and it doesn't take much more to get to the firing point. The heavy brick in the walls of heavy-duty kilns tends to retain heat; thus they are slower to heat. Small kilns,

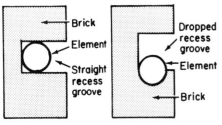

(Above, left) Best heat transfer; no obstruction; elements retained by pins, tend to bulge out of place.

(Right) Excellent heat transfer as retaining lip rapidly heats; keeps elements in place; easy repairs.

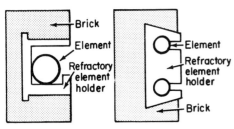

(Above left) Good transfer of heat, elements stay in place, but repairs difficult if ware melts in holders.

(Right) Holder limits transfer of heat. Mechanical protection good, but element life reduced.

Fig. 2–5. Heat transfer and element placement. Courtesy Paragon Co.

because of the amount of space in the chamber, usually heat more evenly than large ones. Polygonal-shaped kilns have fewer cold spots than square kilns because the heat flow is less impeded within the space. In all kilns, evenly spaced elements are important for an even distribution of heat.

Kiln Insulation

It seems logical that a kiln with thick insulation would be more economical to operate than one with less insulation. But just the opposite is true. The whole object of firing is to reach a certain temperature and then shut off the heat. Before the kiln is opened, all of the heat in the chamber must be diffused. With glass, especially in fusing, the kiln must be stone cold before you remove your projects. A kiln that retained heat perfectly would never cool. Insulation therefore is not quite the simple adjunct you may have considered it to be.

The most effective part of this kiln insulation is the first few inches. As more insulation is added to decrease heat loss, heat storage is thereby increased. This means that you need more power to heat the chamber. More power is required to produce this stored heat than would be needed for the heat lost with less insulation. It follows that the most economical operation of a kiln is to have the proper balance of heat loss and heat storage. This is achieved by using the right insulating material *and* the right amount of it. Kilns are insulated with many types of material. Some are good, some better. You should check this out before buying a kiln.

The principal types of insulation are firebrick, block diatomaceous earth, and mineral wool. Firebrick is probably the most common, and often it is the only insulating material. This is usually a light brick, although in this form it has less mechanical strength than the heavier variety. Light firebrick in small kilns allows lower cost, and it is quite satisfactory if protected by a steel case. Block insulation or mineral wool is used in the sidewalls of large heavy-duty kilns to reduce heat losses. The hard block insulation is permanent and will not change form or deteriorate with use. Mineral wool tends to pack down, which means some areas may become overinsulated, resulting in lower efficiency.

The best way to determine the type of insulation is to check the manufacturer's specifications. If you buy a secondhand kiln and it has no specifications, just look inside. Heavy-duty firebrick is buff-colored and quite porous. Also look for insulation behind the brick. In a heavy-duty kiln, this is critical because it controls kiln life. If you are contemplating a large floor-model kiln, pound the side with your hand. It should be firm and

Fig. 2–6. (Top Left) Block diatomaceous earth is reinforced with asbestos fiber. Firm, solid block.

(Right) Firebrick is the most popular insulation because of its low cost and efficiency.

(Below) Mineral wool block has low mechanical strength. Tends to settle with use. Courtesy Paragon Co.

solid. If you want a small table-model kiln, make sure the firebrick is unbroken and thick enough to keep the heat in the chamber, but not so thick that the kiln will take hours to cool. Try the kiln: If heat radiates through the outer walls, forget it.

Differences in Kilns

Your kiln is the most perfect working tool you must own. But the knowledge you must have when you choose your kiln is not always available when you go to buy it. It is easy to become overwhelmed and end up with too much kiln or too little. In either case, it will be a frustrating experience. As a general view, the following types of kilns from the Paragon Co. are fairly standard and all work well for glass.

Group A Kilns

These kilns operate from a 115-volt circuit and, because of this limitation in power, they are limited in size. The sizes generally available (referring to the chamber size) are 6 by 6 inches to 11 inches across by 13 inches deep. Although all operate from a single 115-volt circuit, some require 18 amperes. Under such circumstances, using the base circuit will not allow you to make use of the full capacity of your kiln. Check the amp capacity of your home or studio before selecting a kiln that requires more than 13 amps. These kilns have the advantage of lower initial cost, low operating cost, portability (so you can even take it with you on vacation), and simplicity of operation. The disadvantages are their small capacity, the lack of a switch control, and slow firing in the larger sizes because of the power limitations.

Type 1, perfect for firing jewelry, miniatures, and even copper, is ideal for a second kiln that is to be used for testing or rush-firing. Such a kiln is convenient for the individual doing a lot of work, who wants to test experimental effects. It saves time and materials, rather than firing an entire kiln full of pieces in an arbitrary manner.

Type 2 is used mostly for copper enameling, but we have also used it for glass fusing and painting. For bending or sagging, however, we have found it to be insufficient. The firing chamber is about 8 by 4 by 9 inches. The elements are in the sidewalls and are easily replaced.

Type 3 seems to be the favorite of the hobbyist with limited electric power. This is the tallest and most efficiently shaped kiln in the group. It has full switch control, with insulating firebrick lining protected by a metal case. It is not only good looking, but it does a good job.

Fig. 2-7. Group A kilns. Courtesy Paragon Co.

Group B Kilns

These kilns are made in many sizes and shapes and are very practical for the average hobbyist (if, indeed, such a person exists in this individualistic craft). The average size is 15 inches in diameter by 13 inches deep. Most models require 230 volts, and this is available in most modern homes. Some of these kilns can be used on 115 volts, so check with your salesperson and electrician. Performance in this group is equal to larger professional models of the same type and temperature rating.

Type 1 is an excellent kiln for the accomplished glass artist as well as for the beginner. The firing chamber is 12 by 8 by 12 inches deep. This kiln is equipped with an infinite control, so temperature can be maintained at any level. The door is counterbalanced.

Type 2 is the kiln that is most often seen in the studio of the serious hobbyist. The firebricks used in the lining have a high insulating value and require no additional insulation. This is a medium-priced high-fire kiln that is good for ceramics and porcelain as well as glass. It has full switch control and comes in a stainless steel or a hammertone brown case (at least the one made by the Paragon Company).

Type 3 is also a great favorite of many workers. It has a large capacity and good control of chamber heat.

Group C Kilns

These kilns are the larger floor-standing models, and obviously you need room for one of these. But if you are doing any sort of mass production work and have the room, how can you resist? The capacity in this group ranges from 1.3 to 2.6 cubic feet. The chambers can be as large as 18 inches wide and 20 inches deep. A variety of models are available, from medium and standard to deluxe. Kilns in this group are widely used in schools and in ceramic and glass studios.

Type 1 is 15 inches square by 13 inches deep and has a heating capacity of 2300 degrees F. This is the economy model of the heavy-duty, square, insulated kilns. The sides are made of stainless steel, and there are two switches for even firing.

Type 2 is a scaled-down version of the larger studio or professional kiln, but it includes all the same features. It has a long life with little maintenance and is a good investment for those doing glass sculpture or thick, heavy pieces.

Type 3, probably the most popular of all kilns, is a high-fire porcelain all-purpose kiln. These kilns are 18 inches deep and range in diameter from 18 inches down to 15 inches. This model is insulated with fire-

Fig. 2–8. Group B kilns. Courtesy Paragon Co.

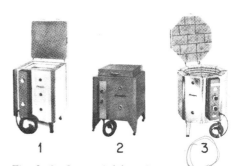

Fig. 2–9. Group C kilns. Courtesy Paragon Co.

brick and may be fired and cooled quickly. Installation is easy and inexpensive. A full-opening hinged lid is standard.

Group D Kilns

We include this group of kilns for the sake of completeness, although it is unlikely that the average hobbyist will go this far into kiln work. These are mainly for institutional or commercial use, but we have found them in stranger places. Kilns in this size group, 3 to 7 cubic feet, should always be heavy-duty because the stresses created by heating such a heavy mass require extra strength. Before using this type of kiln, study the mechanical specifications with care. In these kilns, construction details and quality may vary widely. The general principles in these large units are the same as in the smaller ones, but the potential problems can be greatly magnified by their sheer bulk.

Type 1 is a large ten-sided kiln with a firing-chamber capacity of 7 cubic feet. These kilns are always high-temperature units that will fire just about anything. They always have three switch controls and stacked sections.

Type 2 is a good example of a standard heavy-duty high-fire kiln for general use. Firebrick and diatomaceous block are the insulation.

Type 3, larger than Type 2, is often the first choice of institutions because of its large size, long life, and even temperature rise. This kiln has a counterbalanced lid and is easy to load.

General Principles of Kiln Use

There is no way to predict how any kiln will behave. The enameling kiln is a favorite with us for its price and quick firing ability, but the novice should remember that even with this kiln you cannot assume anything. This is especially true during the cooling process. If you are using two kilns of the same dimensions, do not expect them to cool at precisely the same rate. Trust the pyrometers, not your assumptions. Many large kilns, even after cooling all night, may still be too warm in the morning for the glass to be taken out. The shelves and molds themselves retain heat, and they, too, must cool so that their heat is not transferred to the glass.

Venting and Cooling

Good venting is primary to good results. Glass takes a slow temperature rise, so we leave the door of the kiln ajar when we begin the firing process. We usually don't close the door until the pyrometer goes to about 800 degrees F. During this time, we switch (at about 500 degrees) from low to medium, and from 800 degrees on

1   2   3

Fig. 2–10. Group D kilns. Courtesy Paragon Co.

we switch to high to get to the firing point. This does not hold true for all firings, but it is a good general rule.

Keeping the door of the kiln ajar when starting to fire will not only provide the necessary slow heating of the glass, but it will clear the kiln of possible pollutants, either from the present firing or from a prior one. Such byproducts tend to condense on the firebrick or shelf, and with reheating they can recondense on the surface of your work. This can be disastrous. Cloudiness of the glass is not always the result of overheating: It can come about from something as prosaic as a dirty kiln.

As for cooling, just turn off the switch at the proper temperature. The *average* kiln will lose heat in a sufficiently slow manner to allow for proper glass cooling. Depending on what you are doing, you can crack the door after the pyrometer has dropped to approximately 1000 degrees, making certain that you close it again at approximately 700 degrees. Some glasses (although rarely if they are being fused) will tolerate this shortcut; others will shatter. In sagging or bending, you can get away with this shortcut more readily, depending again on the glass as well as on the complexity of the bend or sag, which adds stress to the glass. With some opalescent glass for lamp panels, we open our top loader directly after reaching the firing point and let the glass cool completely with no problem. But where coefficients of expansion are fairly critical, as in fusing or lamination techniques, you will probably have enough difficulties without looking for more. Here it would be best to be conservative.

Firing Temperatures

Enameling Kilns. In these kilns, you may not achieve complete sagging or fusing until 1500 degrees F. or even slightly above. Without a pyrometer, you will have to keep opening the door to see what is happening (we do this even if using a cone). This process cools the glass and adds to the time involved. In the long run, however, we have found this to be safer and we feel more secure with the arrangement. You might want to have a wired door—that is, elements placed within the door—in your enameling kiln to prevent the notorious "cold spot" that would otherwise exist. In general, a good enameling kiln will sag and fuse glass at about 1400 to 1450 degrees. If you go any higher than this with stained glass, you will almost surely lose color. Most of the stained glass we have worked with will lose a substantial amount of color even at 1400 degrees. This is especially true of reds. If you are working with stained glass, start watching it at 1200 degrees. Once the glass begins to acquire a rosy hue, the kiln should be shut off.

Ceramic Kilns. Most glass workers use this type. The average ceramic kiln will bend glass over a mold at 1175 to 1250 degrees. It will fuse from 1350 to 1450 degrees, and it will sag also in that range depending on the complexity of the sag. Again, stained glass may lose color.

Porcelain Kilns. These are high-fire kilns, and the temperatures are rather severe for glass. The porcelain kiln holds heat very efficiently in its firing chamber and will effectively act on glass at about 100 degrees lower all around than the ceramic kiln. It also takes longer to cool than does a ceramic kiln. On the whole, we do not recommend these for glass work.

Gas Kilns. We have discussed the electric kiln at length because most workers end up with one. The energy provided is cleaner than gas, and the installation of the kiln is cheaper and easier. Gas has other disadvantages, too. Gas kilns retain heat longer than is good for glass after the firing point is reached and the heat turned off. For ceramics, this is no problem. Clay has a wide firing range and a gas kiln has no ill effect. Glass has a very critical firing range, the limitation of which spells success or failure in your endeavor. If you do use a gas kiln, it is essential that you vent the kiln directly after reaching the firing temperature to allow the heat level to drop. If you don't do this, the glass will almost certainly fragment during the cooling process. Gas also contains many contaminants for glass. Sulphur is one, and it can lead to discoloration as well as frosted surfaces.

Wood-Burning Kilns. We have not worked with a wood-burning kiln. A friend of ours built a large one that he uses for both ceramics and glass. This is an outdoor endeavor that appears to us to be a lot of work, although he says it's fun. It depends on your definition. Quite a bit of wood is used to heat the chamber enough to fire glass; the temperature cannot be regulated as precisely as in an electric or gas kiln. The principles of a wood-burning kiln are the same as for any other type.

Hints for Better Operation

1. Never rush.
2. Venting is important; don't overlook it.
3. Since no two kilns are alike, don't try to duplicate a project from one kiln to another.
4. Wherever possible, use the same types of glass for fusing or lamination so that the coefficients of expansion won't conflict.
5. In general, hard, brittle glass requires more heat, soft glass less.

6. Beware of overfiring. This will diminish the effects of colorants by flaking or "frying" them, and it will distort the glass as well.

7. Beware of underfiring. You will end up with improper sagging, unfinished angular edges to fused glass, and immaturity of paints and stains, which will make them appear dull and cloudy.

8. Get a pyrometer for your kiln.

9. Before using any glass or colorants for the first time, test fire.

10. Change all kiln elements when necessary. If you put this off, the uneven heat may produce poor results. (Incidentally, you may be able to clean elements that are not terribly corroded by firing camphor [mothballs] in the kiln to about 1400 degrees. Corrosion will be deposited in the form of black flakes.)

11. Don't use too long a wire from the power source of the electric kiln. It's a good idea not to use an extension cord at all. It cuts down on the power going to the kiln, and hence on its efficiency. Use only the length of cord provided.

12. Any rule can be broken for experimental purposes.

Chapter 3

A Glass-Crafter's Guide to Tools and Devices

All of the tools and devices we will discuss are tailored to perform a new technique or to perfect or simplify an old one. For you, the worker in glass, some may be novelties, others luxuries, and still others essential. The choice is yours. We will also catalog and describe a few of the newer items that bring another dimension to the joy of crafting in glass.

Hand Glass Cutters

The hand glass cutter, the most basic tool of all, for many years never underwent any changes in design. Like the turtle, it was thought that the glass cutter was the end result of an evolutionary progress that required no further adaptations. The standard cutter was, after all, efficient, functional, and very specific. Yet for those of us who teach students to cut glass, we realized that the cutting process was one of the most formidable of challenges, and mainly because of this basic cutter. It was difficult for many older people to hold and difficult to maneuver. Those individuals set in their ways or who never did get the swing of it had to leave most of their glass cutting to a neighbor or, more often, to the teacher.

Most beginners want to hold a cutter similarly to the way they hold a pen. While this can be done with the standard cutter, a certain amount of wrist motion is sacrificed. Considering the influx of people into the craft who are in a hurry to cut glass immediately and who are not partial to an instrument as independent as the standard glass cutter, a change in design seemed called for. This has been done most effectively by Glass Accessories International with their line of Supercutters.

This doesn't mean that the standard cutter is on the way out. The number of people who have trained with

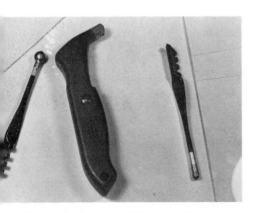

Fig. 3–1. A group of Fletcher glass cutters. Left: a ball cutter, the ball for tapping a score line underneath a piece of glass. Right: a straight shaft cutter. Both show grozzing teeth, shaft, and cutting wheel. Between them is the Fletcher heavy-duty cutter. Note the angle of the cutting shaft to the handle.

it, who use it regularly, and who will continue to use it along with the newer cutters has increased. Rather than replacing the standard cutter, the new cutters are meant to implement it and, where necessary, substitute for it.

First, let's take a look at Old Faithful—the instrument that everyone, lay and professional alike, thinks of when the term *glass cutter* is mentioned. This tool measures approximately five inches from wheel to top of shaft and consists of four parts: the cutting wheel (made either of steel or carbide), the grozzing teeth, the finger rest, and the shaft. For maximum mobility, the glass cutter is held in the first three fingers of the hand, with the thumb pressing from below, the index finger on top, and the middle finger exerting pressure from the side to hold the cutter steady. The shaft is held upright at about a 45-degree angle between index and middle finger. Care should be taken not to allow the shaft to rest backward on the web between fingers; the constant riding of the shaft against this tender part of the hand will chafe the skin. The grozzing teeth, for purposes of balance, are best held down toward the glass. The fingers grip against the flattened portion of the shaft; you should never grasp the cutter at the grozzing teeth, although students invariably often make their task harder by doing this. The grozzing teeth are rarely used in craft work; some glaziers use them to smooth out particularly rough edges of glass, but a grozzing pliers is much better suited to this work. Cutters can be purchased with or without a ball at the end of the shaft. The ball increases the weight and swing of the shaft and is used for tapping a score line. This is its only purpose; it has no effect on cutting or scoring.

Such, in brief, is *the* glass cutter. There have always been some variations in design, mostly in the size and hardness of the wheel, and in the German Diamantor cutter, with a bulkier shaft and a change to a wooden instead of metal one.

One of the first companies to revamp cutter design completely was the company who over the years also did the most to popularize the standard shape. The Fletcher Company's heavy-duty cutter is a complete departure from the delicate, dartlike standard glass cutter. It is a hand-filling, fist-clenching tool that lets the glass know you are there. By using one of the most basic hand motions—the grip—and by providing the proper cutting angle almost automatically. Fletcher solved two of the more nagging problems beginners have had with the standard cutter. The manufacturer claims that this handle shape produces over fifty percent more cutting pressure than the regular cutter. An indentation in the top of the handle allows both pressure and

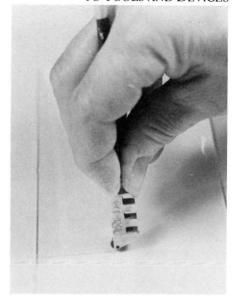

Fig. 3–2. Positioning of the fingers when using a standard glass cutter. The foreshortening of the illustration makes the fingers appear closer to the grozzing teeth than they really are.

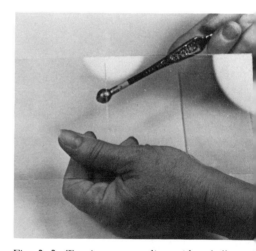

Fig. 3–3. Tapping a score line with a ball cutter. Note the position of the left hand, which supports the glass and grasps both pieces of the glass to be separated. Many beginners grasp only one piece and thus cannot control the other piece.

Fig. 3–4. The Fletcher heavy-duty glass cutter. The thumb provides a great deal of downward force in the position shown.

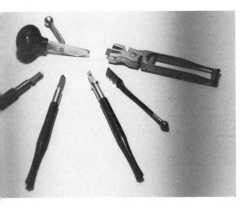

Fig. 3–5. A clutch of glass cutters. Lower left: the family of Supercutters. Right: a standard Fletcher, and above, the Omnibus cutter. Top: Stanford Engineering's "fist" cutter.

Fig. 3–6. For a "catch-all device," the Omnibus glass cutter works surprisingly well. The partial fist grip is comfortable, and the index finger provides guidance. Hidden in the palm of the work hand are the sharpener, scissors, and garden tool.

guidance by the thumb. The nose of the cutter is already placed at a 45-degree angle (the same as the regular cutter, which you must maintain yourself), so all you need do is run the wheel down the glass.

How effective is this cutter, and what advantages does it have over the standard one? For straight lines, we find that it works very well indeed, as well as for moderate curves and angles. The difficulty arises when cutting circles and patterned shapes. Here we find that it is awkward. We are used to the freer wrist motion of the standard cutter, and we miss this mobility. However, after a number of determined attempts, we managed to cut patterned shapes, and we feel that any novice would be able to do this even more readily, not having to unlearn a previous technique.

At the same time, as its name implies, the heavy-duty glass cutter is meant to cut thick glass, such as plate, where a forceful score line is a great help in breaking out the piece. Maximum pressure is achieved by placing the thumb on top of the handle. Here the device is particularly delightful, making perfect scores time after time.

The Omnibus glass cutter, which we picked up recently in a hardware store, demonstrates ingenuity, if not much else. This little tool attempts to be everything to everyone, combining a sharpener for knives, scissors, and garden tools—and, at the reverse end, a glass cutter, almost as an afterthought. But the tool works. You can cut glass with it readily. Most notable is the grip. This cutter is also gripped in your fist, using the thumb or index finger as a guide. It is comfortable, allowing maximum use of the natural curl of the hand, and you can exert quite a bit of pressure on the glass without tiring your arm, a complaint many novices have about the standard cutter. This tool can be manipulated into pattern cutting if you work at it, although a good deal of wrist mobility is lost because of the type of grip.

The German firm Diamantor emphasizes thickening the shaft of the basic cutter and making it of wood to lighten it. In changing the design, the idea was to allow a more effective grip between the fingers, since the thin metal shaft is somewhat difficult to balance. We find that the Diamantor cutter takes up too much room between the fingers, spreading them to such a degree that continual use chafes the skin. Also the wood tends to rub more than the metal. Those individuals we have surveyed who use Diamantor cutters either don't do extensive amounts of glass cutting or hold the cutter like a pen. But our opinion is that it is too short and too light for this technique.

One of the most original glass-cutter designs we have seen is made by Stanford Studio Engineered Products of

Manitou Springs, Colorado. Employing the fist grip, which seems to be the way to go in many cutters, the Stanford glass cutter allows the fist to close around a football-shaped Bakelite handle. Projecting downward from this handle is a straight shaft, at the end of which is the standard wheel and axis. Halfway down the shaft, a metal rod flares backward at an angle of 45 degrees and is capped by a ball. This ball is larger than that on most regular glass cutters, but its function is the same: to tap a score. Because of the way it is placed and its larger size, it can be swung very effectively. The metal rod is used as a support for the thumb during the cutting process. This is done by gripping the handle in the fist and guiding the wheel over the glass, either forward or backward, steadying the shaft with the index finger. A set screw at the bottom of the shaft allows the position of the side rod to be changed to accommodate left- or right-handed cutters. The shape of the handle is supposed to minimize fatigue, and it does do this even after long periods at a stretch. The wheel is carbide, and, since proper pressure is almost automatically applied, it will do a proper job over a long period of time.

Once again, we found cutting patterns awkward. However, with a little practice, the average student should be able to learn to do this readily. The Stanford glass cutter comes with two Allen wrenches (one for the handle and one for the axle), and all parts are guaranteed replaceable.

The Supercutter series by Glass Accessories International is according to many people one of the most dramatic breakthroughs in the scoring of glass. The basic grip of these instruments is a pen-finger grip rather than a fist. This allows more flexibility of the wrist, although this is of course a personal judgment. To give even more mobility, because of the pen grip rather than the three-finger grip of the standard cutter, Glass Accessories modified the heads to swivel either partly or completely. This can take some getting used to. However these tools are relatively easy to use, and with a minimum of practice, even the most extreme beginner can cut glass.

The basic cutter of the group is the Supercutter, and there are enough departures from the ordinary in this item to justify the manufacturer's claim that it is the first professional glass cutter that can be called a new tool. The Supercutter certainly has points of interest that make it unique. To begin with, it is self-lubricating. A drop of kerosene lubricant is injected from the reservoir to the cutting wheel each time the head of the instrument is compressed. As can be seen in Figure 3–11, the reservoir is directly within the handle. This is knurled metal about $\frac{1}{2}$ inch in diameter. Glass Accessories has recently

Fig. 3–7. Stanford Studio's fist cutter in action. The thumb is on the thumb rest, and the pressure is from the palm through the stubby shaft to the glass. It is comfortable for straight lines rather than curves, which tend to be awkward to do.

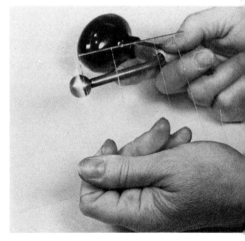

Fig. 3–8. Tapping a score line with the ball of a Stanford cutter. It provides quite a whack.

Fig. 3–9. The family of Supercutters. It's hard to keep up with these prolific cutters. Left: The original Supercutter and the thinner version. Center: the plastic model. Right: the Miracle and Diacutters. It takes practice to get used to these cutters if you are used to a standard cutter.

Fig. 3–10. The Supercutter in action. Most workers use the pen grip just about exclusively with these cutters. It is fairly difficult to hold the original Supercutter in a standard glass-cutter grip, although this may be done with the thinner version.

come out with two variations of this cutter—a Slim-Line metal cutter, which is $\frac{3}{8}$ inch in diameter and thus easier to hold and maneuver, and a Pencil Acrylic pattern, which is the same cutter with a hollow plastic handle. This seems to be the favorite from our survey. It is certainly one of our favorite cutting devices.

All the Supercutters have about $\frac{1}{16}$ inch play between the top of the head and the bottom of the handle/reservoir. This is taken up by the normal pressure exerted when you start to cut glass. If you open the screw-tapper cap about two revolutions, kerosene will be pumped to the cutting wheel through a wick in the capillary tube. Closing the cap stops all flow. Each Supercutter comes with a plastic syringe for filling the handle reservoir with cutting lubricant. If this seems like a lot to do each time you cut a score line, it is. But what a score line! And how easily it is accomplished.

In addition, the Supercutter allows you to change blade shapes, so you can use one cutter for many purposes. Pattern or straight blades are available as replacements on any Supercutter handle. The Supercutter is guaranteed by its manufacturer as follows: "Each patented cutting wheel approaches diamond in hardness and is guaranteed to cut 10,000 meters or approximately six miles of hardened glass."

Glass Accessories also makes the Miracle Cutter and the Diacutter. The Miracle Cutter is basically a Supercutter without many of its advantages, but at a lower price. The attempt here is to catch all phases of the market without sacrificing the unique features. Accordingly, the Miracle Cutter has a wood handle in a brass collar, but there is no lubricating mechanism and therefore no head compression, no screw tap, no tapper. After using the Supercutter, which we did first, it's easy to become spoiled and resent the absence of these features. The shaft of this cutter is thin, from less than $\frac{1}{2}$ inch at its widest part to the $\frac{1}{4}$-inch taper above. It is a nice, elegant cutter weighing about $3\frac{1}{2}$ ounces, compared to the Supercutter's weight of $5\frac{1}{2}$ ounces. It is less balanced than the Supercutter, being nose heavy, but this is probably a plus so far as ease of cutting is concerned. Like the Supercutter, the head, or blade, has about an eighth-of-a-turn swivel, which at first takes getting used to.

The Diacutter is designed in almost all ways like the Supercutter and Miracle Cutter, but it is closer to the Miracle Cutter in construction. The only difference in handle design from the Miracle Cutter is an extra cuff on the brass collar at the lower end to provide a complete swivel of the head. This cutter is supposed to be used exclusively for pattern cutting, and the head is meant to turn to follow every angle of the pattern.

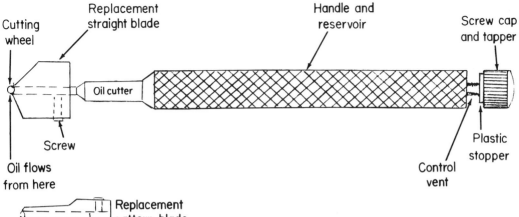

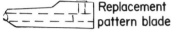

Cutting wheel

Replacement straight blade

Handle and reservoir

Screw cap and tapper

Oil cutter

Screw

Oil flows from here

Control vent

Plastic stopper

Replacement pattern blade

Fig. 3–11. Inside a Supercutter. The engineering is impressive.

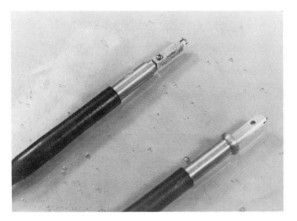

Fig. 3–12. The heads of a Diacutter and a Miracle Cutter: The sleek look.

Fig. 3–13. Cutting with a Miracle Cutter.

Fig. 3–14. Two of the newer cutters on the market. Left: The Cutter, made by the Pro Glass Cutter Company, has a "comfort grip"; you put your finger through the hole and cut. It works well and will enable you finally to get a good score. The cutter is color coded: red is a steel wheel, blue a carbide wheel. Right: Creative Stained Glass Studio's oil-cutter handle, complete with oil cutter as shown. Another interesting variation on the theme of new cutters, and effective as well, it has a stabilizing set screw, an option for the craftsperson who wants maximum control.

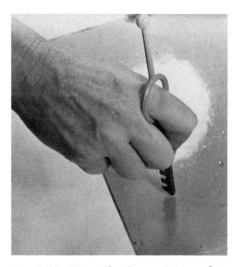

Fig. 3–15. Using The Cutter. It is comfortable and sure, the grip is natural, and the score line is impressive.

Provocative as this intention is, we must confess that we had all sorts of problems trying to get the cutter to do its job—and so did everyone else we asked who had tried it. There is also the assumption that glass workers will want a cutter that serves only one purpose. But not many will. And the Diacutter just doesn't cut straight lines all that well. The swivel arrangement tends to get in the way more than it helps. On the whole, if you can buy only one cutter, and you want one of these, stay with the Supercutter. But, who knows? Perhaps shortly they will make a pattern cutter that will do the job all by itself. Then we will all be obsolete.

Glass-Cutting Machines

There is nothing that these machines can do that can't be done by the individual craftsperson and any hand cutter. But they will do it more quickly and will continue to do the same cuts over and over without getting bored. But the machine is not a craftsperson; it is just another tool, although it can be an important, essential tool if you are involved in certain aspects of glass crafting. And you never know: As small and individual as your operation is now, one calculated to please only yourself, one day it may grow into a business. In this case, you might find these machines essential. Even where you are only operating along strictly hobby lines, you could do worse than invest in one or two of them. They are fun, and they make your hobby even more fun.

Circle Cutters

The "standard" circle cutter has for many been the Fletcher Lens Cutter No. 32. This machine employs a central, fixed pivoting point around which a 3-inch shaft rotates according to hand pressure. The cutting wheel is released from the glass by a spring when the pressure is removed. To the end of the shaft is screwed a replaceable carousel containing three cutting wheels that rotate as they get dull. The length of the shaft being the radius of any circle, the maximum circle you can score with this machine is a 6-inch diameter. The shaft is calibrated for smaller radii. Any circle cutter scores only the glass; you must still break out the circle.

A similar idea incorporating other advantages is the Stanford Precision Circle Cutter. Here the radius of the shaft is 7 inches, allowing for a full 14-inch diameter circle, an important consideration for sagging plates and other decorative glassware. A kit is also provided for a jig-board hold down. This allows you to cut scallops, inversions of the primary cut, and many other fancy radius cuts. These are all "part" cuts. When the

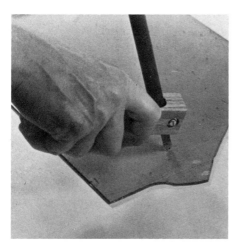

Fig. 3–17. Right: The packaged oil-cutter handle comes with full instructions. You supply the cutter.

Fig. 3–16. Using the oil-cutter handle. This is a fist grip, and it provides a lot of workable pressure onto the glass surface. Another very effective invention.

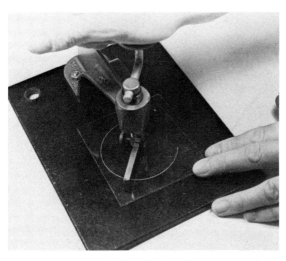

Fig. 3–19. The Stanford Precision Circle Cutter is much larger than the Fletcher, and it makes circles of far greater diameter. It is a substantial instrument, well designed, and well crafted. Surprisingly, though, the shaft is not calibrated. This would be a great convenience because it is awkward to keep measuring the radius with a ruler.

Fig. 3–18. The Fletcher "lens cutter" is limited to fairly small circles. Press down on the handle, turn the wheel, and presto, you have a circle. The shaft is calibrated.

machine is used for this purpose, the operator must use the small knob that is provided directly above the cutting-wheel holder. If you tighten this screw well, it gives a lot of control to the jig-cutting process. You will have to loosen the radial shaft and use the small knob to guide the cut. For jig cutting, you cannot use the large knob on top of the machine, since this would leave you with little or no control. The large knob is used strictly for circle cutting.

An even different type of circle cutter is designed by Glass Accessories International. This Suction Circle Cutter does not use the table-spring load-arm technique of the previous two machines. It is also the largest radial arm we have seen, measuring almost 18 inches. This gives a maximum diameter of 36 inches, which is larger than most hobbyists need. The machine is beautifully designed and easily transportable. It consists of a long metal rod (calibrated, of course) that is attached at one end to a make-or-break suction cup. This is a heavy-duty affair with a strong knurled switch that is easy to work. Upon the metal rod, the cutter slides, encased in a heavy block of metal controlled by a screw. The cutter is swiveled. Pressure is exerted by hand on a cylindrical metal handle. Altogether, the tool radiates workmanship and is a pleasure to use. The suction cup works effectively, and you can knock out circle after circle without becoming fatigued. When not in use, the arm swivels upright and the machine balances without a quiver. This allows taking all pressure off the cutting wheel so as to increase its life. The tool can also be kept upside down, and even then it retains its quiet dignity.

Duplicating (Template) Cutters

Duplicating, or template, cutters are also called "odd-shape" cutters, and more and more of these imaginative devices are appearing on the market. We will limit our discussion to two of them.

The principle behind these cutters is the precise duplication of any pattern into glass over and over regardless of the shape. Therefore, you must have a firm template to follow and a rapid means to transfer this template to the glass-cutting device. Cheapness and ease of making the template are of primary importance. Both the machines we reviewed utilize cheap, easy-to-make templates. Source of power is another factor. Here these machines diverge: One uses hand power (the cheapest), and the other compressed air (not expensive).

Stanford Studio's odd-shape glass-cutting machine runs by compressed air. It has been designed to be as small in bulk as possible and still be effective. Two sizes are available: one with a cutting area of 8 by 8 inches, the other with a cutting area of 11 by 14 inches. We chose the smaller unit because it is easier to transport.

Templates recommended by the company are $\frac{1}{8}$-inch clear Plexiglas. These can be cut with a conventional router, a Dremel motor tool with a router attachment, or with Stanford's engraving unit, which uses a Dremel motor tool as its power source. It is suspended from the machine carriage and thus does not interfere with the plastic chips that get caught under the regular router

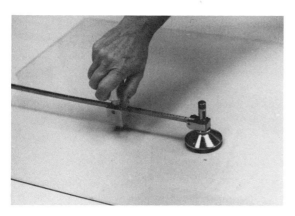

Fig. 3–20. Stages in cutting a circle with Glass Accessories' circle cutter. The suction cup is in play with the back lever up. Only minimal pressure is needed on the swivel knob, which is held by one hand.

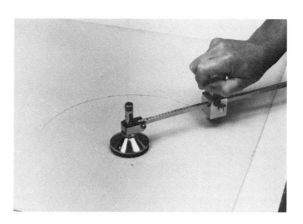

Fig. 3–21. The circle one-quarter cut. The arm of the unit reaches off the table, so stay out of its way.

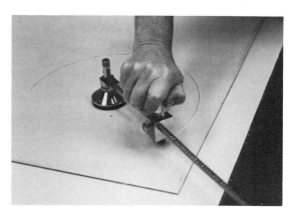

Fig. 3–22. The circle three-quarters completed.

Fig. 3–23. The completed circle, with a precise meeting of the line.

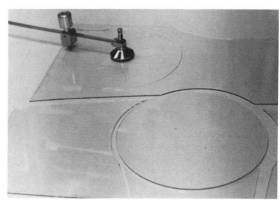

Fig. 3–24. The circle broken out; another circle started. This machine never stops.

Fig. 3–25. Stanford Engineering's duplicator. An impressive-looking machine, it does several complicated operations with amazing vitality. It is also great fun to use. Although it looks complicated, it is easy to use, and you can become an expert in about twenty minutes. One caution: Be sure to cut your template with grooves of the required dimension. It makes it easier for the stylus to follow them.

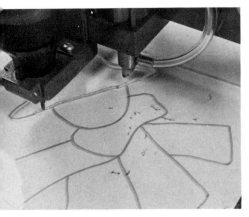

Fig. 3–26. Cutting a template with the template-cutting part of the Stanford duplicator.

bottom plate. In all cases, the cutting bit should be made to cut a 60-degree groove in the template.

Templates are made by placing your drawing or sketch under the Plexiglas and cutting the groove, using the line drawing as a guide. The placement of your template line in relation to the cartoon line will depend on whether you are using lead came or copper foil. You may want to cut inside or outside the line of your drawing. It does take some practice to make a functional Plexiglas template, but once you have the technique down, there is really nothing to it. Be prepared (as in glass cutting) to spoil some Plexiglas. Practice with scraps at first. You can acquire these from your local glazier.

The vee groove you will be cutting into the template will be about $\frac{1}{32}$ inch deep, so you can make templates on both sides of your plastic stock and save money and room. Once the template is cut to your satisfaction, place it in the template board holder. This will accommodate various sizes of templates. Glass is cut when the spring-loaded stylus is depressed in the groove of the template. There is an adjusting collar to prevent the stylus from digging too deeply into the template. Proper adjustment will make the stylus glide in the groove. This vee groove of the template should be lubricated in order to make the stylus glide more smoothly and prevent excessive wear of the template. You can brush regular motor oil (or even STP) on your template and then wipe off the excess. This will leave enough in the grooves. With proper care, your templates should last a long time.

As the template arm moves within the vee of the template, a duplicating motion is provided by the cutter along the surface of the glass. Thus the glass cutter is operated almost by remote control. You move only the handle of the stylus. The pressure of the cutting wheel against the glass is preset. It is adjustable for various glasses, however, and the carbide wheel is easily replaced. The cutting pressure is not a function of your pressure against the template. You can also move the stylus in the template groove as fast as you wish. The cutter will keep pace. We have found that, rather than hurrying, a settled rhythm is best. Once the glass is scored, breaking out the score line is done in the conventional manner. You can, of course, work these break-out lines into the design of the piece, eliminating the need for further scoring once the glass is out of the machine. This greatly speeds up the assembly-line process.

Some people we have introduced to this machine seem leery of the compressed air necessary to run it. Actually, this is no problem. You can use the smallest

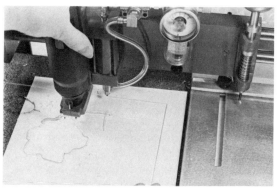

Fig. 3–27. Cutting a simple pattern with the Stanford duplicator. The Plexiglas is routed along predetermined lines. It is simpler to draw the pattern directly on the Plexiglas with a glass-marking pencil rather than hold the pattern directly below the router, where it was awkward to keep in place. No doubt a little practice would alleviate this. It is simple enough, however, to draw the pattern on the Plexiglas; then your outline can't slip, and instead you can concentrate on routing it out. Moderate hand pressure will bring the router head into contact with the Plexiglas.

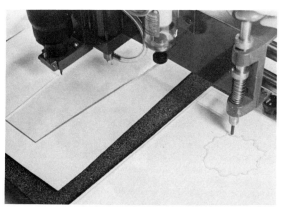

Fig. 3–28. Transferring the routed pattern under the stylus on the right. The glass-cutting head is the one to which the tube is going. Gentle pressure on the stylus knob will bring the glass-cutter wheel directly against the glass with a predetermined pressure. Once your piece is scored, you can easily break it out of the glass by working break lines into your template. The break lines go to the border of the glass for breaking out of the patterned shape in the easiest way.

Fig. 3–29. Stanford's duplicator and a cutting pattern in Plexiglas.

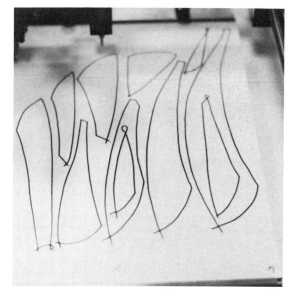

Fig. 3–30. Close-up of the Plexiglas pattern. Note the way the turn of the stylus (center pattern) is designed into the cut, with the small circle on top of the point.

Fig. 3–31. The finished pattern for the scarecrow with possible break-out lines drawn in. The lines are shown only for the hat. Once you have decided where the lines should go, they can be integrated into the pattern and then cut by the machine.

air compressor available that is equipped with a storage tank. We used a Sears compressor simply because we had one on hand, but any cheap compressor will do. It does not make the machine more cumbersome. Air supply should be at least 30 pounds per square inch. This should be regulated at the compressor itself, because the plastic tubing recommended could burst above that pressure. Fittings are supplied with the machine. An air-pressure regulator is mounted on the machine carriage, but it is used only to apply the proper pressure to the cutting wheel. Normally about twenty pounds (or a little more) is required, depending on the hardness of glass or the condition of the cutting wheel. This amount of pressure is not applied to the glass; most of it is consumed by a spring inside the air cylinder that returns it to the "up" position. Only about seven pounds are used to cut the glass.

Our impression of this machine is that it is a high-quality, well-designed unit that will do the job of many hands, if many hands is what you need. It is not for the hobbyist making one-of-a-kind items. But, realities aside, it's fun to play with—and if you are doing any sort of duplicative work, you could well find this unit a constant companion. These machines are hand built, on order only, and delivery dates are variable.

The duplicator from Glass Accessories International uses a different principle for its odd-shape cutting. Here the power is hand supplied, rather similar to the circle cutters, but whereas the circle cutters rotate around a fixed pivoting point, here this area is made variable by implanting a template. Such a jig may be made of plastic, metal, or thin wood. It is held to the shaft by two screws, so holes must be drilled at these spots. The machine will accommodate templates of about $3\frac{1}{2}$ inches in widest diameter. A spring-loaded arm assembly rides around the borders of this jig as the arm is turned by hand. Pressure downward directs the cutting wheel against the glass. The unit is extremely well machined and can be used by the most inexperienced tyro. We have had lines of students just wanting to test this machine, which patiently accommodated some of the wildest jigs they could think up.

We don't mean to imply that this unit is a toy. Far from it. It is one of the most sophisticated cutting devices we have found. A good part of the beauty of the machine is its simplicity. It is designed for the production scoring of glass parts. The replaceable cutting wheel requires no lubrication and is easily changed after miles of scoring by moving the axle retainer and its axle. By loosening the Allen nut located on the top of the unit, the magnification adjustment screw can be used to vary the size factor within two coarse ranges.

Fig. 3-32. The handsome Glass Accessories duplicator. Shown is the guide unit on the base. The machine is cutting a pattern even as you look at it, the guide arm riding around the cardboard template.

Fig. 3–33. The disassembled duplicator shows the basic head assembly on the left. Top right is the cardboard pattern; below it is the plastic pattern holder and the two screws that keep all in place.

Fig. 3–35. Duplicated shapes from the cardboard template.

Fig. 3–34. Close-up of the pattern going back onto the shaft. The pattern holder (the plastic shield) is already in place; the cardboard template will be next, then the two screws that hold it together. Finally, the head assembly screws onto the shaft as a unit.

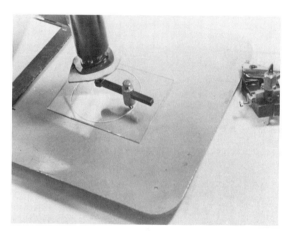

Fig. 3–36. Glass Accessories duplicator with the duplicating head set aside (right) and the circle-cutter attachment placed. A pleasant piece of machinery. Note that the pattern for duplicating is still left in place even though a circle is being cut. This enables a rapid switch from duplicator to circle cutter and back again.

An accessory is the Miracle dry-wheel circle-cutter attachment. This unit, sold separately, easily attaches to the duplicator base unit in place of the duplicator instrument. It can score circles up to 6 inches in diameter; a 12-inch size is also available. A duplicator base, also sold separately, is used with either size duplicator (a 6-inch size is available) or with the circle-cutter attachments. This base provides a cutting board and an adjustable straight edge to aid in holding the glass part for scoring.

There are few things more exciting than seeing something really clever come to pass. Both of these machines easily score high points in this regard. It is worth getting into odd-shape duplicating if only to own and operate one of these. You will find, as we did, that this activity is a privileged experience with so apt and ingenious a helper at your side.

Cutting Boards

As opposed to the odd-shape duplicator, cutting boards provide jigs for duplicating standard geometric figures, allowing anyone to cut over and over small straight shapes such as triangles, rhomboids, and trapezoids. The Fletcher Company has supplied this need with its Horizontal Cutting Board, which will cut glass up to $\frac{1}{4}$ inch in thickness. It is simple and easy to operate and requires no skill. The horizontal cutting board lends itself to either left-hand or right-hand operation and features a long-life cutting head equipped with ball bushings. This is easily reversed for inboard cutting. No outside power source is needed; your arm alone is enough. Multiple copies of irregular shapes are quickly and accurately produced.

The first step here is to cut a cardboard template with scissors and then use this to position and clamp the edge-guide bars. Trapezoidal shapes (two parallel edges) can be produced with a single setup. The edge-guide bars are coated to prevent glass chipping. The cutting board is ideal for stained-glass craft work because it is lightweight and portable. Work-positioning attachments are optional and available to anyone who wants to cut triangles, trapezoids, or any other straight shapes. We like the ease with which the beginner can cut with this board, getting right into designing with glass. It gives the beginner confidence, and it saves time and material. Most beginners usually try to get as many pattern shapes as possible out of a single piece of glass. With freehand cutting, such attempts can end up ruining an entire sheet. With the horizontal cutting board, the beginner can lay out an entire lamp or any geometric shape and cut the pieces with as little waste as possible. The time saved in the cutting phase can be well spent in the decorative phase.

That busy manufacturer Stanford Engineering produces the Pivot Straight-Edge Cutting Board. Like the one made by Fletcher, it can cut trapezoids, diamonds, triangles, and other straight-line shapes. It comes in two sizes, the large board measuring 36 by 24 inches (score line of 36 inches), and the small board measuring 16 by 32 inches (score line of 32 inches). The action here is

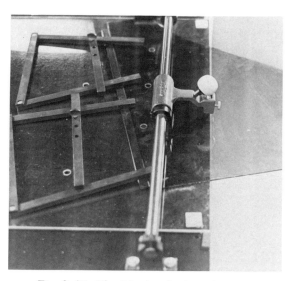

Fig. 3–39. Cutting a triangle on the Pivot Straight-Edge Cutting Board. Almost any geometrical shape can be easily formed, then frozen into position as a template, then changed to any other geometrical shape when you are finished.

Fig. 3 37. The Fletcher horizontal cutting board. The bars at left position and hold the glass at the desired angle. The knob on the right flips down onto the glass and is drawn down the length of the supporting bar, scoring as it goes. The knurled knob on the right above the glass holds the cutter within the assembly.

Fig. 3–40. The Pivot Straight-Edge Cutting Board cuts pieces to a pattern in jig time.

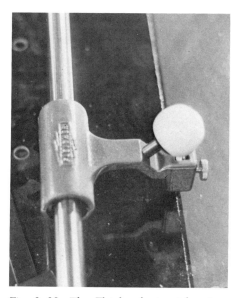

Fig. 3–38. The Fletcher horizontal cutter. Close-up of the score line and the scoring mechanism.

simpler than the Fletcher machine because it is a pivot arrangement using a metal bar to form the angles. This bar is held firmly by screw clamps and so furnishes the hold down as well. A second metal bar serves as a guide to the jig and a brace. The device is quite ingenious and gives accurate cuts time after time.

As a final example, the Cookson and Thode Timesaver is a handy little device—and one of the first on the market—for cutting straight-line shapes without a board as such. The Timesaver uses triangle and straight edge to provide a multiplicity of shapes that can be duplicated so long as you do not change the angle formed by the tool. The straight edge is movable around the perimeter of the triangle, and a combination of these edges forms the guides for your cuts. Thus it is a simple but well-devised unit. Your choice here should be based, as usual, on price range, plus what you want for your money. Essentially all three of these units do the same thing. You choose the degree of sophistication.

Self-Propelled Cutters

We are aware of only one self-propelled cutter, The Great Cut-Up. And speaking of sophistication, who could guess what could be done with rubber bands, a glass cutter, and a hand-turned rod? If you feel that a rubber-band-powered machine cannot be taken seriously (although a spring-loaded one can), you should abandon your snobbism. For spring enthusiasts, the manufacturer offers an option to this machine, but it believes that the rubber-band tension system is superior. It allows an infinite amount of variation of pressures, and the motivating force is easily replaced if a rubber band breaks or stretches out. And it is cheap.

What The Great Cut-Up does is hold and score the glass by itself while you turn a wheel to move the cutter over the surface. If you are cutting a patterned shape, you gently turn the glass so the score lines follow the marked lines. If you want a straight cut, you don't even have to guide the glass; just turn the wheel and the score will appear. How is this done? Simplicity itself. The glass cutter is always held perpendicular to the glass. It maintains absolutely even pressure throughout the score—the net result being a good clean break of the glass. You maintain your pressure with the rubber bands, increasing or decreasing pressure by adding a second rubber band or by changing slots on the central post. You can turn the knob as slowly or fast as you like, although we have found that slow gives better control. And even though you will not hear the sound of the cutter scoring the glass, as you would with hand cutting, you will still end up with a perfect score.

Fig. 3–41. A charming device, the self-propelled cutter called The Great Cut-Up cuts glass by itself. Turning the wheel (left) moves the glass over the rod and under the glass-cutter wheel. Just enough pressure is provided by the rubber-band arrangement to score adequately, so breaking out is no problem. Indeed, this machine scores higher than many of our students for cutting glass.

Fig. 3–42. Cutting to pattern with The Great Cut-Up. All you have to do is turn the wheel and guide the glass.

If you are cutting a pattern, the pattern pieces should be transferred to the glass by tracing around them with a permanent marker, rather than taping them to the glass. With a little practice, you can soon learn to score the glass on the inside edge of the tracing, which will give you perfect fidelity to the pattern piece. This will save you a lot of time by not having to grozze, and it will provide cleaner lead or foil lines because of the superior fit of the pieces. Because of this even score, deeply curved cuts can often be broken out in one piece.

Aside from these technical advantages, The Great Cut-Up makes life a lot easier for those people who can't seem to master hand glass cutting (older people finding this particularly difficult). It allows them to score glass sitting down, thus lessening fatigue by eliminating tired fingers, arms, and legs. Individuals with arthritis are especially made welcome into the glass-cutting craft by The Great Cut-Up, which does the work that they could not possibly do themselves.

Of course, this machine is not for everyone or for all glass scoring. If you can score accurately freehand, you would just be slowed down by it. If you have many straight lines to score, you would be better off using a cutting board, or the freehand-and-ruler technique. The same is true for breaking down large pieces of glass to pattern or cutting circles. Nor should this machine encourage you to avoid learning to cut by hand. At the same time, it can be at the very least a security item; at the most, it can be a production device, permitting you to get into the decorating phase of glass crafting more rapidly. It is among the more versatile of all the new machines, despite its deceptively simple exterior.

Glass Routers

Glass routers and grinders, all motor driven, produce odd shapes—curved as well as straight, inside curves, pieces containing holes, multifaceted pieces, sinuous shapes, shapes simple, and shapes as complex as a piece from a picture puzzle. These machines are technically "shapers," and they all work by holding the glass against a spinning central rod that is embedded with abrasive particles. Unlike the duplicators, these units are not particularized for turning out the same shape over and over, although that can be done. Instead, they are meant to produce pieces of glass that technically cannot be cut because the scored lines would not be able to be broken out of a single piece. Some of the shapes produced by these machines would require several pieces of glass cut the ordinary way to provide the same effect. The closest you could get usually to matching one of these pieces would be by slow and lengthy grozzing with a pliers, which, three out of five times, would take several pieces of glass before a final product would emerge unbroken.

A diamond router therefore is really an automatic grozzer. It incorporates a diamond grinding wheel to do the work otherwise done by hand. The wheel, whirling round at high speed, grinds the edge of the glass to the ordained design. It does this rapidly, and, depending on the precision of the tool, accurately. Diamond grit is used as the abrasive medium.

Since glass does not always respond well to transfiguration, we have selected several machines to provide examples. But before we get into specifics, let's look at some generalities.

First, diamond shapers—that is, glass routers and grinders—are not dangerous. Obviously this is strictly an individual opinion, since anything is dangerous if misused or used carelessly. If you abide by the few rules for safety, however, you can operate your grinder with no more risk than you would find from your dishwasher. As a novice in the craft, you will have power at your fingertips in a medium that now lets you start right in and create, to invent intricate shapes that not even a cutter experienced in the field for years could duplicate by hand.

Second, one might assume that because diamonds are involved, such machines are prohibitively expensive. Not so. The diamonds are industrial ones, either mined or man-made. The diamonds make up only a

Fused panel   *Anita Isenberg*

Fishbowl
Anita Isenberg

Glass rose with leaves
Seymour Isenberg

Medallion   *Kay Kish*
Bird   *Anita Isenberg*

Poinsettia candleholder   *Anita Isenberg*

Indented shield   *Anita Isenberg*

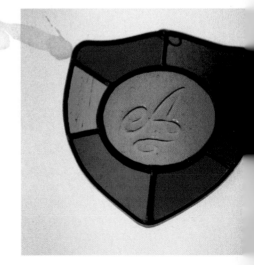

Bathroom mirror
Anita and Seymour Isenberg

Glass flowers in vase
Anita Isenberg

Branch with leaves
Seymour Isenberg

"Old Cheyenne"   *Marie Snell*

Fused figurines
Anita Isenberg

Scarecrow and wheelbarrow
Anita Isenberg

Fused glass abstract
Boyce Lundstrom,
Bullseye Glass

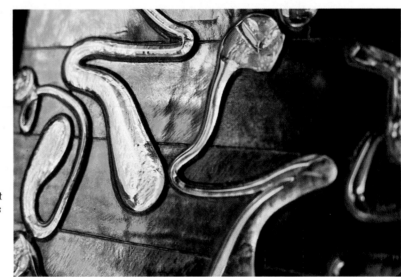

Fused glass abstract
Boyce Lundstrom, Bullseye Glass

Fused Christmas wreath and tree
Anita Isenberg

"Lilies of the Field"   *Barbara Saull*

Decorated dish   *Marvin Riddle*

Bird dish   *Charles Cantor*

Flowered candy dish   *Marvin Riddle*

Lion plate   *Seymour Isenberg*

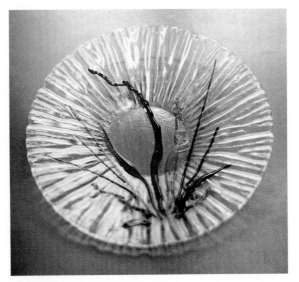

Dish overlaid with colored glass rods   *Anita Isenberg*

Flower motif plate

Fig. 3–45. Grozzing with the Glastar grinder. The protective shelf is in place. The thinner top grinding wheel is also fixed with particles on top for putting holes of its diameter in glass. This is the grinder we use in the Projects Section for the Flower Wheelbarrow. We keep plastic under all grinders to protect the working surface from moisture.

Fig. 3–43. Grozzing with the Glasscrafter grinder. Even the most delicate piece (in this case a glass flower) can be ground with no fear of breakage.

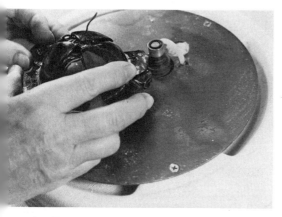

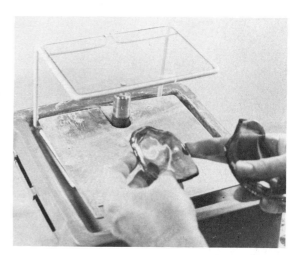

Fig. 3–44. Close-up of the same flower against the grinding wheel. Note the different diameter working surfaces on the wheel. Water for lubricating is kept in the reservoir directly below the top holding plate.

Fig. 3–46. Close-up of the Glastar grinder showing the pattern cut in the glass. It is smooth and precise—and fast.

small portion of the grinding surface of the router. This little bit tends to go a long way, however; even a small amount of diamond will cut a surprisingly large amount of glass. For instance, a few carets of industrial diamond crystals will grind several hundred pounds of glass into powder.

The functioning surface of any routing tool is the head. Here you want dependability and precision. Both factors depend on the bonding of the diamonds to the metal forming the base of the mechanism. Two basic methods are used to bond diamonds onto the router tool. One is to electroplate the diamond crystals onto the head; the other is to impregnate them in a metal matrix around the tool. There is a great difference of opinion as to which method provides the best tool for the money. On one hand, electroplating provides only a single layer of diamond crystals on the core, and as these wear away you must replace the head. On the other hand, the impregnation method uses temperature and pressure to bond a mix of diamond and metal powders to the core, which gives several layers of diamond crystals. As one layer wears away, another is revealed. All the same, the electroplating method seems to hold up best for glass work. Even though the life of the wheel is shorter, you get a truer cut with the single wearing surface. While impregnation may last longer as a cutting surface, it is not the *same* cutting surface.

Let's look at some of the advantages of these diamond routers:

1. *Speed and precision of acquiring the shape.* Since you are dealing with one distinct activity, you come up immediately with your shape, as opposed to an odd-shape cutting machine, where you still must break out your score lines.
2. *Salvage of glass.* Practically no breakage.
3. *Ease of operation.* There is no comparison to hand grozzing. Hand grozzing always involves risk of the glass fracturing at a critical point. This can happen with the router, but it is far more unlikely.
4. *Time saving.* As opposed to almost any other procedure.
5. *Precision.* Even the novice can produce a piece of glass containing intricate cuts.
6. *Adaptability.* Although glass varies in hardness, any glass that is typically used in a studio or hobby workshop—plate, single or double strength, imported or domestic glass, cathedral or opalescent—is suitable for shaping with the router.

That these are practically self-governing machines doesn't mean you shouldn't take care. You must be careful that the diamond router doesn't scratch the glass, for instance. Keep all work surfaces as clean as possible when the machine is in use. Don't use your machine as a novelty: Each time you use it, the router bit tends to wear and the diamond particles begin to flatten. This causes an increased load on the particle bonding, which eventually lets go of its hold on the worn-out diamond.

Glass is a poor conductor of heat and tends to expand irregularly. Therefore, simply to grind glass against any surface would be disastrous in the long run. The heat of friction would cause the glass to crack. It also causes increased wear on the diamond head. The way out of this is to supply a coolant. Special water-based coolants have been designed that help to decrease friction and wear. These coolants also make the grinding process smoother and provide the ground edge of the glass with a better finish. Most diamond routers are supplied with a coolant sponge or wick, which rests in a reservoir that is filled with the coolant mixture. Many routers simply use water, although check with the manufacturer of yours to see what is recommended.

Safety Measures

Getting cut by placing your hand against the diamond bit while it is revolving is a logical conclusion. Why so many workers test their machines in this fashion is puzzling—but they do. Probably it will not be the diamond crystals that do the cutting: They are too small. More likely you will get cut from the glass powder embedded in the bit from previous work, or from the sharp edges of the bond. What does the job on your finger is of little consequence; the point is to keep your hands off the router bit.

One way to keep the router from attacking you is to place it on a flat, sturdy surface. We have seen workers balance it on what amounts to a seesaw. It also helps if the surface is water resistant, because of the considerable amount of splashing when you work. Any quality router should be electrically grounded: That means it comes supplied with a three-prong plug. Don't try to get around this by adapting it to a two-prong plug. The grounding is an essential safety measure.

We discourage the use of gloves with the router as we do with any glass work. Especially with machines, gloves give a false sense of security, are bulky, limit flexibility of the fingers, and cause more accidents than they prevent. Eye protection is another matter. Always wear something over your eyes when you use any wheel, belt machine, or device that can send glass flying. Particles of glass in the eye are no fun. And don't depend on your eyeglasses to protect you. Glass can slip under the lenses and still get into the eye, as well as scratching your glasses. Safety goggles should be kept with the machine. They can be slipped on over your regular eyeglasses. Some routers come equipped with, or offer as an option, a sturdy eye shield. While this is a worthwhile addition to your machine, we suggest that you wear safety goggles as a matter of course. Where your eyes are concerned, you can't be too careful.

Always wash your hands after working with your router, especially before handling food. This is another reflex action you should develop. It is surprising how many people forget to do this.

Maintenance

Bit changing should be a smooth, easy activity. With many routers, alas, it is not. A quality router should have removable bits, but not at the expense of your sanity. One of the major difficulties with these units when they first came on the market was in removing the old bit. Today, manufacturers have overcome this, but check this feature before you buy a router.

Diamond-router bits occasionally need to be cleaned (or "dressed," as it is called). An electroplated bit should *not* be dressed because the "dressing stick" will remove important parts of the single layer of material and ruin the head. This is one of the reasons why it is important that you know which kind of head you are using. A head that is made by the impregnated method may be dressed—and should be—because here you have more than one layer of material. The procedure in dressing is to hold the edge of this special dressing stick, which has been soaked in coolant, against the head as it turns. Do this lightly at first, then with increasing pressure, until the diamond starts to abrade the dressing stick. Ask your dealer about this procedure.

Dressing the head removes the glass particles—glass dust, actually—from within the interstices of the cutting head. If you don't do this, the particles will build up and smear over the bond. The diamonds—and the cut you will be trying to accomplish with them—will be ineffectual. Dressing allows the wheel to cut freely and cleanly once again. You will know if your wheel needs to be dressed because the diamond bit will begin to cut more and more slowly. Since the tendency of the worker at this point is to increase the pressure of the glass against the wheel, excessive chipping may begin to occur on the edge of the glass. If you are using an electroplated head, this is the time to replace it.

The average coolant wick should last anywhere from six months to several years, depending on how frequently the machine is used. Replacement sponges are available from your dealer. The sponge must be natural or acetate. Don't ad-lib with a piece of cotton: The fibers will get caught in the router bit.

A good router requires very little overall maintenance. The main feature of maintenance is to clean the machine daily after use to remove all of the glass dust. Use a wet cloth to wipe off the work surface and remove any built-up glass from around the router and the head. The coolant should be changed once a week, whether or not the machine is being used regularly. Most workers we have talked to do not do this—out of sheer laziness, as they admitted. It is also important to keep the motor bearings oiled. Individual machines have directions to tell you where they are and what type of oil to use.

Even with the best of cleaning, you may find that when you turn on the router after not using it for several days it won't cooperate. Check to see if the machine is plugged in. More than half the time, that's the trouble. If it still won't go on, with the switch off and preferably with the machine unplugged, turn the router shaft by hand several times, first one way and then the other. This will free the glass dust that has probably built up around it. It should work after this.

A quality router should not overheat even when it is used for long periods. It will get warm as you use it, but this should be no cause of concern if you have lubricated it according to instructions. Even if you haven't replaced the water-coolant mixture for some time, it shouldn't make a difference to the machine. If the diamond head is properly manufactured, it should not rust, nor should coolant damage the machine base.

The primary concern of beginners who are learning to rout is the diamond head. It sounds expensive, ominous, and daunting. Be realistic: Everything wears out in time. Your diamond head may wear out in some areas and not in others. If very smooth areas begin to show in the bond (under direct vision, not under a magnifying glass), or the cutting becomes erratic, the diamond bit is probably worn out. Don't keep it around for a memento. You can't afford to junk up your workshop, a common error. Dump the core and get a new bit. It is possible to have the old core rebonded, but it hardly pays. You can get a new head for less money. By the time any of these bits go, you should have gotten more than your money's worth in use.

Routing Procedures

There are only a few basic routing procedures, and each one can be modified by individual variation and technique. However, a few points are worth going over if you've never worked with a router for glass crafting:

1. *Pressure.* You supply this. You must hold the surface of the glass against the rotating cutting edge of the head. The more pressure you supply, the deeper and faster the cut will go. The more pressure, the more friction—and the greater the possibility of breaking the glass, especially if it is a

large, fragile piece. The less pressure, the slower the cut, but the more facility you have to maneuver the glass where you want it, and the less likelihood of breaking the glass.

2. *Stability*. Glass can be held against the head from any angle. If you are angling the glass against the head, hold it as steady as possible and use less pressure than you might otherwise use, since the glass may wobble. If you hold the glass flat to the head, you can use more pressure because the glass is more stable, being supported by the plate of the machine.

3. *Chipping*. One reason why large chips are created is because the protruding edge of an irregularly cut piece of glass crumbles rather than grinds against the head. Usually this happens with very thick glass. The lack of support of this thin shelf is what causes the problem. You can overcome this difficulty in one of two ways. The first is to lay the glass with the protruding edge up, tilt the piece forward at about a 45-degree angle, and feed it with moderate pressure against the head. Or, second, lay the glass flat against the plate of the machine with the protruding edge down, and feed it against the head in this manner. Either way, you will expose a minimum of the surface with as much support as possible. In either method, you should exert minimum pressure until the protruding surface is ground away.

4. *Placement*. A diamond router can be used anywhere, but they can cause a mess, so it is best to use it in an easily cleanable location. You will end up enjoying it more.

5. *Guidance*. Where straight lines are being routed to polish off excess chips of the glass edge, it is best to use a guide and not trust a freehand technique. You are dealing with a whirling circle; the slightest slip of your hand will cause the machine to dig out a portion of your straight edge. Just the slightest bit will ruin the edge, and it is hard to tell by eye alone if this is happening. You will find out quickly enough, however, once you hold up the glass. Now you are faced with another restraightening procedure to get out this indentation. You can keep this up until you have reduced your glass to powder—or you can use a straight edge.

6. *Duplication*. Where you have two pieces of glass in which the intricate cuts are the same, you can do them both together. This will not only save extra work, but it will assure you of exactness. We use masking tape to hold the pieces together firmly. This keeps them from creeping apart dur-

ing the grinding process. Where more than two pieces have to be cut and the glass is thin, try taping the three pieces together. We do not recommend this if the glass is fairly thick—that is, double strength or plate—but semi-antique and picture glass can be sandwiched in this manner.

You can cut a pattern with a router in two ways. The first way is to trace the pattern onto your glass blank with a glass-marking pencil. These lines will usually stay on the glass as you work, unless you smear them pretty heavily. Just use them as a guide while grinding. The second way is to tape the actual pattern, cut from pattern paper, onto the glass and (using this as a guide and going slowly while exerting little pressure where the cuts are the most intricate) grind to the paper edges. Don't go *into* the paper edges. With care and practice, you can duplicate patterns very precisely with either of these methods.

Note: We are indebted to Inland Craft Products Co. for much of the above information.

Glass Grinders

It is difficult to choose "the best" glass grinder because there are so many. Grinders have all but duplicated themselves over the past few years, so we have selected those that we feel most comfortable with.

The first is made by Glastar. Like the other grinder companies, this one is highly reputable, quick to respond to questions, and courteous in the extreme. The Glastar cutting head is a solid one-piece unit that attaches to the motor shaft with a set screw. This is a critical feature: If the head is held to the shaft strictly by pressure (as is the case with some units), you may have trouble getting it off when it comes time to replace it. It is better if it is held by a set screw, but don't be too sure it is. This set screw must be precisely ground and fitted or the head will wobble during operation and cause erratic cuts. The Glastar head is simple to replace; the set screw is precisely fitted, so there is no wobble of the head. The screw stays tight throughout the grinding process, yet it will turn without inordinate force being applied when you want to replace or change the head. The cutting head, motor shaft, and set screw are all made of stainless steel, and the cutting head is guaranteed against the diamond surface peeling off. Glastar uses the electroplating technique to attach the diamonds to the core of the head. They claim the diamond cutting surface will last between 100 and 150 hours: That means each head will grozze thousands of pieces of glass. We used ours for about that length of time and find the head still effective. And we haven't experienced any trouble with the mechanics of the machine.

The diamond cutting head is $\frac{3}{4}$ inch in diameter so that it can be used to grozze small inside curves. An even smaller head, available as an accessory, can be mounted directly above the primary cutting head without removing it. The diamond surface of the head extends $\frac{3}{8}$ inch above the table, so when the bottom half of the diamond becomes worn, the head can be lowered to provide a new cutting surface. As the head rotates, it pumps water into the sponge, which is mounted directly behind and against the cutting head. The wet sponge keeps the diamond cutting surface clean and cool and ensures against flying glass dust (or at least it minimizes this hazard). The head is driven by a 3,200-rpm motor with permanently lubricated ball bearings. The off/on switch (a must in any of these machines) is mounted conveniently on the front of the unit and is totally insulated to avoid any possible shock hazard. The water system (water is the coolant by itself) has no seals to wear out, so there is no leakage. A 7 by 7 inch metal table provides a smooth working surface free of obstructions, making it possible to shape very large pieces of glass.

Optional equipment is available, such as an eye shield, an adjustable straight-edge guide, a small grinding head, and an extra-smooth grinding head. The item that we find especially useful is the adjustable straight-edge guide, although all the items are designed for flexibility of use and comfort. The straight-edge guide allows you to grind straight edges to exact dimension, accommodating rectangles from $\frac{3}{8}$ inch up to 4 inches in width. For instance, if you have cut a rectangle oversize, you can set the guide to the correct width and push the glass between the guide and the cutting head, thus grinding the glass to the right size and making the sides perfectly parallel.

We feel that the eye shield should not take the place of safety goggles. It helps mostly in keeping glass dust from scattering throughout the work area, although with any of these machines we have not found this to be much of a problem so long as the proper sponge is used against the head.

The small grinding head is very nice to have. It is $\frac{1}{4}$ inch in diameter and is designed for work on very tight inside curves. It is the smallest cutting head we know of, and it has diamonds covering the top surface as well as the sides so that it can be used to grind a hole in a piece of glass: A cute trick, and a useful one. The extra smooth grinding head is a luxury item. We have found little chipping of the glass with the regular head. By controlling the pressure of the glass against the well-engineered head, you can get a fine, smooth cut that needs no improvement. However, if you want an extra smooth head to make up for sloppy technique, it is available. You always pay for poor technique one way or another. The extra smooth head cuts more slowly than does the standard head. An optional foot switch is also available. Glastar has a limited one-year warranty that does not cover wear of the diamond grinding surface.

A second machine, although not second in capability, is the Glasscrafter Mark IV. This is an advanced model in a line of units put out by this company. Here the grinding sleeve is a fused diamond/metal matrix. This means that the diamond particles are distributed throughout the thickness of the grinding ring. To achieve maximum grinding efficiency and life expectancy, Glasscrafter advises the following:

1. Adjust the sleeve up and down often along the shaft to equalize the wear. Extended grinding with the sleeve located in one position will groove the sleeve, create grinding problems, and seriously shorten the life of the sleeve. Each time an adjustment is made, add a few drops of oil in the top of the sleeve and motor shaft to prevent sticking and corrosion.
2. Make sure that the grinding sleeve is getting adequate water from the sponge. Clean the sponge periodically. Remove it and wash it in warm water.
3. This unit also uses water as the coolant. To get your machine ready for use, pour a cup of water into the trough, dampen the sponge, and make sure that it is against the grinding sleeve. The basin should be washed out periodically to prevent excess silica build up. You can remove the surface plate for hand cleaning.

   When cleaning this or any other electrical unit, be careful that water doesn't get into the motor. Always wipe the shaft of the motor clean, and even turn the machine upside down to get all the water away from the motor. This holds true for the electrical plug as well.

The Glasscrafter comes equipped with two hole cutters. This is a fascinating and practical activity that may be worth the whole cost of the machine to you. One option on the machine is a straight-edge guide, or fence, to help maintain an even border. Instructions for its attachment are included.

A word about cutting holes in glass with these machines: This can be dangerous if you don't follow the instructions that come with the machine. We found one suggestion, of putting clear tape over the section of the glass to be worked on, a necessity. The tape holds onto glass chips as well as the core portion of the hole. When doing a large cutout, make a number of holes, then score and break out the inside sections.

Another fine machine is the Wizard, made by Inland Craft Products Company. This machine has been engineered to be simple to operate and yet be highly durable. No assembly is required. It is an electrically grounded machine and should be used as designed: That means the three-pronged cord plug should not be adapted to a two-prong socket. The machine should be used on a flat, rigid surface. A height of 42 inches is sufficient for most workers. A splash guard is set up behind the water-coolant reservoir.

Before this unit is plugged in, 8 to 10 ounces of water should be put into the reservoir. The Wizard manufacturer recommends using their own water-soluble coolant, available from the dealer.

The Wizard has an extensive array of router bits. You can acquire just about any shape you can think of to grozze the glass form of your dreams. Each bit has more than half an inch of usable diamond surface. According to the manufacturer, this is the most usable diamond provided with any grinder on the market today. By adjusting the bit up and down on the shaft, you should be able to get three or four usable grinding surfaces, depending on the width of glass. Adjustment of the bit on the shaft is accomplished by loosening the set screw in the bit with the Allen wrench that is provided with the unit.

The Wizard grinder is constructed of heavy-duty glass-filled polymers. The motor is a 3,400-rpm, 115-volt, 60-cycle split-capacitator unit. It has permanently lubricated ball bearings and a stainless steel shell. We suggest, as does the manufacturer, that you use its water-soluble coolant. It makes the machine run and work very smoothly, and the bit cuts more efficiently because of the lack of friction, which increases the life of the diamond head and makes the cleanup easier. This specific coolant also prevents seizure of the bit to the motor shaft because the coolant acts as a corrosion inhibitor.

We have used all three machines, and we have watched others using them. Each is a superior product. Individual variations may appeal to some workers and be disdained by others. The Wizard, for example, was designed with a "lift-off" top system, which we like very much. When the reservoir of the machine needs to be cleaned, the work surface is simply lifted off. There are no screws or bolts to remove or get lost. This makes cleaning a simple procedure, not a cumbersome task. The Wizard is available with a soft rubber work surface that can be temporarily or permanently attached to a "lift-off" work surface. This special surface prevents scratching when grinding soft or antique glass. The Wizard also has a simple to use, premounted straight edge that can be purchased as the primary lift-off work surface with the machine, or as a secondary lift-off surface at a later date. In short, these are three fine machines.

Foiling Machines

The art of copper foiling is an intrinsic part of crafting in glass. Many workers, in fact, use copper foil almost exclusively, relegating the leading procedure to large windows. At the same time, foiling can be tedious, and the tedium can lead to a sloppy procedure. Foiling machines have two purposes: (1) to cut down the foiling time, and (2) to make precision folds of copper over the glass edge instead of irregular, sloppy folds.

All these units work on the principle of feeding the foil from the roll into a grooved wheel that forms it evenly over the glass edge. As this wheel is turned, either by hand or by electricity, the foil is advanced, the backing is stripped away, and the glass edge is neatly trimmed with the metal. To a greater or lesser extent, these machines also crimp the foil tightly and smoothly to the glass. Here handcrafting is more effective than the machine, for in no case is the copper edge finished as well as by hand. But, considering the time saved, the small difference is hardly noticeable.

Foilers are available in all price ranges, from motor driven to hand operated, from single- to multiple-size copper foil, from wood to plastic. There are too many to review, but we will mention a few that we've found to be the best.

The Mark II and the Foiling Process

As a prototype, we will use the Mark II Foil Wrapping Machine made by Lamps Ltd. This quality unit comes completely assembled (an important point) except for two reels, two hold-down arm assemblies, and four wood screws. These are bagged separately in the packing box. Extra washer shims are provided around the forming wheel shaft. There are two sets of wheels on this machine; both are mounted with washer shims installed between the wheel halves. Each forming wheel (the wheel that applies and crimps the copper to the glass edge) is really a half-wheel made of soft but durable plastic. Separations between wheels allow for different size foil widths to be used. Washer shims are used for the separations.

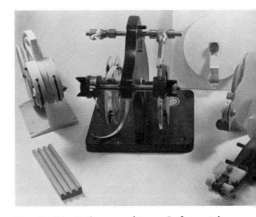

Fig. 3–47. Foiling machines. Left to right: Sunshine Glass Works, Lamps Ltd. Mark II, Diegel's Foil-O-Matic, Stanford's unit and the machine from Philadelphia Resources.

While many workers consider a copper foiling machine a luxury, we disagree. A Tiffany-style small pieced lamp or window could be done in far less time with the assistance of one of these machines than if you hand foil all the pieces. In addition to saving time, the foiled pieces come out so evenly that they give a truly professional touch to the entire project. And this result is worth it whether you are foiling several hundred pieces or a mere dozen. The Mark II exemplifies what a good foiler should be. Most important, it allows for proper groove setting for the different thicknesses of glass.

In the Mark II, when the forming wheel wears appreciably, the washer shims can be removed to maintain the correct gap dimension. A proper gap dimension will allow for a slight wiping action against the glass by the sides of the wheels. Try this before using any foil. If the glass must be forced into the slot, or if there is a tight wiping action against the sides of the glass, the groove is too narrow. Some copper foiling machines do not have any accommodation for this. The glass wobbles in the groove, and the machine will not give a precise overlay of copper. Other foilers have two wheels, preset, for the most common widths. We prefer half-wheels that can be set for individual glass thicknesses. Once you have adjusted the width of your wheel to the width of the glass, you can't help but get the ultimate foiling result. Once you have set the width of your wheel to the glass dimension, it becomes a simple matter to foil continuously. If you change to another glass width, just take out or put in the appropriate number of shims.

To start the foil-wrapping operation in almost all the machines, but especially in the Mark II, advance the copper tape to $\frac{1}{2}$ inch beyond the cutting edge of the hold-down blade. This is done by pressing on the blade with the index finger of one hand and rotating the wheel with the other hand, turning one of the wing nuts of the wheel containing the foil. You now have a small area of foil exposed and ready to use. Hold your glass piece in one hand, place it onto the foil (which has its sticky side up, the backing peeled off), and press down into the slot of the forming wheel. The sides of the wheel will crimp the foil evenly to the glass sides, and the bottom of the slot presses the foil directly to the glass edge.

Now, guiding the glass with one hand, use your other hand to turn the wheel simultaneously as you turn the glass against the forming wheel. In this process, you are feeding tape (foil) at the same rate that you are turning the glass piece to receive it. You can use both hands on the glass piece if you prefer, pressing down on the forming wheel as a pully, which will cause

Fig. 3–48. The Mark II by Lamps Ltd.

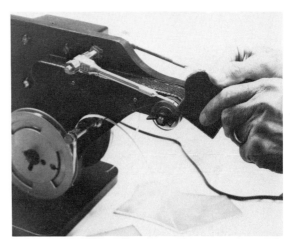

Fig. 3–50. The Mark II in action.

Fig. 3–49. The foiling process is a simple one, if you have a good foiler. Here is Lamps Ltd. Mark II. Copper tape (foil) stretches from the feed wheel to the forming wheel. The backing is automatically removed. The copper foil wraps and crimps automatically around the piece of glass as it is hand-turned between the forming wheels. We have best results when the forming wheels are pliable.

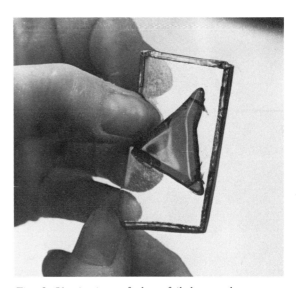

Fig. 3–51. A piece of glass, foiled around three edges, as it comes from the machine.

the wheel supplying the foil to turn on its own. The foil pulls the wheel round as you use it. It is essential that the foiling machine be attached securely to a table or it will tip over. For the Mark II, there are screws and mounting holes in the base for this purpose. Most foiling machines have this accommodation, but look for it before you buy.

Hand foiling with the Mark II (or any foiler, for that matter) uses very little energy. However, electric models, complete with foot pedal, are also available. Whether motor or hand driven, the process of foiling is exactly the same. The only difference is in the prices of the machines and what extra attachments you want.

Although many workers sit down to foil, we tested all units from a standing position, since we find that this gives a better sight line of the work. We prefer to look *over* the forming wheel rather than *into* it. A high stool will provide comfort and vision. We don't suggest sitting in a chair with your eyes below the forming wheel. This allows you to hold the glass at a slight angle, which eventually will result in foiling too much on one side or the other. Remember to hold the glass as vertically as possible. This is much easier to do if you are viewing it from the top edge of the forming wheel. Both large and small pieces of glass can be used. Choose the method of wrapping that suits you most comfortably, whether using both hands on the glass or one hand on the wheel to guide it.

Once the glass is almost completely wrapped with foil, you should proceed more slowly, leaving about $\frac{1}{2}$ inch of glass edge unwrapped. With the Mark II, you can use your index finger to press down on the knife blade, pull upward on the foil, and sever it. The loose end remaining can be fastened down by hand to complete the wrapping cycle. There should be a slight overlap of the ends of the foil, but there should be no gap. A little practice will give you the feel for it.

As we mentioned, the problem with all foiling machines is the loose crimping of the edges of the foil against the glass. While the foil is pressed down adequately enough to grab the glass, it usually has little ripples in it. This means that you must smooth it down by hand, using the flat edge of a knife or similar object. Small tools called "crimpers" can be used to press the foil evenly. All foiling machines we have seen are a bit shamefaced in this regard.

Other Foilers

A device that is very effective in flattening the foil against the glass is Diegel Engineering's Kwik-Krimp. While this is not a foiling machine per se, it can be attached to Diegel's Foil-O-Matic machine, or it can be held by hand. It crimps and seals applied foil in one sweep of the unit. Like the Mark II, this unit deserves a favorable rating. It is less luxurious than the Mark II, but it has many of the same features. The paper backing is automatically peeled off the foil and guided away from the work area. It can be set to fall into a waste basket. Reels to hold the foil are adjustable for $\frac{3}{16}$-inch, $\frac{7}{32}$-inch, $\frac{1}{4}$-inch, $\frac{5}{16}$-inch, and $\frac{3}{8}$-inch foil sizes. Specially designed guides hold the glass firmly in position so as to minimize as much as possible the off-centering of foil along the glass edge. According to the manufacturer, the worker has to manipulate only the glass and the foiling takes care of itself. We have found this to be the case. The unit will maintain the centerline with the foil. This means that even if you have never foiled a

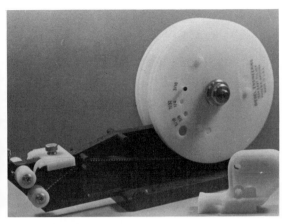

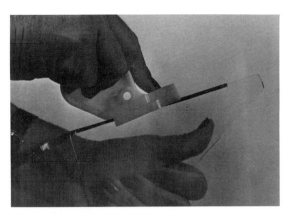

Fig. 3–52. Diegel Engineering's foiler and Kwik-Krimp.

Fig. 3–54. As the Kwik-Krimp is pushed along, it automatically flattens the foil to either side neatly and effectively. It works equally well on curves.

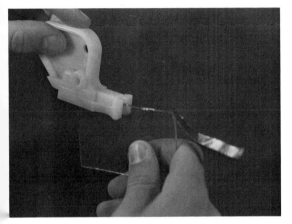

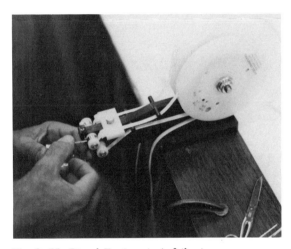

Fig. 3–53. The Kwik-Krimp in action. Copper foil is applied to the glass but is not folded down along the edges. The Kwik-Krimp has a groove that fits over the glass edge and the copper foil.

Fig. 3–55. Diegel Engineering's foiler in action.

piece of glass before, you can come out with a fine, professionally wrapped piece. This is true despite the hard plastic rollers with precut grooves for the difference in glass (foil) sizes. Some workers may prefer the soft form rollers with maneuverable spacing.

Some of our students found the directions confusing. There are five diagrams, several of which seem redundant, and the plethora of arrows and figures are more daunting than helpful. We think you'll be happy with the machine once you use it; it's easier than the diagrams make it look.

The hand-operated Copper Foiling Machine by Sunshine Glass Works is a low-price instrument but a formidable one. It dispenses both $\frac{3}{16}$-inch and $\frac{1}{4}$-inch copper foil, removes the backing as it operates, centers and crimps the foil over the edges of the glass, and does

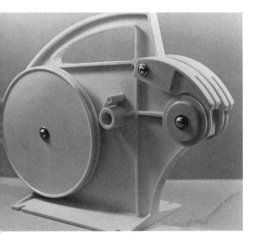

Fig. 3–56. Sunshine Glass Works' foiler

Fig. 3–57. Stanford Engineering's foiler.

Fig. 3–58. Philadelphia Resources' foiler.

straight lines, as well as inside and outside curves. The foil backing is removed by a backward-thrusting straight edge. The waste backing, however, comes back over the supply wheel and can tangle. The forming wheels are plastic, as in the Diegel machine. However, a rubber bushing in each wheel provides a "give" to the glass. Spaces between the forming wheels are fixed for the two sizes of foil. Over each wheel are guide slots that pivot to allow easy access to the foiling wheel. The bushings are the same size both for the narrow and the larger forming wheels. A wider bushing in the larger space would be more desirable, though.

Sunshine suggests that for ease of wrapping and best results, the glass edges should be ground lightly to prevent the glass from cutting through the foil. In fact, this is a good idea with all foiling machines. There is also the possibility that some foil that is wrapped on cardboard spools may not fit the supply wheels. If so, you should peel off one layer of cardboard from the inside of the spool and refit it. Don't remove too much or the fit will be too loose and the roll will joggle.

To use the machine, peel the backing from the end of the foil and feed it through the edge of the splitter. Copper foil (adhesive side up, as usual) goes under the straight edge of the wedge, or splitter, and directly to the foiling wheel. The machine is designed basically for $\frac{1}{8}$-inch glass. For best results, use copper foil gauge .0015 to .002.

The Sunshine machine doesn't have the versatility of the other two, but it works well for what it claims to do, and its low price and stability are attractive. We tested it on a number of our students and other workers, and the consensus was that it was a good buy for the money.

Stained Glass Design's Elite "1" is an automatic foil-wrapping machine that can step up the production of mass-produced items. It is a durable, precision-made machine designed and developed for stained-glass craftspeople by stained-glass craftspeople. The Elite is constructed of solid, heavy-gauge aluminum with a tough anodized gold finish. The motor, high quality and built to last, comes equipped with a foot clutch that allows you to have both hands free to hold and wrap the glass. The complete Elite "1" package includes three wrapping (forming) wheels that, according to the manufacturer, are designed to give the best possible wrap of foil on glass. Forming wheel sizes are for $\frac{3}{16}$-inch, $\frac{7}{32}$-inch, and $\frac{1}{4}$-inch foil.

The Elite "1" is similar in operation to the Mark II automated unit. Both are tough machines that do a good job, although we wish the Elite did not turn the backing back onto the feed wheel, a tendency that many of these foilers have. It would seem more logical and more satisfactory to turn the backing toward the floor. All the same, this is a highly recommended unit and one that will do a fine job for you if you want automation.

Probably the foiler with the least amount of frills is that made by Stanford Engineering, called simply the Copper Foil Dispenser, which consists of a single wheel with anchoring screws. It is strictly a hand-powered unit designed to allow "foiling without foul-up," since the foil tension is set by tightening the axle to individual preference. The feed wheel (there is no forming wheel) can be set to different widths to accommodate the different sizes of foil: The dispenser will hold $\frac{3}{16}$-inch copper foil and up. Crimping as well as tape application must be done by hand. The wheel acts simply as a dispenser. This is about as basic as you can get, and some may feel it's too basic.

Philadelphia Resources manufactures a Glass Foiler, which is somewhat more complex than Stanford's. It is basically the same idea, but it has a forming wheel and a boss to separate the backing. We do not agree with the manufacturer's boast that it is the most advanced glass foiler on the market, but it may suit your purpose if you want a compact unit with more working parts than the Stanford. This unit also has a "metal cutter" to cut the foil when you have finished the foiling process. Interchangeable feed wheels with firm rubber bushings are available for different sizes of tape.

In addition to the assembled machine are hard plastic forming wheels for $\frac{3}{16}$-inch, $\frac{7}{32}$-inch, and $\frac{3}{8}$-inch copper foil. Each wheel consists of two color-coded halves, and the colors should not be mixed. The machine must be mounted on a steady table or, if portability is desired, on a piece of board. It is too lightweight to function otherwise. If you want to fix the machine to a table, fasten the body so that the forming wheel hangs over the edge of the surface. This will allow you to wrap long pieces. To wrap long, curved pieces, you should have a work surface with open space beneath its top so that the glass can swing under the table while being wrapped. The machine we tested worked well and provided reasonable accuracy. Our original fear was that the retainer wheel (the wheel holding the copper foil roll) would come off, since it is held only by the pressure of the bushing, and by this alone it must cling to the roll of foil. However, this did not happen when we used the machine. At the same time, we feel this bushing must be a source of wear and eventually the wheel may become loose. Some type of screw-in device might better serve the purpose. At least, it will provide a more scientific approach, to say nothing of added security.

Fig. 3–59. Anderson's hand lead chopper is razor sharp, so we keep it in a sponge, edge first. It balances on the T-crossbar when used with came lead.

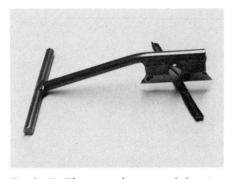

Fig. 3–60. The came chopper angled against a piece of lead came.

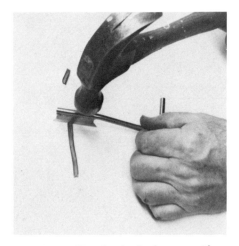

Fig. 3–61. Hit the lead chopper with a hammer sharply and watch the lead come clean.

Lead Cutters

Lead cutters will cut lead came, reinforcing rods, and reinforced lead to specific sizes and angles, and they do this more readily and accurately than a leading knife. This doesn't mean that the leading knife is obsolete. Whether or not you use a lead cutter, the leading knife remains an essential tool. Lead-cutting devices are useful for those workers who cannot supply the force to cut came with a knife. The reason may be age, arthritis, a disability or handicap, or sheer frustration at continually crushing the lead with the knife. They also come in handy for the person who cuts so much came—for lamps or windows, for example—that cutting it by hand becomes impractical. We've cut a lot of lead came in our time, and small dimensions usually aren't a problem, except for the extra time involved. However, spending the day cutting the heavy stuff—$\frac{3}{4}$ inch round H, or $\frac{1}{2}$ inch, or hacksawing reinforced came—can be exhausting. These devices will not only cut the came faster than you can do it by hand, but they will maintain a proper angle right through the came, thus doing away with the usual trimming. And they won't crush the lead. Thus time and patience are well served.

Lead Choppers

Several imaginative choppers are available for doing easy cutting. Two of them are made by the same company: Anderson's Stained Glass. The more simplified variety of lead chopper is ingeniously straightforward. In effect, it is a sharp cutting edge within a balancing handle. You place the edge (a commercial razor blade) atop a piece of lead came at whatever angle you desire, hit the top smartly with a hammer, and, presto, there's your lead, cut neatly and without crushing. This device can even double as a lead knife. It can be used during the "leading-up" operation just with hand pressure. A slight wriggling back and forth will drive the blade through lead up to and including $\frac{1}{4}$ inch with little difficulty. Blades are replaceable.

A note of Warning: It is a good idea to keep several sheets of paper under this hand chopper to preserve the table surface. Heavy cardboard is even better. Our experience with this device proves its efficacy. Most workers we tried it on were delighted; all were impressed, especially those working on a large lead production for standard lengths and angles, as for lamp production. But this chopper is equally useful and efficient when you are doing one length at a time. If you have a number of lengths to get ready, all you need is a jig.

The Anderson Electric Lead Chopper works on the

same principle as the hand chopper. Considering the increased cost of this machine over its more modest cousin, it is more applicable to mass-production work. All the same, it is nice to have around the workbench because of its sheer effectiveness, to say nothing of what it does for one's self esteem and morale. Even the part-time hobbyist can save time for more creative labor with this device.

The machine is designed so that a powerful 40-ounce solenoid pushes the blade through the came as the pushbutton is pressed. The blade retracts automatically as the button is released. A hold-down bar is provided to position the came for cutting and also to act as a safety guard. The blade cuts instantly. The unit is factory set, and no adjustment or maintenance is required. We have used ours in the studio for more than a year with no difficulty whatsoever. This instrument is especially a great help for older people who cannot muster the strength to cut lead came with a knife, or who might even have difficulty using a hammer with the hand-unit chopper. If you teach glass crafting that involves leading or are considering doing so, you might want to have this machine in your studio for your students. It will make their apprentice work professional in appearance by giving their leading the proper angles and lengths without crushing the came.

Blades for the lead chopper are easily replaced, and spares are included with the unit. Actually any utility-knife blade of $\frac{3}{4}$ inch height can be used. Blade life may average from three to six months with moderate usage. With fairly constant use, we find that blades wear out after about two months. Our overall impression of this machine is that it is for the serious worker or teacher. It produces more work with less effort. The safety factor is always something to consider in any machine using power and a sharp blade. Since there is no off/on switch on the model we tested, we suggest you leave the machine unplugged when it is not in use. For ease of operation, it is easier to keep the unit ready for use, but several times when we did this, we brushed up against the unit and set it off. The electrical unit is 6 by 7 by $8\frac{1}{2}$ inches high. Shipping weight is $6\frac{1}{4}$ pounds.

Saws

Window Works offers an attractive device, the CS-1 Lead Came Saw. A circular steel blade 3 inches in diameter is attached to a small motor, which in turn is attached to a wooden handle hinged to an upright. The whole thing is lifted to a height of $\frac{3}{4}$ inch, allowing plenty of room for the came to be slipped beneath. A button conveniently located on the handle sets the saw in motion; the weight of the motor furnishes all the

Fig. 3–62. Anderson's electric lead chopper, showing the guiderails from the top.

Fig. 3–63. The guiderails from below. The blade comes down with a short, quick slash.

Fig. 3–64. The electric-saw came cutter from Window Works. This handsome unit works as well as it looks.

Fig. 3–65. Window Works' came cutter. The off-on button couldn't be in a more convenient place.

strength needed to do the cutting as you gradually lower it. A plastic shield surrounds the work area to some extent, but you should wear safety goggles all the same. A wooden peg furnishes a stop guide for the came to be sawed. The machine is handsome—made of wood, not plastic—and is a welcome addition to any work table. Angles or straight cuts are easily accomplished, and if you have trouble cutting came by hand, you might try one of these clever inventions to make your glass work more pleasurable.

Pliers

There are a great many tools on the market for glass crafting, and each is effective in its way. But the Diamond Tool and Horseshoe Company's tools are extra special in that they are so finely made, so easily employed, and so friendly to the hand. They are high-quality precision tools especially designed for glass work, and their cushion grips add that little extra bit of luxury to their use. It is a measure of the importance of the glass hobbyist market that such tools are now being produced in this country by a company of the stature of Diamond Tools. Years ago, no American factory would consider making tools for the glass hobbyist.

Of the excellent pliers Diamond makes, one of our favorites is its 8-inch Running Pliers (No. RP–8) for breaking out long scores where breaking in any other way would probably fracture the glass. The pliers have precision jaws curved to allow an even squeeze on both sides of the score line. You line up the score with the guideline on the upper jaw, as usual, set the set screw in the top of the pliers to provide the proper amount of pressure, enough to grip the glass firmly, and squeeze. What's so different about this? Not only does it work, but you have absolutely even pressure to both sides of the score. You come out a winner each time. The hand has an innate wisdom; for those of us who have spent years working with our hands, this "touch" is our most reliable antenna. Diamond's tools appeal to this "hand sense."

Also available—and recommended by everyone we've tried them on—are the nipping pliers to cut lead came. We use No. S–54 RGP. We have found that using nippers on came is difficult to do without crimping the lead. These nippers do not crimp to any appreciable degree, and their flush cutting as well as the trimming and mitering of corners make them just about indispensable.

Three types of glass pliers from Diamond are worth trying. The first is a 6-inch curved-jaw glass-breaking pliers (shown upside down in the Diamond catalogue), No. GC–6. These pliers are as good in precision, wear,

67

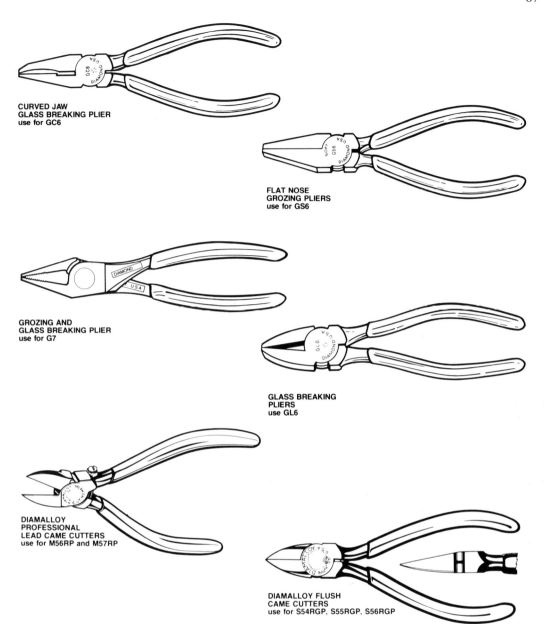

CURVED JAW
GLASS BREAKING PLIER
use for GC6

FLAT NOSE
GROZING PLIERS
use for GS6

GROZING AND
GLASS BREAKING PLIER
use for G7

GLASS BREAKING
PLIERS
use GL6

DIAMALLOY
PROFESSIONAL
LEAD CAME CUTTERS
use for M56RP and M57RP

DIAMALLOY FLUSH
CAME CUTTERS
use for S54RGP, S55RGP, S56RGP

Fig. 3–66. Diamond Tool pliers.

68

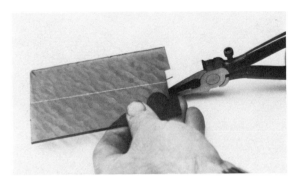

Fig. 3–67.

Fig. 3–68.

Fig. 3–69.

Figs. 3–67, 3–68, and 3–69. Working with Diamond Tool's running pliers. It isn't the amount of pressure that does the trick; it is how you apply it. These pliers help.

Fig. 3–70.

Fig. 3–71.

Figs. 3–70 and 3–71. Diamond's nipping pliers.

Fig. 3–72. Grozzing with Diamond's grozzing pliers. At one time square, the edges have been rounded off with the pliers.

Fig. 3–73. The Diamond grozzing pliers in action, rounding the corners even more. These pliers have strong teeth, but the object in grozzing is to grind, not break, glass. These pliers don't let you forget that.

Fig. 3–74. Breaking with Diamond's breaking pliers. A piece of glass is scored across, the breaking pliers in position to the line.

Fig. 3–75. The glass is neatly snapped at the line, the breaking pliers pulling out and down.

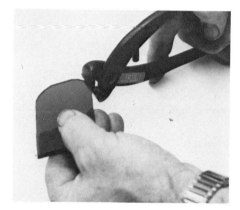

Fig. 3–76.

Fig. 3–77.

Figs. 3–76 and 3–77. Another interesting hand device, Glass Accessories' glass nippers. Instead of grozzing glass, these jaws bite it. The trick is to take small nibbles rather than large chunks. If you handle this tool right, you will have little difficulty in nipping away at rough surfaces or rounding corners.

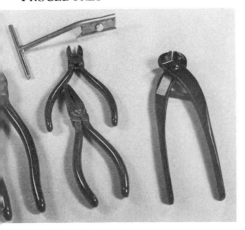

Fig. 3–78. Some of the newer hand tools that you may want to consider. Each in its own way is a delight.

and grozzing ability as the imported German grozzers most of us have for years considered to be the best available. They can also be used as glass-breaking pliers if you want to incorporate two tools in one and save some money.

Two other pliers made by Diamond are for glass breaking. We prefer the 7-inch grozzing/glass breaker for breaking rather than grozzing. It is similar to the standard glass pliers, with a wide jaw and serrated areas for only *rough* grozzing. These pliers are good for pulling off long strips of glass from a score. For grozzing inside curves and other convoluted surfaces, you are better off with No. GC–6. Wide jaws in a grozzer tend to chip, rather than grozze.

Another pair of pliers is a 6-inch smooth-jaw glass breaker. It lies midway between the GC–6 and the G–7. The design of the jaws gives a good bite to grasp glass that is to be broken out of a circle or wide curve.

Chapter 4

Instant Glass Cutting:
No Strain, No Pain, No Mess

Probably the procedure that tends to keep some people in search of a hobby from going into glass crafting is the cutting of the glass itself. This process has developed into a mystique. Other than being afraid of glass, many people are in awe of it. Have you ever cut a piece of glass in front of someone who doesn't work with the material? The individual may well be amazed to see how you score and break out the piece with apparent ease. Of course, you don't tell the person how long you have practiced.

If you've never cut a piece of glass before, there is no reason why you shouldn't try your hand at it. It's fun. With a few basic instructions and a little effort, you can certainly learn to score and break out simple cuts. And for more complicated cuts, a new device will allow you to do it in practically no time.

Keep in mind the long definition of glass in the Introduction. As a frozen, uncrystallized liquid, glass has no grain, so unlike wood, there is no proper or improper way to score it. Many beginners working with glass think that certain stained glasses have a "grain" because of the pattern impressed on its surface when it is rolled. But this is not true. Of course, not all glasses cut with equal ease, but this has nothing to do with a grain.

Cutting glass is an imprecise term. When you run a sharp edge with a glass-cutter wheel over a glass surface, you are plowing a line through part of its width. *Scoring* glass is really what you are doing, and scoring is the first part of two basic techniques used in all glass cutting.

Scoring Glass

For demonstration purposes, we will use a Fletcher carbide cutter, although any cutter will do. Glass cutting is an art: If you take pride in the way you do it and not look on it simply as a means to an end, you will accomplish more in quantity and quality. A good glass cutter learns to use wrist, hand, fingers, and elbow to advantage.

If you use a standard Fletcher cutter, the "proper" way to hold it, according to the manufacturer, is to place the glass cutter between the first and second fingers. The thumb supports the cutter on the underside. Keep your wrist mobile; don't tighten up your arm during the scoring motion. The wrist is the key. If it locks because you are nervous or trying too hard, the motion will be unnatural. A little practice in holding the cutter is all that most people need. However, if you have trouble with the standard cutter, try any of the others we discussed in Chapter 3. If you at least understand the principles of using the standard cutter, using any other one will be that much easier.

The cutter should form about a 45-degree angle with the glass. The handle of the glass cutter should not rest on the web of the fingers. At first, practice the position on a piece of paper rather than on the glass itself. The glass can be distracting if you are just learning. Once you think you have the movement down, then go to the glass.

Even with the cutter in the correct position and moving it correctly, you may find cutting the glass difficult at first. Therefore, select your practice glass with some forethought. Plate glass is soft and fairly easy to score, but you won't be able to break it. Single-strength glass, thin as it is, is often very tough and can be deceptive. Double-strength glass is probably the best to practice on. You can score and break it with ease after less than half an hour's practice. Be sure to use a good size piece. A piece 4 by 5 inches is adequate. For long cuts, you will want a larger piece. We've seen students busily practicing on shards of glass. The idea is not only to score, but to break out the glass. You'll have trouble with both procedures if you practice on slivers.

Before touching the glass with the cutter, make sure that the glass surface is clean. Soap and water will clean glass better than most of the cleaners on the market, which tend to leave a film that interferes with good scoring. Newspaper is fine for wiping down any glass; when you hear the paper squeak over the surface, you will know the glass is clean. And remember to clean both sides. Dirt on the table side can still form a pressure point and shatter the glass as you score. And if there is dirt or grit on your glass, it will not only ruin the cutter wheel, but it will act as a fulcrum and, as you score over it, will crack the glass.

You are now ready to make the score or cut. Place the glass on a flat surface. It doesn't matter whether you cut directly against a wood tabletop or whether you position your glass upon a surface with more "give" to it. We suggest that you pad the cutting surface with several thicknesses of newspaper or an old carpet. It is critical that all splinters of glass from any previous cutting be brushed away before you use the surface. And, remember, don't brush them away with your hand.

To make a straight cut, draw the cutter along a straight edge only once. Don't go back and forth over the score line, and don't stop and start the cut in the middle. Draw your glass cutter over the surface in one complete sweep. We start at the top edge of the glass and draw the cutter down toward the body, allowing the cutter to run gently off the bottom edge. Other workers prefer to go in the opposite direction, looking "over" the cutter wheel as they push the cutter away from them. Either way is practical; it depends which is most comfortable for you.

For a straight edge, you can use anything that will allow the cutting wheel to score effectively. A metal ruler with a cork backing is fine if it doesn't hold the axle of the cutter so far above the glass that the wheel barely touches. Either use a wheel with a larger diameter or a thinner straight edge. We've seen students in the excitement of the moment go through all the motions perfectly—holding the cutter precisely, positioning the glass, calculating the movement—in short, doing everything but scoring the glass. Remember the cutter wheel must come into sufficient contact with the surface to provide the proper score line. But this doesn't mean that you must use extreme pressure.

It is best to stand up when making the score. The most efficient use of the body is accomplished in this position. The proper amount of leverage can be put onto the cutter from a standing position far more easily than when sitting. Calculate your worktable height to this position. About 36 inches from the floor is about standard. If you are exceptionally tall or short, compensate accordingly. Standing up also allows you to distribute the weight of your body toward the cutting. Too many experienced glass crafters have the notion that cutting glass means muscling it. In fact, the opposite is true. Specific, calculated pressure rather than brute force is the secret to good glass cutting. This produces accurate results over long periods of time without wearing you out.

Pressure in glass cutting comes mostly from the shoulder, down the arm to the wrist, and then guided through the fingers to the cutting wheel. If you are right-handed, you would stand with your left side turned slightly into the table. This will put your right side slightly away, allowing room for your arm to pass alongside your waist. Standing flat-footed in front of the glass would put your body directly in the way of your arm whether you are pushing or pulling the cutter. Your left foot would be toward the table, your right slightly out and paralleling the left. You will develop modifications of this position for yourself as you go along. Stick with what is most comfortable and most effective.

If, during scoring, glass spray flies along your cutter, you are pressing too hard. On the other hand, if you have only a faint scratch after running your cutter down the surface, you pressed too lightly. With any cutter, good scoring is a matter of practice. A good score line should be readily apparent to a fingernail. It doesn't take long to establish the proper feel to your arm to know when a score will be good or poor.

Breaking Out the Score

Cutting the glass, of course, is only half of the idea. You must now break the glass apart. Before you begin to break the glass, you should practice scoring straight lines, curved lines, deep lines, sinuous lines, faint lines, curves, and circles. In short, you should be familiar with all twists and turns of the cutter so as to mobilize your wrist and acquire a hand sense for the proper angle and pressure that will allow you to obtain the maximum work with the least amount of effort.

Depending on the type of glass, breaking out the score lines can be easy or difficult no matter how good the score. Some stained glasses are particularly psychotic in this regard. The point to keep in mind is not to be discouraged if your break line and score line do not always match up. Every glass worker has this trouble every so often. Having a good score line to begin with does modify the problem, but it doesn't always solve it.

Let's assume that you have a good score line and are ready to break it out. After you have become proficient with score lines, whenever you score a piece of glass, you should break out the score immediately. This is a good safety precaution. If you have several scores in the same piece of glass and attempt finally to break out one of them, the glass may be so weakened that it breaks unexpectedly somewhere else. You can get cut this way.

There are several methods of breaking out score lines.

The Fulcrum Method. The best fulcrum is the glass-cutter handle, but one without a ball. Lift the lower end of the glass and place the end of the score line over the end of the glass-cutter handle. Put down-ward pressure on both sides of the score using a thumb of either hand. The glass should break clean. If not, your score line may not be deep enough, or the glass may be too thick. You can't redo a score line. If the glass is too thick, you can apply more pressure (a dangerous technique) or try another method of breaking it out.

The Tapping Method. Holding the glass in your left hand (if you are right-handed), with support from your fingers to either side of the score line (very important), tap the score line from below. Make the taps count. Don't let the glass swing with the taps; hold it firmly. You should never tap from above; that is, directly over the score line with the glass on the table. Whacking away at it in this fashion is unaesthetic, unscientific, and unprofitable. The glass should shatter indignantly.

When tapping a score, use the ball on the end of the cutter shaft if you have one. Using the plain cutter-shaft end is useless. You can use the teeth of the cutter as a tapping tool. But never tap with the cutter wheel unless you enjoy buying new cutters. As you tap, check the score from time to time against the light. If you are accomplishing anything, you will see the score begin to "run." This extension of the score through the glass is an indication that your tapping is succeeding. You can easily see the irregular edge flash back the light. Don't keep tapping that same area; move along the score. Once the score has run its length, the two pieces of glass will easily separate. If the glass is thick, as with plate, and the score has run but the glass has not separated, use the fulcrum method. This will work readily on the weakened score line. Since tapped edges usually break out unevenly, they should be grozzed or sanded before being used.

Hand Breaking. If the glass is of a reasonable size, tip it from the table so that you use the top of the table as a support for the back part of the glass. The procedure for hand breaking is the same whether the piece of glass is small or large. Place the thumb of either hand to either side of the score line. Make certain that you curl your other fingers into a fist—don't let them circle the glass. Then exert pressure downward. The force is a pulling/bending motion that will run the score line and separate the two pieces of glass. Never break glass by hand where you have any part of it nestling in your palm. Always break glass over a table, not over the floor. This protects your feet. The safety rule is to keep as much of yourself away from the glass as possible.

The Tabletop Method. This is a variation of the fulcrum method, and it works only with straight cuts.

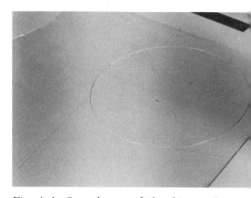

Fig. 4–1. Several ways of "breaking out" a circle. You should have made an adequate score, either freehand or with a circle cutter. To get the best result in smooth edges and the entire circle in one piece, draw extensions of the circular line, as shown, to the borders of the glass with your cutter and break the pieces out individually.

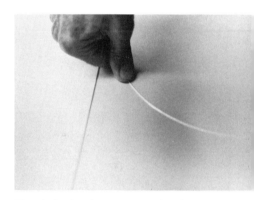

Fig. 4–2. Another option to breaking out a circle is to run the circle using your thumb, first turning the piece upside down and then applying pressure to the score line.

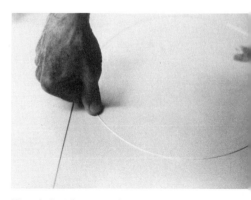

Fig. 4–3. The score line runs almost completely around the circle at this point.

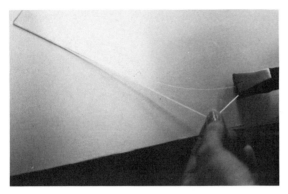

Fig. 4–4. Use running pliers to run the line . . .

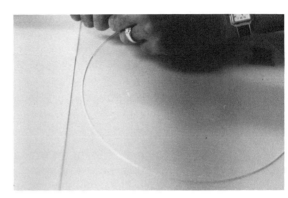

Fig. 4–7. When you are finished . . .

Fig. 4–5. or use the end of a pencil . . .

Fig. 4–8. and when you have broken out the score . . .

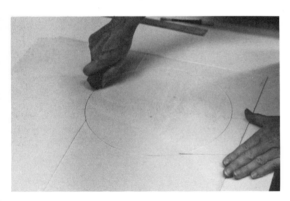

Fig. 4–6. or a block of wood.

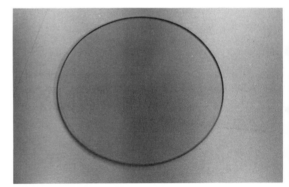

Fig. 4–9. you have this.

Once the cut is made, position the glass over the edge of the table so that the score line is directly over the edge. Now pick up that part of the glass that hangs over the edge and, holding the part of it that is still on the table with your hand for support, bring down the raised edge smartly. The glass should snap apart at the score line. Remember to keep your feet away from the glass during this operation.

Breaking with Pliers. Running pliers are used for long, straight cuts. The idea is to use the curved jaws as a fulcrum. The score line is sighted along the line on the upper jaw of the pliers. The set screw is regulated to the proper amount of pressure to be applied, and the pliers are squeezed. If the pliers are good, the glass will break. Breaking pliers are used to grip the excess glass and pull it away from the score line with an outward/downward breaking motion. Grozzing pliers are used to nip or file away small areas of glass along a score or to break out inside cuts or other multiformed shapes for pattern cutting. For more about pliers and their use, see our book *How to Work in Stained Glass.*

Cutting Circles and Patterns

The trick in cutting circles is not so much in scoring the circle as in breaking it out of the glass. Scoring is accomplished by following the pattern with the glass cutter used in the usual way. Once the circle is scored completely, lines are cut from it to the outer glass edges so that from the perimeter of the circle radiating score lines carry the break stress to the points where pressure can be applied. These score lines are broken out successively until the circle itself is completed. The score lines can be broken out by hand, although it is usually better to use glass or grozzing pliers. You should break out small increments of the circle at a time. Your free hand supports the unbroken portion of the glass against the tabletop. That part of the circle being worked on should project over the edge for gripping easily with pliers. It's a good idea to keep a waste basket under your pliers to catch the glass scrap.

For patterns, any stiff paper will do that is rigid enough to support pressure from the glass cutter. If a pattern is to be used only once, you should be as particular in your choice of paper as though it were going to be used over and over. A lot of sloppy work is otherwise brought into the act. You certainly don't want the edges of your paper to become ragged and shreddy as you work. The glass-cutter wheel should be flush against the border of the pattern, physically riding against it. The axle will thus be traveling over a small area of the pattern margin. With a complicated pattern, it is best to cut the more difficult shapes first. Then if

Figs. 4–10 and 4–11. Breaking out score lines by hand: Plate glass is used to demonstrate.

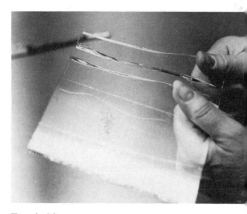

Fig. 4–10.

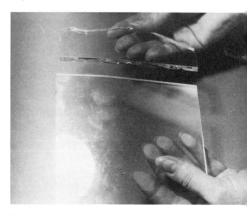

Fig. 4–11.

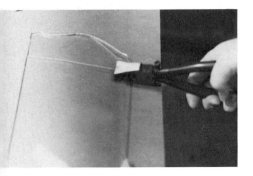

Fig. 4-12.

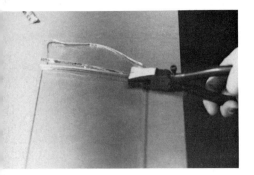

Fig. 4-13.

Figs. 4-12 and 4-13. Breaking out score lines with a running pliers.

the glass breaks, you have wasted less time. Each score line that follows a portion of the pattern should be broken out before the next score is attempted. Grozzing pliers are particularly handy in pattern cutting.

Practice free-hand cutting by making a geometric drawing—a square or a triangle or some curves—and placing it under some clear glass, try to follow the lines with your glass cutter. This is meant for practice only, and it should never be substituted for standard pattern cutting with the actual cut pattern atop the glass. But practicing in this way will allow you to follow an actual pattern more deftly.

Save all your glass scraps; you'll never know when they will come in handy. For some projects, you can use glass chips and glass grindings from scraps. Glass chips are easily made by rolling scrap glass in a piece of cloth and hitting the mass with a hammer until the chips are the size you want. Continuing the process even further gives you glass grindings. These are especially useful if made from different colors of stained glass. You should be able to get stained-glass scraps from any local studio. If not, colored glass chips are sold by many hobby shops.

Venetian "tube" glass, or *millefiore*, is a type of glass "bead" that is composed of many colors. When heated, this bead tends to flatten out into a whorl of colors. The range and mix of colors you will get depends on to what extreme these beads are melted. The end result can be quite dramatic. These attractive beads can be used in a number of ways—from little ancillary touches to complete works.

The Glass-Cutting Workshop

"How much room do I need?" This is one of the most frequently asked questions by people who want to go into glass crafting. As you will see, even this problem has been solved. However, our answer remains the same: "As much as you can get." Under ordinary circumstances, the amount of room you have for your hobby is limited to what you can reasonably take over. Certainly you don't want to work in a closet. The average glass hobbyist works in a basement. This is generally adequate so long as you make the space comfortable and have good ventilation and lighting. You will need a sturdy worktable with a good-size top. A top can be made from a sheet of $\frac{3}{4}$-inch plywood, 4 by 8 feet (as it comes). This size will comfortably handle your tabletop kiln in one corner, provide a nice working space, and leave room for projects in various stages of completion. It should also allow you room for a tool rack. The more room you have to work, the better able you are to keep things neat. This way, at a critical moment, you won't have to hunt for a tool buried under all sorts of debris. Don't spread out just because you have a lot of room, though. Keep things in order.

A stone or concrete floor is best for glass cutting. Try not to work on a carpet. No matter how neat you try to be, chips of glass will find their way to the floor. With a cement basement floor, this won't matter. You will feel them underfoot and can sweep them up with ease. Glass will eventually mar a wood, tile, or plastic floor.

Care of the Glass Cutter

The craftsperson who really cares, cares about tools. If you maintain them in good working order, they will never fail you. This is no less true for your glass cutter than for the most complicated piece of machinery. The cutting wheel is the central point of this instrument. When it is not in use, keep the glass cutter in a solution of light oil and kerosene—about half and half. We put some steel wool in the bottom of a small baby food jar, then add the kerosene/oil mix. The cutter wheel rests on the steel wool, thus keeping the wheel off the surface of the glass. In addition to protecting it, this keeps the axle from accumulating grit; a buildup of grit can eventually freeze the wheel. Unless the wheel turns freely, a glass cutter is quickly ruined. Never use turpentine as a lubricant; it will deposit sticky residues over the axle.

A Portable, Self-Contained Glass-Crafting Unit

For the apartment dweller, student, or person with limited space, or for anyone who dislikes cleaning up and yet would like to work with glass, or for anyone who wants an additional work area, Morton Glass Works has come up with a unique idea. It is a portable worktable that has built-in cutting and breaking equipment, a surface that disposes of glass chips so they won't get on the floor, self-adjusting borders for panels, and a jig for duplicating shapes. In addition, the whole surface can be used on a lightbox to give you an idea of color selection as you work. And, with all of this, it is also simple to use.

A white plastic cutting board approximately $\frac{3}{8}$ inch thick is divided into $\frac{1}{2}$-inch squares, which form a grid almost as deep as the board. Cutting is done on top of the grid, so all glass debris—powder, chips, grozzed pieces—falls through the squares and is kept off the surface of the board and prevented from falling on the floor. The squares are used as individual locking arrangements as well for a series of blocks that fit into them firmly. These can then be used as borders for any shape, which means that nails and special boards to

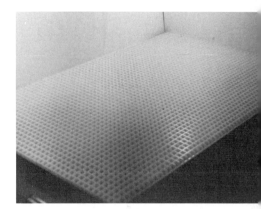

Fig. 4–14. The cutting board of the basic Glasscrafting unit.

Fig. 4–15. Close-up of the cutting board showing trapped pieces of glass within several of the squares.

Fig. 4–16. A piece of glass being cut on the board. You can use the lines as they show through beneath your glass as a guide to straight lines or curved lines between these underlying surfaces.

Fig. 4–17. Holding/measuring blocks that come with the cutting board. Each item is slotted to lock into place on the board automatically.

Fig. 4–18. Positioning a piece of glass, using the measuring block, gauge, and holding blocks.

carry the work in progress are unnecessary. In addition, smaller blocks carry pivot points that can also be locked in place within one of these ubiquitous squares. This allows for the scoring and breaking out of shapes that otherwise could be done only with a grinding machine— and probably not so well or quickly. Since this unit is new and allows so much flexibility in cutting, let's take a closer look at it in action.

Fig. 4–14 shows the plastic cutting board. Because the board is made of hard plastic, the glass moves smoothly and easily over it without scratching. Scratching is further alleviated because there are no chips of glass anywhere on the surface; they have been trapped within the squares to keep the entire area neat and clean. When you are finished working on the board, all you have to do to clean up is turn it upside down and tap on the under surface, thus releasing the trapped debris into the trash.

Fig. 4–16 shows a piece of glass being cut on the board. You can exert all the pressure you want without indenting the surface or breaking the glass. Normal cutting pressure, of course, does not demand great weight on the glass, but we have put more than the normal pressure on the board just to test it, and there is no problem. The board also comes with two holding/ measuring blocks (Fig. 4–17), each equipped with a sliding-scale bar that locks into position with a wing nut. The square grooves on the under surface of these blocks lock into place on the board.

Fig. 4–18 shows a piece of glass ready to be cut to proper dimension. Left-handed workers would reverse the block setup. It's quicker than nailing pieces of wood, and it's neater and much more effective for special cuts. You can even use any of the longitudinal or horizontal lines formed by the squares as straight edges. These are easily seen through clear glass. In Fig. 4–19, a larger piece of glass is being squared off before being cut for pattern. The arrangement of the blocks is fairly arbitrary, and so is the number you may want to use. Fig. 4–20 shows an easy way to cut lamp panels using a variable jig.

Some very tricky cuts can be done with the Glass-crafting board. Using the breaking buttons that fit into the squares on the board (Figs. 4–21 and 4–22) takes a little practice, and you must have a proper score line, but the end result is amazing. And these shapes are not just curiosities. Foiled into a pattern, or fused to an underlying piece of glass, they can have a dramatic effect. Figs. 4–23—4–30 show some of the stages in producing these cuts; Figs. 4–31—4–34 show some of the results.

Fig. 4-19. Squaring off a piece of glass.

Fig. 4-20. Using the variable jig. The angle formed by the metal bar to the plastic straight edge is changed by moving the wing nuts. If you are cutting out a lamp, you would vary your cutting from right to left, just turning the glass from one side to the other.

Fig. 4-21. With these "breakers," you will get some of the oddest shapes you've ever seen from glass.

Fig. 4-22. The buttons fit into the squares with pegs.

Fig. 4-23. The glass is scored in the usual way. This is a thin piece of glass being cut with one of the Supercutters.

Fig. 4-24. The cut is almost complete. The piece of glass is steadied on the cutting surface with gentle pressure. The surface is not at all slippery.

82

Fig. 4–25. Once the cut is made, we use the special "breaking" block that comes with the unit. Note that the block has a slight inward curve at either end.

Fig. 4–26. The end of the block is brought down on the piece of glass, which has its end placed on the button, as shown in Fig. 4–25. The score line is placed over the center of the slope of the button. Pressure is exerted downward with the block so that its curved surface cradles the glass, with most of the force focused upon the score line.

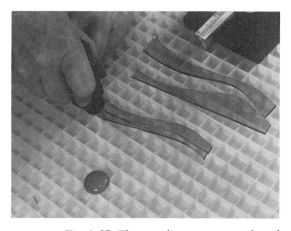

Fig. 4–27. The score line runs accurately and almost instantly down the glass.

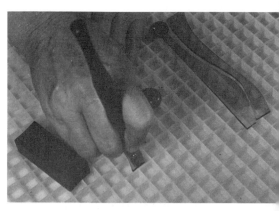

Fig. 4–28. This is the same procedure on an even thinner piece of glass. The scoring begins . . .

Fig. 4–29. once again, pressure is exerted . . .

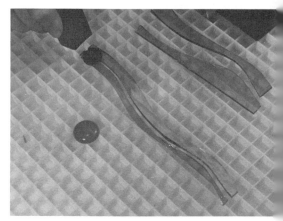

Fig. 4–30. and, again, a fast, true break is made running the length of the score line.

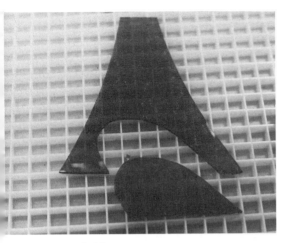

Fig. 4–31.

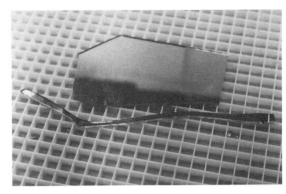

Fig. 4–33.

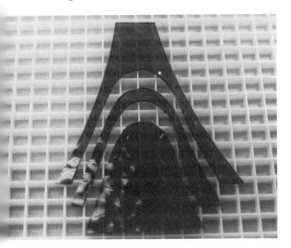

Fig. 4–32.

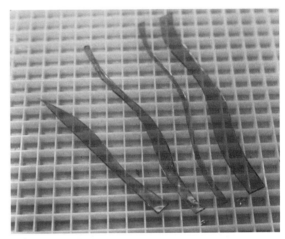

Fig. 4–34.

Figs. 4–31, 4–32, 4–33, and 4–34. Some of the "impossible" cuts that can be made in glass using the Glasscrafter's board:

As you can see, the old idea that cutting glass is a mystical endeavor limited to the very few is no longer able to compete with the simple, safe, and effective methods available today. There is a glass cutter to fit every hand and every pocketbook, every strength and every weakness. And even if you live in a small apartment, you can still find adequate space to work with the compact Glasscrafting unit. In short, for the worker in glass, there is every reason to forge ahead. You never know what you can do until you try.

PART II
Glass to Glass

Chapter 5

Lead, Solder, Foil, and Glue

Much of what we have to say about these materials and their applicability to glass crafting is detailed at length in our book *How to Work in Stained Glass*. However, we will present some new information as well as offer an overview of each item.

Lead

Lead is used in several ways in glass crafting: As sheet lead to cut out ornamental designs, as lead for melting with a torch or in a kiln to fill a mold, and, most often, as lead came to border glass objects. Here it is used in channeled lengths both to provide a finished edge and, within the body of a work, to hold the different pieces of glass together. In stained-glass work, since each glass is a different color, the only way to change colors is to change the glass.

There are many ways to bond stained glasses together; lead is one of them. Lead came comes in six-foot lengths and is available from any supplier of stained glass (see *Sources of Supply*). While it also comes in variable thicknesses, we will deal mostly with the smaller widths. U and H leads refers to the type of channel: a U having only one channel for use as a bordering lead, and an H meant to fit two pieces of glass together, the rim of each piece in an opposite channel.

Solder and Flux

The beginning glass worker sometimes confuses solder with lead. Soldering, however, is a means of uniting two metals, using heat and an alloy to bind them. The metals must be amenable to "taking on" the solder (alloy). In glass work, we use a tin/lead mixture for solder, either 60/40 (preferably) or 50/50. A heat source is also necessary that will quickly bring the surface temperature of the metals at least 100 degrees above the

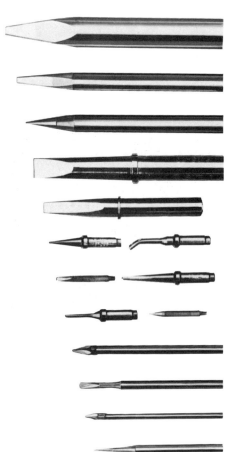

Fig. 5–1. Some of the soldering-iron tips that can be used for glass crafting. Not all of these are applicable, but all are at least possible. These tips are of the "set-screw" variety. This is better than the "screw-in" type, which tend to freeze in the iron. (Courtesy Plato Products)

melting point of the solder. This allows the solder to flow and the metals to absorb it. Flux, another substance you will need, is a chemical that cleans the surfaces to be soldered and helps the solder penetrate (wet) them. Flux used for glass usually contains oleic acid or ammonium chloride. There are a number of fluxes available, however, and many manufacturers have developed offshoots of either or both of these standard agents.

The most common heat source for soldering is the soldering iron. These tools have the advantage of small tip size, instant heating, safety, and ample heat output. Most workers using an iron, especially with lead, will also use a soldering-iron control.

The Soldering-Iron Control*

Lead melts at 620 degrees F., whereas 50/50 solder melts at 420 degrees. Whether you have a 40-watt iron or a 400-watt iron, if you plug it in and leave it for twenty minutes, the tip temperature will exceed 900 degrees. If you then touch that iron to your lead, you will quickly burn a large hole in it. That is precisely what the soldering-iron control prevents.

One of the newest (and the best) soldering-iron controls is made by Glastar. This control, like any other on the market, doesn't control the temperature of the soldering iron: It controls the power to the iron. You, the worker, control the temperature of the iron by first finding the right temperature as the iron heats up. Once you find this, the control allows you to lock it. Then if you solder at a consistent rate, the iron will not overheat. Unfortunately, many workers cannot find a constant rate, and that is what makes it so difficult to control the temperature. One seems to be forever turning it up or down. However, here are a set of rules to follow when using your soldering-iron control. If you follow them carefully, you will have no problems with burning lead or getting a proper bead on your copper foil.

Finding the Proper Soldering Temperature

1. Cut a 6-inch piece of $\frac{1}{4}$-inch flat lead and a 6-inch piece of solder. Flux one side of the lead and lay the solder on top of this fluxed surface.
2. Plug your iron into the control and set the control to Full. Wait about two minutes.
3. Place the flat face of the soldering-iron tip on the solder and hold it firmly against the solder and lead for five seconds.

*This information is adapted from material published by the Glastar Company and reprinted with permission.

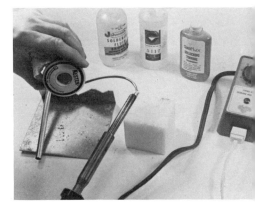

Fig. 5–2. Soldering necessities. (Left to right) a roll of Kester solder, specially formulated for stained-glass work; a flux brush and an Esico iron resting on a soldering-iron stand; a Kestart Tinning Block; and the Glastar Soldering-Iron Control. (Top) Three different fluxes that work well: Johnson's, Gardiner's 5117 flux, and Taraflux, all for stained glass.

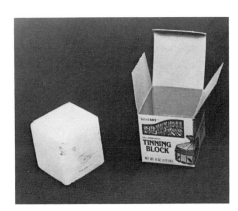

Fig. 5–3. The Kester Tinning Block, made by the same people who make solder, is a handy item. This is a salammoniac block that allows you to clean and tin your iron quickly in one operation. Have the soldering iron as hot as you normally do in soldering. Then apply the flat surfaces of the soldering iron to the Kester Tinning Block in a back-and-forth movement with a little solder present.

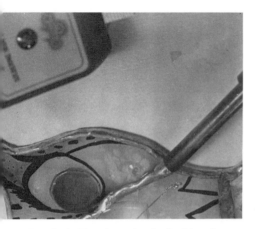

Fig. 5–4. Drawing a bead of solder along a copper foil joint with the Glastar Soldering Control Unit. The unit maintains the iron heat at a constant temperature, allowing beading to occur.

4. If the solder melts rapidly and flows out to form a smooth puddle (and if you don't burn a hole in the lead after the five seconds), your iron has reached the right temperature. If this happens, you are lucky. If it doesn't, keep the control on Full. Remember, each iron is different; you may have to change control settings for another iron.

5. If the iron melts slowly through the solder, or the puddle of solder is mushy rather than liquid, your iron is still too cool. Wait twenty seconds and try Steps 3 and 4 again, using a 150-watt or larger iron. This may require six minutes or more to heat up. If the solder is still too cool, repeat the twenty-second wait until you are successful. Here time is the variable. You might want to get a more efficient iron if the wait is too long.

6. If on the initial test you burned through the lead, turn your control to Off, wait twenty seconds, and retest. If the iron is still too hot, repeat the twenty-second wait until you are successful.

Keeping the Iron at the Proper Temperature

Once you have attained the proper temperature, turn the control to the number indicated in the chart. The setting on the control depends on the wattage of your iron:

Wattage of Your Soldering Iron	Setting on Control	Exceptions
60 watts or smaller	—	control not required
80 watts	75	—
100 watts	60	—
Weller W-100	—	control not required
120 watts	50	—
150 watts	40	—
175 watts	35	—
200 watts	30	—
300 watts	20	—

As soon as you set the number on the control, start soldering your project. You don't have to hurry, but don't linger between solder joints. Move along at a steady pace. If the phone rings as you are soldering, turn the control to 20 when you leave; but when you return, don't touch the iron to your project. Repeat the test in Step 4 first. The iron may have become too hot during your absence. Once the iron is back to the right temperature, turn the control to the proper setting and continue soldering. After you have soldered for a few minutes, you may have the feeling that the iron is either too hot or too cool. Despite your inclination, don't turn the control up or down. Leave it alone and follow these steps:

1. If you think the iron is too hot, go back to the five-second test in Step 3. If it is too hot, try to increase your soldering speed. You may have been dawdling without realizing it.
2. If you think the iron is too cool because your solder joints are a bit lumpy, lay the iron down for twenty seconds. Then start soldering again. You may be trying to solder too fast, or you may not be leaving your tip on the lead long enough. The tip should be in contact with the lead for approximately two or three seconds in order to heat it enough to accept the solder.

After you have completed several projects and have had several hours' experience soldering, you will find that your soldering speed has increased considerably. If you must stop several times during a project to let the iron heat up, change the setting on your control. Increase the setting by 10s until you can maintain the correct temperature for your rate of soldering. The time you put into checking the iron against the control and vice versa will be more than made up to you in time saved as you work, to say nothing of unburned lead and frustration.

As far as soldering without a control, there is no question that it can be done. In the long run, however, you will probably waste more time and materials than if you just purchase an inexpensive Glastar control to begin with.

Foil

Copper foil is sold in rolls of 36 yards (usually) in just about any width from $\frac{1}{16}$ to $\frac{1}{2}$ inch. One side of the roll shows the copper; the sticky side is covered with a paper backing. It is this surface that is wrapped to the glass rim. Once two pieces of glass are foiled, they can be soldered together. In this respect, foil is very much like lead; however, there are important differences between these two metals so far as glass is concerned:

Differences in Soldering Process. While both foil and lead must be fluxed before they can be soldered—and the same flux can be used for both—it is usually easier to solder foil than lead. The copper foil will not burn regardless of how hot your iron gets. Lead, of course, will melt right away from the overheated tip, leaving a hole. This usually cannot be fixed (although some students insist on trying, making the end result a real disaster), and the piece must be releaded.

Differences in Aesthetics. When correctly applied, foil gives a thin, delicate line between the glass. Lead came, even as narrow as $\frac{1}{8}$ inch, provides a heavier line.

Fig. 5–5. Applying a special patina that turns solder a copper color. It is applied with a soft brush at top left. The transformation is almost instantaneous. The coppery hue can be made even deeper by reapplying the patina, and it is longlasting. ALLNOVA, the manufacturer, also makes chemicals that will turn lead and zinc coppery, and this without any preparatory "tinning" of their surfaces.

Fig. 5–6. The ALLNOVA chemicals for changing the color of lead, zinc, and solder.

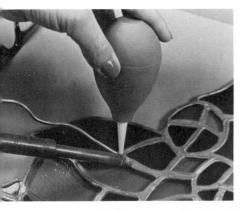

Fig. 5–7. Using the Hexagon "solder lifter." This bulb allows you to unsolder your mistakes. The joint is heated with the iron and the molten solder is sucked into the tube. Pieces of solidified solder that collect inside the tube can be released and reused. A nice recycling touch.

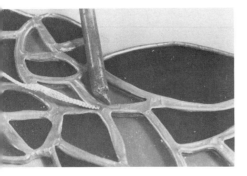

Fig. 5–8. Soder Wick, another solder lifter, works by picking up molten solder and allowing it to flow onto the surface of the lifter. Thus the unwanted solder is removed from the joint.

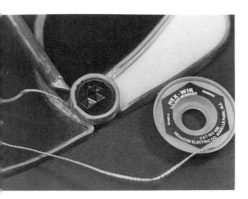

Fig. 5–9. Hex-Wik works in the same way as Soder Wick, but it is considerably thinner. Solder cannot be reclaimed easily from either of these wicks.

In addition, lead is not flexible enough to take the sharp bends and angles of multicurved pieces of glass that copper covers so readily; consequently, it may look overcompressed in areas where it has been forced into tight inner curves, and it will bulge in other places. Lead came when used as a border should be carefully designed so as not to "come away" from the outside edge. It may well do this since, unlike copper, it has no sticky surface to provide adherence. A little glue judiciously applied can help if there isn't too wide an expanse of border.

Differences in Technique. Many beginners gravitate toward foil because they think it is easier to use than lead came. In fact, both methods have their problems, and foil will actually reveal mistakes in glass cutting that can be hidden in the deeper channel provided by came. To get a proper foiled edge, whether the foiling is done by hand or by machine, the rim of glass must be absolutely smooth. Bumps and ridges advertise their presence loudly when you begin to join the pieces. Foiling and leading present different challenges, involve different effects, and establish different nuances. These are the factors, rather than ease (or sloppiness) of procedure, that should determine whether you use one or the other.

Glue Chipping

The saying "The more things change the more they are the same" applies to the art of glue chipping as well as to most other aspects in the crafts field. Common at one time, glue chipping of glass was buried under the "progress" of modern architecture. The delicate tracery that shows up so beautifully in many old windows was traded in for articles that could be mass produced. But glue chipping definitely has made a comeback, and today it is stronger than ever as a decorative design used with clear glass.

The process is a simple one. A coating of glue is applied to a sheet of glass. As this dries, it shrinks and begins to lift itself away from the glass surface. The tension exerted on the glass surface pulls away a small chip of glass, rather like peeling skin. Since the pull of the glue over the glass surface is uneven—in some areas strong, in others weak—there is a marked variance as to the amount of flaking or chipping that will occur. It is this variance that produces the characteristic pattern with its delicate veinings and traceries, like some ghost moving within the surface. A great deal can be done with this feathery texturing for design effects. But there's more to glue chipping than meets the eye.

Not all glass can be treated in this way. Then, not

all glue is good for chipping. In fact, modern glue is purposely made not to shrink and curl—the very properties that one requires to chip glass. Factors such as temperature, humidity, cleanliness of the glass, and preparation of the glass play a part. These are hardly insurmountable obstacles, but many workers try to ignore them in favor of the "quick result." Quick results are usually costly: Glue chipping is a lengthy process.

The first step is to select your glass. We use the pale cathedral glasses whenever possible, but we're also fond of clear glass because of the mysterious effects that occur by the subtle breaking of the light as it comes through. For glue chipping to have the maximum effect, the glass should be prepared to allow the glue to grip. The best way to do this is to use sandblasted glass. Glass can be sandblasted quite inexpensively. The Yellow Pages is a good source if you don't have your own sandblasting setup. The glass surface can be roughened in other ways, too. One is to mull some Carborundum grit over the surface. This grit is available from Sears. We use a porcelain mortar and pestle used for grinding paints. If you don't have this kind of equipment, you could try an electric sander. But be careful that the glass doesn't fly up at you. It is possible to glue-chip glass that hasn't been prepared with a roughened surface and still have interesting things happen. However, the glass must be absolutely clean if you are going to try this.

The glue you use must be an animal product. Glue comes in flakes, which must be heated, or, in smaller quantities, in liquid form. Hyde Glue is our favorite of the liquid variety. If you are going to use glue flakes or powder, you will have to boil them in a double boiler until they liquify. The amount of glue that you spread on the surface of the glass has a direct effect on the amount of chipping that will occur. Mix water with the dry glue at a ratio of 3 to 1 for a very thin mix, or 2 to 1 for a thicker, more average mix. Let the mixture sit until it becomes gelatinous; then heat the mixture in the double boiler until it is watery. Optimum temperature is about 160 degrees F. Do *not* let it boil: The best way to prevent this is to stir constantly. Try to get all the air bubbles out. When you aren't stirring the glue, keep the lid on the double boiler; otherwise you will lose temperature.

When you think the glue is ready, brush it fairly briskly onto the glass. It will tend to "set up" as you work, so you have to be alert. Try to get the glue to flow over the glass with equal consistency. If you pile more glue on one portion of the glass than another, you will have an unequal chipping proportion. If you have a large area of glass to cover, you might consider pouring the glue on and spreading it rapidly with a brush. Any fairly stiff-bristled brush will do. We use a wallpaper brush for large areas. Try to keep the glass as level as possible, and try to maintain the consistency of the glue depth.

Once you are satisfied with your application of the glue, let the glass sit for at least twenty-four hours. The glue will harden and become clear; at this point, it is exerting a lot of pull upon the glass surface, so try not to handle the glass roughly. Note that none of the glue has actually begun to pull off yet; there is still too much water in it. The glue must be allowed to dry even more, and the best way to do this is to apply heat directly above the glued surface. We have found that a standard electric floor heater is the most effective. We have used hair dryers as well, but you have to spend time standing there passing the dryer over the glass. A lot depends on how much surface you are chipping. The electric heater will do the trick if you have a fairly large surface.

Place the heater so that it radiates over the surface, and turn on the fan so that the hot air blows at the glue. You will begin to see the glue lifting away from the glass; the chipping process has begun. Your technique, the amount of glue used, the humidity, and the amount of heat on the glass surface determine how much chipping occurs. Inevitably, not all of the glue will come off the glass; you may have to hand chip some with a spatula. Remember these glue chips contain glass, so don't wipe them away with your hand. Once most of the glue is off the glass, you can clean the surface and examine the effect you have achieved. If you want a finer texture, repeat the process.

Fig. 5–10. An example of glue chipping within a piece of beveled glass. Courtesy of Nervo Studios.

Chapter 6

Fusing and Other Surface Modifications

Fusing two or more pieces of glass with heat is by no means as simple as it sounds. It can be done edge to edge, surface to surface, or as a three-dimensional sculptured technique. The problems inherent in the operation, however, become equally multidimensional because glass must be fused to that of a similar type. Even clear window glasses have this idiosyncracy, preferring glass of the same batch. And fusing different colored or stained glasses is almost, although not quite, out of the question. The different colors and types of stained glass have problems melding and cooling at the same rate. It's that coefficient of expansion again. Because one piece of the fused glass cools more slowly than the other, stresses are created and the piece cracks. If the stresses are great enough, it will shatter. Let's look at some of the effects that can be gotten using fused glass as the essential technique.

Fusing Different Types of Stained Glass

In Fig. 6–3, we cut several panels from the same design so that we could use different glasses. The design was calculated for fusing rather than for leading or foiling. The base is a rectangle, and the tree trunk, branches, and inhabiting owls are laid out to pattern. For the owls, we used glass globs flattened on one side. You can acquire these in most hobby shops that stock glass supplies. For the eyes of the owls, we used two millifiore beads. The beaks are small glass chips from the scrap pile.

Three panels were cut and laid out. Panels 1 and 2 have a gray Kokomo glass base, and all the panels used the same Kokomo red/gold streaky for the trees and branches. The idea is to show the different effects that can occur with a mixture of different colored glass. The pieces were all cut and placed into position on the glass

Fig. 6–1. Fused glass using similar and disparate pieces for color. No painting was done. Left: a small brown bottle fused to a circular piece of Wismach amber glass. This cannot always be done without the circle cracking, but we found a piece where the expansion coefficients matched. Top: a piece of clear glass with fused stained-glass elements placed in a design. Because we limited the surface coverage (and with luck), the piece did not crack. A hint: use a tint. Deep colors are often more difficult to fuse to clear glass. Right: a simple fused bird using all Kokomo blue-tinted glass. The glass was all from the same batch, so there was no problem with fusing.

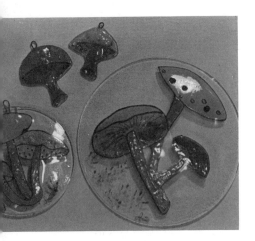

Fig. 6–2. Fused items of the same kind of glass. The color is painted on the fused elements. Fusing and paint maturation occur at approximately the same temperature.

background temporarily with Elmer's glue. On the first panel, instead of a glass chip for the beak, we used a dab of powdered glass-stainer's paint (Intense Black from Reusche).

All pieces were fired at similar temperatures (1350–1400 F.) for experiment and cooled overnight (about 12 hours). Despite this lengthy cooling process, cracks appear around the juncture of the millefiore eyes in panel 1 (Fig. 6–3A). These were the only cracks to appear in this panel, which otherwise manifested a reasonable tolerance to accepting the different colors of glass. Had we annealed this panel at 750 degrees for perhaps an hour, this may not have happened. A way to avoid these cracks without annealing is to do a double firing: the first to fuse the globs to the underlying glass, the second to fuse the millifiore to the glob at considerably less heat than for the first firing. But this is usually more trouble than it is worth, and it may not work. Whenever possible, we try to cut down on, rather than increase, the number of firings. Sprinkled over the background are flakes of snow. This is dry enamel white paint (Drakenfield) held upon the surface and fused. The paint nicely smooths out with the heat. This first panel was fired to 1475 F.

Panel 2 (Fig. 6–3B) was fired at 1500 degrees F. The same cracks appear around the glass globs, the most difficult part in all three panels to fuse properly. Note the more extensive rounding of the glass that forms the trunk and limbs of the tree. This can be used as an indication of the amount of heat applied, since glass edges tend to round with overheating. These borders should be rounded to produce the proper fused effect. Using no fusing whatever, but merely bonding the glass pieces together with epoxy, gives square-cut borders on all the pieces just as they are cut. This is a totally different effect from that produced by fusing. A good fused result, which depends as much upon the design as upon the technique and choice of glasses, must provide a homogeneous melding of these glasses. The result should be a single piece of glass that makes a statement. Bonded pieces make an entirely different statement. Every glass craftsperson should appreciate this fact. This is not to decry bonded glass, which can be dramatic, but to differentiate between it and fused glass. This is a source of confusion to many beginners and even to some who are no longer beginners.

A great amount of heat will tend to round the edges of glass, whereas a small amount will barely round them at all. But going too high in temperature will not only round the edges of the glass, but will cause the individual pieces to shrink as the glass begins to pull together. Consequently, they will pull apart. Panel 3

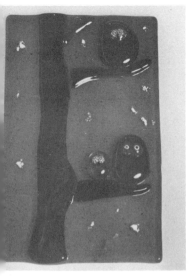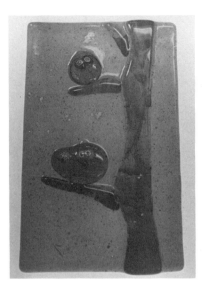

Fig. 6–3A, B, and C. Three owl panels that we tried as an experiment in fusing slightly different stained-glass elements.

(Fig. 6–3C) shows this effect. Here we took the heat up to 1550 degrees F. and then, as with all the panels, cooled it slowly with no annealing. Note how the limbs have pulled away from the trunk of the tree, how raised the overlay is, and how rounded the borders are. Note also how the millifiore beads spread out as they melted.

The glass globs used for the owls were streaky colors, the basic color amber with red with emphatic streaks. After heating, these globs became opaque, the streaks were more or less preserved, and then changed in color to different shades of red to become even more emphatic. The opacity is a heavy mix of gray to orange. This fascinating transformation provides a good lesson: You can never tell what will happen when you heat streaky glass, and especially streaky globs.

Unfortunately, the high heat also took its toll—this panel has a heavy crack running up from the base of the background glass. Annealing might have prevented this. Oddly enough, the globs show no cracks around or through them, which is the case in the first two panels. Note that in panel 3 the high heat not only made the translucent globs opalescent, but it burned out the "snow" that we sprinkled on the surfaces of all the panels. If you try for one effect (in this case transforming translucent globs to opaque), you may lose others. Remember that these are experiments in fusing *different* kinds of stained glass. It is risky, but the dramatic possibilities make it worth trying.

The main secret to success lies in the annealing process. When fusing different types of stained glass, if you hold your kiln temperature at about 750 degrees F. for perhaps an hour and then allow the heat to fall at its

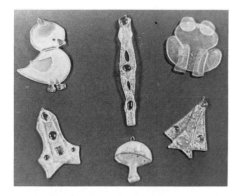

Fig. 6–4. Painted fused-glass pieces, either double- or single-strength window glass of the same type.

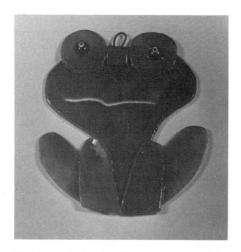

Fig. 6–5. A slightly different variation of the frog in Fig. 6–4. All the pieces were painted; little glass eyes were fused in place, and the mouth was stick-lighted by scraping away some of the paint with a stylus.

Fig. 6–6. A fused fish from window glass, painted and lettered. Fusing was no problem.

usual progression, you may get away without fracturing any glass. If you don't have a kiln that will maintain a specific temperature, you will have to sit with it and manipulate the annealing temperature by hand. This is one reason why we suggest that when you purchase a kiln you should check to see if it has this additional advantage.

Fusing *similar* types of stained glass can be a much simpler process. You can then paint those elements to make them discriminate. Figs. 6–4 to 6–7 show a variety of objects where the pieces of glass have been completely fused.

Stages of Kiln-Fired Glass

Glass that is subjected to heat goes through a whole series of physical changes. Now that you understand some simple fusing techniques, we will go into more detail about what happens to the glass when it is heated. Since glass goes from a "solid" to "liquid" state with sufficient heat, and since liquids tend to move from higher to lower levels, glass also will move. This surprises many workers, who insist on thinking of glass as a perpetual solid. The ability of heated glass to move, if only in tiny increments, can ruin a project. Since control is essential in glass crafting, it is important to keep this idiosyncrasy of glass in mind so that you will achieve better results. Glass will move even on a flat surface; it may "crawl together" or it may spread out. It goes through contortions, changing structure in gross or microscopic stages, depending on the amount of heat it is subjected to.

As glass is heated from room temperature to about 900 degrees F. (using double-strength window glass), it begins to expand. To the eye it remains unchanged, however, and the unwary worker will say, "Nothing is happening." On the contrary. The coefficient of expansion is in full control. From about 900 to 1100 degrees, although it still shows no visible changes, the glass surface is "moist" enough so that low-fire enamels, which mature at this temperature, will fuse to it. Such colorants are extremely touchy about temperature, and they will begin to fire out once their heat ranges are exceeded. In this instance, the glass blank becomes receptive to fusing, even though to the eye it has not changed at all.

From about 1100 to 1200 degrees, some stained glasses may begin to sag. Window glass will begin to "accept" the medium-fire paints such as glass-stainer's paints and silver stain. Silver stain, as opposed to almost any other paint, becomes more intense the higher the temperature goes. From about 1200 to 1350 degrees, some stained glasses (reds, caramel opals, some browns) will begin to lose color. This may or may not return as the glass cools. Many of the reds will turn orange, and many caramel opals will lose much of the brown color and give a faded result. At about 1350, double-strength window glass will begin to sag, and plate glass may already have sagged. Single-strength window glass, however, may show no change.

From about 1350 to 1400, the critical temperature for many glasses, it is wise to watch the kiln carefully. At 1400, it is already too high for most stained glasses, which may begin to distort at 1375. Double-strength window glass is not yet unhappy at this temperature, although its edges may begin to blunt and pull in slightly from the heat. From about 1400 to 1450 degrees, most window glasses will have assumed the shape of the sagger or bend. Fine detail from the mold or sagger will not yet appear on the glass. Stained glass at this temperature is usually a mess, convoluting into a mass of colored shapes with holes and bubbles, which heal and reappear as the glass literally "boils."

From about 1450 to 1500 degrees, most of the shaping of window glass has been completed. However, fusing of elements to the surface (such as leaf stems) may still be incomplete. Lamination of glasses should have taken place, however, since this is a fusion of surfaces only, not an actual melding of one glass into another.

From about 1500 to 1800 degrees, window glass will continue to "pull in" its margins. The amount of shrinkage that occurs depends on the size of the glass. Surprisingly little takes place in pieces of glass measuring in the area of 5 by 6 inches. Window glass can take very high heat without much distortion if pieces no larger than this are used. Smaller pieces are even better. If you are using a mold from which you want to transfer fairly fine lines onto the glass, you can go even higher than 1800 degrees F. with very little distortion of the glass. We have gone up to 1900 degrees to mark small pieces of glass with mold characteristics. Experimenting with your kiln is the only way to find out what you can do to achieve the results you have in mind. On an average, the firing temperatures will vary from 1080 degrees (low-fire enamels) to 1450 degrees for fusing, laminating, and sagging. Somewhere in between these temperatures should be optimum for you, your kiln, and the particular glass you are using. Higher temperatures are certainly possible and even inevitable in some work. When choosing a kiln, it's a good idea to keep this in mind.

Fusing Bottles

In fusing small bottles, we usually choose clear or frosted bottles because they are easy to work with and

Fig. 6–7. Only two pieces of glass were fused to form the body and tail of each fish in this sculpture. One is painted on the tail surface, another has small glass chips fused to his tail, and the third has splotches of paint on his. The bottom fish, camouflaged among the shells, is almost clear glass except for the eye. The shells make a perfect background. We fused stiff wire to the bottom surfaces of the fish and wove the wires into crevices in the shells so that the fish would appear to be swimming.

Fig. 6–8. Fusing glass with a torch. The pile of glass crushings is held with Elmer's glue. A strand of nichrome wire was placed within the pile. The piles were transferred to the charcoal block and the torch applied.

Fig. 6–9. Small clear bottles fused to clear glass to use as holders for glass flowers.

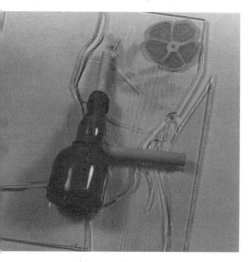

Fig. 6–10. This is what can happen when coefficients of expansion don't match. We tried to fuse a small brown bottle to a piece of window glass. One porcelain rod was placed in the top of the bottle to keep the neck open, and one at the neck to tip it forward. The glass first cracked at these two areas of strain. As we took it from the kiln, it began to break in other areas as well, notably at the base of the bottle against the glass.

usually fuse well to clear glass. We save our airplane cocktail bottles for this purpose. For the project in Fig. 6–9, the bottles were placed on the surface of the underlying glass and held with Elmer's glue. They had been already decorated with decals. (See the Appendix for decaling techniques.) Before firing all the bottles, we test-fired one. The result, carried to 1350 degrees, showed good fusing of the bottle to the glass. We kept it from sagging or folding by filling it with kiln wash. No cracks or fracturing of the underlying glass occurred either, so we went ahead and made a decaled panel of small bottles to use as flower vases. This makes a unique window display.

You can try the same project with brown bottles, fusing them to regular window glass. This is often possible without fracturing the glass, but you have to be lucky. Since the coefficients of expansion are so different, you may run into problems. It helps if you anneal at about 800 degrees F. for an hour. If you are unlucky, something like what happened to us in Fig. 6–10 is possible. Here a small brown bottle fused perfectly to a piece of double-strength window glass. The window glass has been given an interesting granular texture from the firing, although this is faintly shown in the illustration. This is a result of its lying on the kiln wash on the shelf. To prevent sagging, we filled the bottle with kiln wash and kept the mouth open with a porcelain rod. Another rod was used to prop the neck. But despite our careful planning, it didn't work.

Fusing Colorants

Colorants are used for glass in order to avoid the problems inherent in fusing different colored glasses. Usually the colorants used are low-fire enamels (firing at about 1080 degrees F.). Whether or not such colors can be mixed to produce different hues and tones depends on the manufacturer. Glas-O-Past can be mixed, and so can Onita's paints, which, however, are high fire (1400 to 1450 degrees F.). Any colorant should be test-fired before using.

Colorants can be applied to the surface of the glass or used in laminating. For laminating, the colorant is sandwiched between two layers of glass to preserve it. Some paints, such as granular copper enamel used for metal enameling, are made for metal and not glass. These are tailored to a metallic coefficient of expansion and usually will come off the glass surface. Laminating effectively prevents this. Many problems can be alleviated or enhanced by the amount of copper enamel that you use. A small amount powdered over the glass surface may behave, but as you add more and more, the expansion coefficients will create an antipathy, and your project will be ruined. Even in the laminating process, the enamel can still show areas of crackling here and there, but at least it can't flake off the glass entirely.

Using Copper Enamel

Considering the wide variety of glass paints available, it seems odd that some workers refuse to budge from the copper enamel approach. One reason is that people simply have used it for a long time and see no reason to change, since they feel they have worked out all the problems. Another reason is that the different hues and tones that can be achieved with copper enamel cannot be duplicated with other paints. Still another reason is that copper enamel can be effective if it is used correctly.

If you are going to laminate copper enamel, don't apply so much that lumps and bumps appear in the design. The finished surface will be uneven to the touch and will distort the reflected light. The upper glass blank will have to allow room for this. Also, the two blanks may not match up, and this can exaggerate the end result if sagging into a mold also occurs. Keep in mind, as well, that by laminating material you are effectively trapping any byproducts of the firing. In fact, even fumes from copper-enamel binding agents may exasperatingly interfere with the lamination, causing a permanent staining or spotting of the glass or actual bubbles between the pieces. What you need is a binder that will remain practically inert during the firing process. One of the best is baby oil, which fires out well and binds the copper enamel to the glass effectively.

Before you begin the laminating procedure, clean both glass blanks thoroughly. When they are dry, pick up the lower blank by its margins. Pour a small amount of baby oil in the center and spread it evenly over the surface with a clean sponge. Take your time and make sure it is spread over the entire surface. Once you are satisfied that it is even, put the bottom blank down and wash your hands. This process is too often overlooked, yet it is a necessary one. No matter how careful you are, some oil will have gotten on your hands and they will be slippery. We have seen more than one expensive bottle of colorant dropped because of slippery hands.

When your hands are clean and dry, sift the copper enamel over the surface of the bottom blank. We buy our copper enamels with several screen bottles; these small cover screens can be interchanged from one colorant bottle to another. It makes the process much more convenient than using a strainer. You can sift either heavily or lightly, depending on the effect you want, but don't sift *too* heavily or the enamel will interfere with the layering of the glass. If you want a bubbled

Fig. 6–11. A laminated plate with whorls of color in a separated, staccato format within the two layers of glass. The enamels were sifted in. (Courtesy Sydenstryker Glass)

Fig. 6–12. Interesting effects of lamination, using enamels to form a pattern. Here a doily was used for a stencil and the colorants sifted into the interstices. The doily was removed, the top blank was put in place, and the piece was fired. (Courtesy Sydenstryker Glass)

texture, sprinkle a few drops of water onto the baby oil and let most of it evaporate. What remains, since water and oil don't mix, will compact and form spaces within the coating of oil. If you are using mica flakes, sprinkle them on very thinly; they, too, can cause bubbles to form within the laminate.

Designing with Copper Enamel

An automatic depth is provided with copper enamel, since it is used in a three-dimensional process. You can enhance its effect by using other glass colorants on the surface to blend with the copper enamels below. You don't have to be a great designer to do this; many abstracts can be created by sprinkling colorant almost at will. Once it is sprinkled, however, it is impossible to remove (or almost so) without washing off the entire surface and starting over, so you must have some design in mind first. However, you may enjoy this freedom from restriction and come up with some interesting free-form results.

Rather than oiling the entire glass blank as described above, you can paint various designs on the surface with a brush and then sprinkle on the copper enamel. The portion of it that falls on the painted oil design will stick, and the remainder can be blown off or tapped off. If you use this technique, though, make sure that you don't use too much oil; it will run when you try to get rid of the excess enamel. If you use just enough oil here, you will find that the colorant will harden into these lines, leaving the excess free to be blown away. Another way to get the excess oil is with a dry paint brush or a Q-tip, although this can be a painstaking process. To control precisely where you want the colorant to fall, use a mask or stencil. This is painstaking, too, because you have to go through the work of making the item, and it usually isn't worth it for one design. However, you may discover some "natural" stencils if you look around you. A doily, for example, can be used nicely to furnish a design.

Fig. 6–13. Stencil designs that we use for copper-enamel sifting onto the lower blank. The dry powder can be sifted or worked in wet, as shown in Figs. 8–14 to 8–19.

Once you have your "lower" design set, you can enhance it from above with other colorants using an outlining blank, a background (or more applicably, a foreground) white, or any other color that will add to the total drama. The colorants can be translucents or opaques; it all depends on your feeling for the design.

A word of warning: Even though copper enamel colorants are "protected" by being laminated, like many other colorants they can change hue and tone during the heating process. Generally the original color returns, but occasionally it does not. So that you won't be unduly surprised by the result, test-fire them first. Once you have done this and accept their idiosyncracies, you may want to stick with the products of one or two

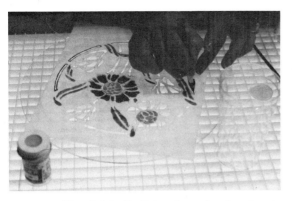

Fig. 6–14. Outlining from the stencil onto the glass using a Wrico pen.

Fig. 6–15. Sifting colorant onto the lower blank of a plate using an 80-mesh copper-enamel sifter. Many copper enamels come in sifter jars; these cost more but are worth it.

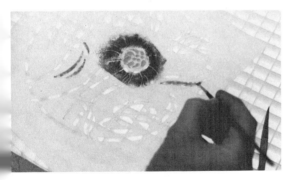

Fig. 6–16. Brushing the enamel into the interstices of the stencil is more tedious than sifting the powder, but some workers prefer to do it this way.

Fig. 6–17. The circle of decorated glass with the stencil removed. Baby oil or gum arabic holds the powder in place on the glass.

Fig. 6–18. The glass resting on the sagger with the top layer also in place. The piece is ready to be fired.

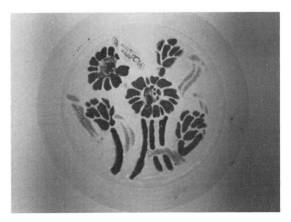

Fig. 6–19. The finished plate, sagged, painted, and laminated.

manufacturers. So much variation exists between products that if you use too many different ones, you will spend all of your time test-firing them. This is also true for glass paints from different manufacturers. Although a good manufacturer is always ready to investigate a customer's complaint, often it is the customer and not the manufacturer who is doing something wrong.

Ceramic Glazes

We are not that enthusiastic about using glazes on glass. Usually they are just too much work. We get delicate shadings mostly from glass paints, although we have seen lovely effects done with glazes on glass, both surfaces of the glass enhancing the other. Glazes can be built up on glass through repeated firings, but you should fire each layer separately, rather than combining two or more. A nice effect of depth can be created, provided you don't put on so many layers that you get cracking and peeling from trapped air or dirt or fumes from the kiln. After applying a layer of glaze to glass, allow it to dry thoroughly before firing. If you insist on adding another layer and firing both at once, the result will be a smeary surface, no matter how dry your bottom layer is.

Glazes can furnish a matt effect to the glass, modifying the light coming through and softening a layer of paint on the other surface, thus adding depth and character to the piece. Unfortunately, we find that this technique is almost always abused, either because the glaze is used so timidly that it barely has an effect, or it is used to excess. You could achieve the same result with less work by using a single layer of colorant expressly designed for glass.

No doubt there is a place for glazes in glass painting, but each worker must decide how large a role it should play in his or her technique. The basic problem, of course, is that glazing is a ceramic technique that does a very specific job. As a glass technique, its use can vary from the nebulous to the overbearing. And keep in mind that it is a lot of work when so many glass paints can establish an emphasis more readily.

Nonfire Glass Paints and Glass-Stainer's Paints

Special nonfire paints designed for glass furnish quite specific effects. An example of what can be done with nonfire paint is shown in Fig. 1–3, where the glass is used as a canvas. No fusion has occurred but the painting is "permanent" so long as it is not subjected to harsh abrasives or mishandling. We have had this painting for ten or twelve years, and the colors still have not cracked, peeled, or faded. Nonfire paints are ideal for those who would like to paint on glass, both for the novelty of the effect and to learn a new technique. Nonfire paints offer a good introduction to painting on glass because you don't need a kiln.

Glass-stainer's paints are kiln-fired paints, and they comprise the majority of paints used in glass painting and decorating. Two examples of these colorants are shown in Figs. 6–20 and 6–21. In the first, "trace" lines outline the features. We used a Hancock black paint, but any dark glass paint can be used. This type of paint can also be used to provide decor, as shown by the two pieces of glass used for the hair, where a brush texture provides a highlight pattern. This is a rough, stylized indication, and it can be softened considerably by painting with matt paint on the back side of the glass. Fig. 6–22 shows the partially completed head. All painted elements are fused directly into the underlying glass.

Fusing Colored Glass to Clear Glass

Many workers say that fusing colored glass to clear glass cannot be done. It *can* be done, provided you take care to anneal properly and avoid excessive conflicts between the different coefficients of expansion. Let's go through the process step by step:

1. With a circle cutter, or freehand, cut a circle about 11 inches in diameter from a piece of clear double-strength window glass.
2. Make sure all surfaces are smoothed and even.
3. Select and prepare a sagger for the design you have in mind. (See Chapter 14.)
4. Cut about twelve strips of colored glass no more than $\frac{1}{4}$ inch wide. Because this size is difficult to cut, you may want to use a glass-cutting board, or you can use shards of glass broken at random. One of our students used colored glass stirrers, which you may be able to get at a bar or in a hobby shop that sells glass supplies.
5. Glue the pieces of stained glass over the surface of the clear glass with Bond or Elmer's glue in an abstract design. One popular design is a fanning arrangement.
6. Place the glass blank with its stained-glass design over the sagger and put it in the kiln.
7. Fire to approximately 1350 degrees F. You will have to keep opening the kiln to have a look. The stained glass will begin to fuse before the clear glass will begin to sag. Once the sagging seems to be complete, turn off the kiln.
8. Maintain annealing at 750 degrees F. for one hour, and at 500 degrees for fifteen minutes.

Fig. 6–20. Trace lines give detail to a glass blank. Here clear glass and a tinted stained glass were used.

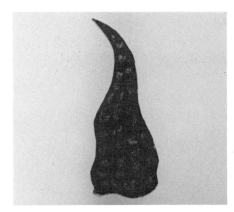

Fig. 6–21. Texturing glass with glass-stainer's paint gives an impression of hair. This is a simple but effective technique.

Fig. 6–22. A partially completed head showing the outline painting and some texturing of the hair.

Fig. 6–23. A sagged plate with fused stained-glass elements on the surface.

Fig. 6–24. A mushroom medallion by Kay Kish, made from clear glass and painted.

9. Do not remove the glass until the kiln is cold. You will have a unique and beautiful plate of fused glass similar to the one in Fig. 6–23.

Fusing Clear Glasses

Fused shapes are probably the most popular types of fused glass, especially from a commercial aspect. The shapes are usually of animals or fruit because the designs are simple, and perhaps because they are so familiar that no matter how stylized they can still be recognized. Most of these shapes are cut from either single- or double-strength window glass and are decorated or colored with glass enamels. Because the shapes are simple, they provide no cutting challenge. Instead, it is the whimsy of design and color that makes the statement. And they are easy because the fusing occurs only over small portions of the glass.

With a fused glass panel, pieces of glass are embedded on a base of glass. Of course, the more glass used as an overlay, the more stress that is placed on the base piece—and this means problems with coefficients of expansion, annealing, and design. So keep your projects simple in the beginning. As an example, here are step-by-step instructions for making a medallion using clear glass. The piece in Fig. 6–24 by Kay Kish is a favorite of ours, and we love to use it for teaching purposes.

1. With a circle cutter, or using a pattern, cut a circle from double-strength window glass about 3 inches in diameter.
2. Using the pattern, cut the appropriate number of pieces and make sure all edges are smooth.
3. Decide what colorants you want to use. We like Drakenfield enamels or Onida translucents in light blues and greens, but choose your own if you want.
4. When the painted pieces are dry, place them on the glass blank. We prefer to keep this piece clear, although you could add colorant to it. (It is a good idea to crimp a gold finding to the top of the item if you intend to suspend it. This will fuse into the glass during the firing process.)
5. Place the piece in the kiln and fire to about 1400 degrees F.
6. Since all this glass is the same, except for any color added, you should have no trouble getting it to fuse. And your final result should look like the picture.

Fusing Stained Glass to Stained Glass

To make a fused panel of different types of stained glass, you should select pieces that are similar enough so that the differences in annealing times and coefficients of expansion will not create internal stresses and cause the piece to shatter. With stained glass, try to select glass of basically the same type in tone and texture, and certainly of the same manufacturer. While this is no guarantee of success, it is at least a reasonable place to begin.

For the turtle panel in Fig. 6–25, we selected cathedral and opalescent glass. The background square of glass has overlays amounting to perhaps one-half of the surface area. To give a dramatic effect, we used a subdued background color, a cathedral amber, and fused it with opalescent glass. Because there were differences in fusing heats, we spent a lot of time finding glasses that would stay together long enough to take a picture. To get even this far, we brought the kiln to 1475 degrees F. and allowed it to cool with two periods of annealing: the first for one hour at 950 degrees; the second for one hour at 750 degrees. The kiln was then cooled for twelve hours, and the piece was taken cold from the kiln. Even so, a few cracks are discernible, but the piece has held together.

Our "fishbowl" projects in Fig. 6–25 were considerably less time consuming. For the fishbowl on the left, we laminated two pieces of stained glass of the same type to form the base of the bowl. The bottom piece represents the water, the top represents the curved surface of the bowl. To this we fused other stained-glass elements to represent fish, bubbles, weeds, and gravel. The different hues of stained glass fused with no problem whatsoever. Even the red for the fish, as well as the crushings used for the bubbles and the gravel, fused well with no cracks. The piece was taken from a cold kiln and placed in another. We used Kokomo glass, and because the glass was all the same, we had successful results.

The fishbowl in the center of Fig. 6–26 is similar in design, but this one we laminated, using two pieces of single-strength window glass. No stained glass was used at all. We ran a piece of copper wire between the surfaces to serve as a hanger and to delineate the curved surface representing the top of the bowl. The fish was cut from clear glass and sprinkled with copper enamels of different colors. The base is clear glass. A copper enamel sprinkling on the surface came out well as the seaweed. The bubbles are small pieces of clear glass. The only colored glass used were red glass crushings for the gravel on the bottom of the bowl.

There are several things to keep in mind regarding fusing and laminating. First, it doesn't pay in time or materials to try to force different glasses together. Eventually, some manufacturer will make glass specifi-

Fig. 6–25. A turtle panel with stained glass fused to stained glass.

Fig. 6–26. Three "fishbowls."

Fig. 6–27. The bottom blank on the left, the upper blank on the right, with the formed elements glued in place before firing. Note the placement of the hooks in the bottom blank.

Fig. 6–28. The "fishbowl" on the left in Fig. 6–26, with the fish and other elements fused to the surface.

Fig. 6–29. The laminated "fishbowl" in the center in Fig. 6–26, with the fish between the glass surfaces.

Fig. 6–30. Disaster in the kiln, the result of incompatible coefficients of expansion.

cally for this purpose, perhaps by changing the silica content, but to date we know of no one who has done this commercially. While it can be done eventually by hit and miss, why bother? Second, you are *probably* safe in using different colored glasses from the same manufacturer for fusing—but even here we wouldn't overload the surface of the base glass with too many elements. And, third, paint your glass pieces after fusing all the same kind. Of course, this isn't the same as using colored glass, but it is the only *safe* way to prevent what happened to us in Fig. 6–30!

Texturing

The surface of certain brands of colorless commercial glasses can be patterned aesthetically by painting, poking, indenting, or abrading almost to your heart's content. Let's look at a few of the items that can be used for texturing effects.

Crushed Glass or Glass Pieces. You should keep a collection of all the pieces left over from various projects, and for more dramatic texturing, mix the colored glass remains among the clear ones. Glass crushings can also be purchased from several suppliers (Blenko Glass supplies some colored crushed glass). You can use colored or clear glass pieces as fused elements to the surface of a base piece of glass. And, if you use small pieces of stained glass, you probably won't have too much difficulty with the expansion coefficients.

The smaller and the finer the crushings, the better. We make our own and get pleasing textured effects depending on the size, color, and amounts that we use. The simplest way to crush glass is to wrap shards in an old rag and hit the bundle with a hammer. Not much force is necessary—a few tappings will do nicely. Of course, you should tap against a fairly hard surface. We use a piece of steel beam that we keep for the purpose, but you can use a rock or a board if it is well supported. Unwrap the rag to get an idea of the different sizes you have achieved, then hammer them again if you want finer crushings. In a surprisingly short time, you will have a great variety of glass crushings, from powder to shardings. When employing them on a surface of glass, use Elmer's glue to hold the larger pieces in place; use gum arabic for the powder and small particles. To be as efficient as possible, we divide our glass crushings into sizes and keep them in small containers. They always come in handy.

Sand. Since glass is mostly silica, the major component of sand, you are really using glass to texture glass in this instance. Sand will texture well without adhering to the glass. The amount and type of stippling it will produce will vary with the size of the sand grains and the type of sand being used. We keep several varieties that we have gathered from beaches. Sometimes the unknown impurities will add their own texture to the glass, even if some of them burn out in the firing. Very coarse sand is good for large emphatic markings on the surface. This actually gives an indenting rather than a stippling effect.

Kiln Wash. This material acts like sand in a way, but it provides a crosshatching effect that is quite different and can even look like a glass frosting. It is softer than sand, although like it, it does not combine directly with the glass. If the glass gets hot enough, kiln wash will leave a very delicate but distinct texturing. If you don't want this effect, you shouldn't have kiln wash in loose form on a shelf if you are taking the temperature up high and want to keep your glass surface smooth.

Carbide Compounds. These compounds are gritty and will leave punctate marks in the glass that can be quite distinct from all but the coarsest sand. They come in different sizes of "grit," and each size produces a slightly different dimpling of the glass surface. We get ours from Sears. You want to be careful that you don't overdo the technique and provide accents that will override the main theme.

We also use carbide compounds to grind the center of our palettes for painting. This technique can also be used over glass, giving a haze either to selected areas or to the entire surface. This effect is different from the haze acquired by sandblasting or by acid etching. We like to employ it at specific areas of the glass, controlling the frosted effect, if necessary, at each area in a different manner. This forces the light to show differently at each portion of the glass. It is a simple process and requires none of the paraphernalia of sandblasting or any of the dangers of acid etching.

Whiting. In a dry state, whiting can be used as a separator. If the glass gets hot enough, the whiting will impress a soft texturing effect upon it.

Mica. Mica can be powdered or flaked. Of the two, we prefer to work with the flaked. Powdered mica, like powdered asbestos, should not be inhaled, so be sure to work in a well-ventilated area if you use it. Flaked mica is heavier than the powdered variety and not so readily inhaled, although you should still have plenty of ventilation when working with it. Flaked mica will not only texture the surface of the glass, but will embed into it to provide faceted surfaces that reflect the light, thereby giving the glass a gleaming appearance.

Indenting the Glass Surface

Imprinting glass to a certain depth and pattern results in *indentation*, an indelible sculpturing that involves a planned distortion of the glass. You must keep in mind that glass "moves" when heated, so be careful not to include any undercuts that will lock the glass in place. Indenting is not meant to become embedding. Remember also that you don't want your finished piece of glass to be lopsided; there must be room in the kiln for the glass to form a steady base. Separators are important here, and any of the mold releases will do. We use Co-Sep, a dental product that we also use for leaf making (available from dental supply houses).

Materials such as wire, clay, and cast iron will indent glass. Each, of course, has regulations of its own for glass. The best thing is to keep it simple. If you attempt to put too much fussy detail onto the glass blank, you will find the end result disappointing. The viscosity of glass is too thick to respond well to fine lines. What you will end up with is a blurred design, rather than a complexity of patterned lines.

Fig. 6–31. Indented, molded glass pieces. The molds don't have to be complex to be effective. Often the less complex, the better.

Indenting with Wire

Of the three "stamps" we like to use for indenting, only wire can be shaped and used practically at a moment's notice. And you can create with it first and then transfer this to the glass. Clay must be formed and kiln-fired, and cast iron has to be used as found. Wire has its own sculptural quality, and all sizes can be used. The heavier the gauge, the more positive the indent will be. The smaller the gauge, the higher you may have to raise the temperature in the kiln to get the viscosity of the glass thin enough to permit the indent. Don't make the wire design so complicated that you have all sorts of closely knit curves and crossings. This will leave the glass puzzled and unable to sag between all these turns and twists. Always lay the glass level over the wire, making sure there are no wire surfaces jutting up to permit the glass to slew over when it is hot and in motion. Shaping your wire can be done by hand with needle-nose or regular pliers.

Fig. 6–32. Pieces of bottle glass indented and decorated.

It is possible to sag a piece of glass into a mold while simultaneously indenting it with wire. Here you must be careful not to use too heavy a gauge, because this will prevent the glass from sagging. You may want to do this purposely to achieve a design; used as spokes of a wheel, wire will permit the glass to fold down between these straight lines. You must heat the kiln to about 1700 degrees F. for this to take place. However, if you want the wire to bend with the glass and form an indent in the sagged area, use a fairly thin piece of wire that will not be rigid. It may be best to remove the temper from the wire by heating it in a flame and then plunging it into cold water. Another factor that helps to make the wire amenable to bending as the glass is heated is to glue it firmly to the bottom surface of the glass. Make certain that the glue is dry before putting the project into the kiln.

You can bend your wire first, right into the shape of your mold, and allow it to sit there while the glass folds onto it from above. Here again, it is best to remove the temper from the wire to get a closer conformity to the mold shape.

Indenting with Clay

You can get far more distinguished, imaginative shapes with clay than with wire. For adding fine lines to a basic clay sculpture, wire can be used as an additional indent. If you are not familiar with using clay, a little practice will have you turning out objects that, if not masterpieces, can be used effectively for indenting glass. If you find that one craft at a time is enough, you can purchase small pieces of greenware at any ceramic shop, fire them in your kiln, and then use the pre-formed object as an indent. Always use a separator with any clay model, and allow the kiln to become stone cold before removing either clay or glass overlay. With proper care and handling, your clay indent can be used over and over.

As opposed to wire, clay has advantages and disadvantages. It is not as "direct" an approach, requiring always the secondary step of heating prior to use. Clay also requires that a separator be used, whereas nichrome wire and copper wire don't, since they won't adhere to the glass. Before using copper wire, brush it to a gleaming hue with a wirebrush or steel wool and be sure all surface oxides have been removed. Clay models also require some going over before use, mainly to see that no separator has plugged up an area of the model.

Always make sure, if you are using whiting or any similar "particle" separator, that you have an even consistency of the water-separator mix. It is possible, of course, to use a dry separator with a clay indent and just sift the material over the surface. We are never entirely comfortable with this technique, however. Invariably, we miss a spot or two or get too much separator on areas. And we always regret not having taken the time to mix the separator with water, brushing it on and allowing a proper drying time. Hurrying almost always leads to problems.

Indenting with Investment Material

Investment material, as described in Chapter 9, is a fine indenting material when it is used to transfer the form of an object to glass. A broach or pin of a practical design can be impressed into the modeling, an indent formed, and the glass heated over it. The design should be practical, though, with no curves and peaks or hills and valleys. This would result in an exercise in futility.

Investment material does have drawbacks. A free-form indent implies that the worker actually models it. Such a procedure is best done with clay, where you have the proper time to get your idea into tangible form. Once you add water to investment material and complete the mix, you have roughly about five minutes until it hardens. If you add too much water in an effort to increase this modeling time, you will find that the material becomes too runny and can't be worked at all.

The average indent, whether clay or investment material, should rise no more than $\frac{1}{4}$ inch above the modeling surface. If the indent is raised much more than this, more heat will be required to get the glass to "run" properly. In addition, more distortion is possible. These processes are not so discernible when you heat glass in a mold, where it is in an entrapped state. An indent has no borders to contain the glass, and it is more vulnerable to overheating and distortion. Thus you should keep the indent just high enough to impress the glass.

Indenting with Cast Iron

It is difficult to be creative with a cast-iron indent because you must use the iron as you find it. However, there are good designs all around you, from numbers to initials to entire words. Although many impurities are removed when cast iron is made, this doesn't mean that it will take the firing without changing any of its characteristics. In fact, it is very idiosyncratic in its behavior—one of an identical pair of numbers or letters firing perfectly, the other developing rust stains and other blemishes that transfer directly to the glass.

Any metal objects that are to be used as indents should be prefired to test their stability. Most metals will react to kiln heat, whether by oxidation or by pitting. As with clay, use separator on the metal indents and allow it to dry well; you may need several coats to get a proper thickness. Again, we like to use the dental separator Co-Sep, a good release agent for just about any metal. This material flows on well, grips the metal base securely, and dries rapidly. You need wait only an hour before firing.

Improving Your Indent

No matter how effectively you work out your design, and no matter how careful you are in following our guidelines, there will be occasions where your indent will be a disappointment. This is usually because it doesn't show up well enough in the glass to provide the dramatic effect you anticipated. The outlines of the pattern may be hazy, inner surfaces blurred, and (most disastrously) from certain angles the pattern may disappear from the surface entirely. This may be because of the way the light falls on the glass and the angle from which you are observing it; nonetheless it is dismaying to find all your work going for nothing. But don't fret. By its nature, an indent in glass is meant to be subsidiary to the glass, a fringe benefit rather than a foreground insistence. If you aren't satisfied with this delicate ghostlike quality, you can do certain things to improve your indent. More often than not, dissatisfaction with the appearance of the indent occurs in clear rather than colored glass, the tones of the latter carrying through a dramatic effect of its own and emphasizing the indent against the color zone. Even in colored glass, however, you may find the indent less provocative than you wish. If so, you can touch it up with glass enamel paint and refire it. You needn't refire over the indent since you will be using a low-fire glass enamel, which matures at about 1080 degrees F., considerably lower than the sagging temperature of the glass. This will certainly make your indent stand out.

Rather than simply touching up, you can color in the entire design. However, if you find this necessary, you probably have chosen a poor design, although you might want to do it even with a good design. It depends on your judgment. With clear glass, you can silver stain the indent and, refiring, come up with a golden glow over the design that can be breathtaking. You can use a bold outline alone for the borders of the design, allowing the eye to take in the rest, or you can add touch-ups of paint to it within this bordering emphasis. Part of the fun of indenting is what you do with the design afterwards. But you should never make it so obtrusive that you lose the subtleties. We often put a stained-glass border around an indent. This combines two different forms of crafting in glass within a single finished project.

Overlays

Rather than indenting the glass from below, overlays give a surface effect. You can use many different materials for overlays. Among them are:

Crushed Glass. The texturing effect of crushed glass used on the lower surface as an indentation for design can be quite different when it is applied to the upper surface. Depending on the amount of heat that is applied, the glass crushings will melt and fuse together. The sizes of the crushings—from powder to actual glass

Fig. 6–33. Improving the indent with a stained-glass border. The original indent, although clear, lacks drama. Now the focus is on the indent.

Fig. 6–34. Improving the indent with paint or colorant. Left: touches of colorant and a millifiore have been added. Center: a second piece of tinted glass has been fused to the back, throwing the indent into relief. Right: a design has been painted contrary to the indent.

chunks—enhance or diminish this effect. The larger the crushings, the more heat you will need to fuse them onto the surface. In areas where a bold emphasis is desired, glass crushings can be very effective, rather like the result of a palette knife in oil painting. You have to be careful not to overload the surface of the base glass, especially if you are using colored crushings, or they will shatter because of the different expansion coefficients. You can also use clear glass crushings and individualize these areas afterwards with paints or stains. This effect should be used sparingly; it is all too easy to overuse it.

Paints, Glazes, and Stains. These are overlays in the strict sense of the word, but since they blend into, rather than rise from, the surface, we do not group them here. See Chapters 10 and 13, where they are discussed in detail.

Enamel Threads. These are a lot of fun to use and can provide a fine "cobwebby approach" or a tangled mass of color through which the base glass is only occasionally glimpsed. You must watch your heat when using these threads. We use them mainly with a torch, where it is comparatively easy to see if too much or not enough heat is being given to maintain their raised effect on the glass.

Capillary Tubing. These are tiny but perfectly shaped glass tubes used in doctors offices and scientific laboratories. They can have an extracurricular life as glass overlays. Because of their perfect shapes, they can be cut into sections that will form neat, orderly designs. The tubing is usually "hard" (borosilicate) glass, so it has to be taken up to about 1700 degrees F. in the kiln to get it to fuse to the glass surface (also borosilicate). But the extra energy is worth it for the flexibility you now have to form design overlays that are precise and professional looking.

Capillary tubing is easily broken by hand after being nicked with a triangular file. Don't try to break this seemingly fragile tubing without first using the file. The tubing can break indiscriminately and, small as it is, give a nasty cut.

You can color this tubing prior to firing if you use a high-fire paint such as Onida's. Mix the paint into a liquid state and dip one end of the tubing into it. The paint will rise within the tube to its entire length—a capillary-action technique that justifies its name. It is always necessary to glue any design formed by this tubing to the base glass; otherwise you will end up with a free-form pattern no matter how careful your unglued arrangement was prior to firing.

Glass Threads. You can spin your own, of course, and make your threads as thick or as thin as you wish. The threads can be used as an overlay design similar to capillary tubing or combined with it for variety and rhythm. Such thin threads can be readily laminated, more so than even the extremely thin capillary tubing. When laminating glass threads, it isn't as essential to watch the heat degree for degree, since the threads are more or less protected and will usually provide the right effect even if slightly overheated. If you are using them on the surface, however, overheating can melt them away. Like capillary tubing—and like just about every type of overlay—the glass threads should be glued to the surface before firing and allowed to have their glued portions thoroughly dry before any further steps are taken.

Millifiore. This Venetian tube glass is one of our favorite overlays for abstract design. The more heat applied, the more the color spreads. These "beads" can be used as an overlay on a base glass or as fused elements, bead to bead, in a fusing/casting process to form bowls or flat hanging designs. An interesting project is simply to arrange a number of these beads side by side in a pattern, making sure they touch one another. Be sure the kiln shelf is well coated with separator, then apply heat. The result will be an interesting multicolor display.

Jewels and Globs. If not too large, these will fuse to the glass blank surface quite well, although care must be taken to anneal them well to avoid cracking the base glass. Avoid reds, which almost inevitably cause trouble.

Chapter 7

Lamination: Working in Depth

Lamination implies the layering of glass—usually two, but possibly three, layers—with some "foreign" substance sandwiched between the layers. Some of the purposes of laminating are:

1. To achieve depth.
2. To enhance the thickness of the finished object.
3. To entrap material within glass that would not otherwise adhere, for whatever reason, to the glass surface.
4. To protect material within the glass surface that would be unduly subject to wear from the surface.
5. To "marry" metals such as wire mesh or small rods to glass to form a stable design.

There are other, more individual reasons, for laminating glass—not the least of which seems to be the novelty of the technique—but the ones we discuss here comprise the basis of the endeavor.

General Laminating Principles

There has to be, if not a relationship, at least a truce between the glass that is doing the laminating and the material that is being laminated. Fusing must be able to occur without staining, mottling, or fracturing the laminated material or the glass itself. There are materials that seem to cry out for an artistic evaluation, but physically they cannot be laminated. Fabric, organic matter, and plastic must be test fired to see what remains. If the residue is ashy, or if it will mar the surfaces of the glass, it should not be used. Material that will burn out if applied to the top surface of a piece of glass will certainly burn out in the laminate as well. Laminating something does not automatically preserve it. This may be true when plastic is used as the protective covering, but it is not true with hot glass.

Laminating does not prevent a substance from burning. If it would burn in the open, it will certainly burn in the kiln.

Laminating should be done with similar types of glass. It isn't feasible to laminate stained glass to plate, or plate to a different manufacturer's (or even, in most instances, to the same manufacturer's) double-strength or single-strength glass. You will likely end up with a general mess.

The purpose of laminating, whether using two blanks or the casting/fusing technique, is to come up with a project that cannot be done as well with any other technique. Cold laminating, using glue rather than lead to bind glasses together, is also a valid statement under certain circumstances. Obviously cold laminating is easier than the kiln-fired method because there are no expansion coefficients to worry about, and just about anything goes. And very dramatic effects can be created. It is up to the individual craftsperson to decide whether it is the end result or the technique that is most important. We feel there is no shame involved in a compromise between the two.

Colorants for Laminating

Although glass stains and paints for surface work are available, one never tires of seeking the ultimate effect that is at once personalized and, often, unexplainable. The color ranges provided by copper enamels will not always match those of glass enamels, and it may be just this color that you want. Copper enamels flake and peel off the glass surface. Thus they must be laminated. Caught and sealed between two glass surfaces, they cannot separate from the glass. Interesting effects can be achieved using ceramic or copper enamel colorants for lamination and glass enamels on the surface. The depth and range of hues seems to reverberate into space when the right colors are toned into one another. Laminated copper enamels are usually used in granular form, sifted onto the lower blank.

Materials for Laminating

There is a general temptation to sandwich all sorts of items between glass. However, not all of them work, and perhaps not all of them should. But here are a few that are effective.

Silver Foil. This can be quite dramatic. When used as a background, foil gives a textured, steely look to the finished project and an opacity to the paints and stains applied to the surface of the glass. This is not to say that silver foil should cover the entire surface; rather, it should be used with discretion to make a statement *through* the glass. Often we cut silver foil into interesting designs using stencils and then laminate these designs between the blanks. This is a quick, simple, yet effective display that even a beginner can do. No one need know it's your first effort.

Silver and Gold Flakes. Some workers use these flakes to add sparkle within the laminate. But a little goes a long way.

Ceramic Overglazes. Some overglazes are metallic, others are not. Interestingly, many of the colored hues fade when laminated; the color, as well as the oil these glazes are prepared with, tends to burn out. In order to avoid fading, one might try to prefire these substances before the actual laminating is done. It may or may not help. Metallic gold or silver overglazes can be placed either within the laminate or on the top surface of the glass. These overglazes can be used for outlining as well as for general coloring.

Ceramic Underglazes. These are delicate agents and are probably best used within the laminate rather than on the surface, where they will be subject to wear and tear. A certain amount of texturing of this material is possible; like matt paint, you can texture with newspaper, brush daubings, or fingers to get interesting swirls and waves of color that will deepen or lessen the amount of light coming through. Texturing also can add to the three-dimensional effect, which is so much a part of the lamination technique.

Stained Glass. This can prove to be too thick for laminating. Since it comes in a variety of thicknesses, it might be best to use the rolled rather than the blown type. Even here you don't want to use too much because of the variance of expansion coefficients. Occasionally we prefer stained glass in order to get it into a more workable thinness, taking the material up to 1450 degrees F. or even to 1500 degrees to allow it to flow into interesting patterns. The annealing process when laminating with stained glass must be accomplished very slowly. You will need patience to laminate this material satisfactorily. On the whole, we have found that Kokomo and Blenko stained glasses give the least trouble with expansion coefficients.

Mica Flakes. These fluff up during firing and raise the glass blank, or at least that portion of it directly over them. Thus they are good for forming design bubbles. The more substantial the mica, the larger the bubble—up to a point. Clumps of flakes still look like clumps, and they tend to lie sullenly within the laminate as dirt spots.

Sand. The lamination of fine or coarse sand either sprinkled over the surface of the lower blank or arranged into design formations works well. It can be used alone or in combination with other materials. Because sand is nondescript in color, you might want to add colorant to it before or afterward.

One of the best methods of laying down sand is to apply a thin layer of gum arabic to the lower blank in brushstrokes. Then sprinkle the sand over it. The grains that fall on the wet gum will stick, the rest can be brushed away. If you want to apply sand over the entire area of the blank, use baby oil rather than the gum. The quantity of gum necessary to cover the blank produces a great deal of waste material and fumes in firing out, enough to prevent the two blanks from sealing evenly. We have tried birdcage gravel as well as sand to see if we could get any extraordinary effects. But robbing our parakeets proved to be for the birds; the final production was fairly uninteresting.

Shells. Although seashells tend to crack in the kiln, small ones can be laminated if you don't raise the heat too rapidly and if you anneal slowly. The effect is often kitschy but if used sparingly, it can provide a rather endearing design formation. A combination of shells and sand is almost too logical to be true. And, of course, glass is the inevitable extrapolation from sand.

Metals. Any kind of mesh is fairly easy to laminate. You may want to only partly laminate a metal, allowing fringed ends to protrude beyond the glass for soldering to whatever project you have in mind. Screen shapes or mesh can also be cut into designs, either plain or painted, and laminated to make an interesting geometric pattern. Many metals do not take coloration well, however, especially when heated. You can still use color on the upper blank to give a tinge and depth to the embedded screening or mesh. This technique can be combined with any of the other laminating materials.

The oxidation of metals can be a problem. As they are heated, many metals form an oxidation coat over their outer layer. This is known as fire scale. The amount of oxidation formed will depend not only on the amount of metal surface exposed to the air, but on the type of metal that is being used. Fine wire forms less fire scale than does heavy wire. Copper wire forms quite a bit of it; nichrome wire forms very little. You might find the transformation of the metallic surface a good design element.

Wire Lamination

Whenever we work with wire and glass, we are always tempted to just twist the wire into some sort of free-form design and then laminate it to see what it will look like at the end. Usually it doesn't look very good. It

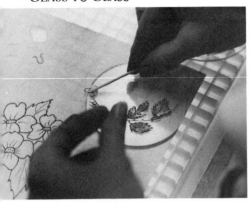

Fig. 7–1. Laminating the hook to a medallion. The hook is glued to the back surface, and a small piece of glass is placed over it. The glue will burn out in the firing. Turn the corners of your hook up as shown; this will lock them securely in place.

Fig. 7–2. Gluing the hook. Note the amount of glue used; don't be stingy here. The glue stabilizes the hook and keeps it straight through the firing.

Fig. 7–3. The beginning of an investment casting procedure. To prevent flow of the investment material under the metal flower, it must be fixed. Here we use Styrofoam with a pocket cut to fit the model.

is always best to plan your design in advance. On a piece of paper, draw whatever convolutions you want the wire to assume, and look at it before twisting the wire. Can the wire withstand the various twists and turns? Will the glass be able to accommodate them?

If you think the design will work, fix the wire to the lower blank with Elmer's glue to make certain it doesn't move during firing. Also, make sure at this point that it doesn't project so much above the lower glass surface as to prevent the upper blank from seating properly. In many cases, the wire will become detached where it is supposed to adhere. You might put a weight on it to hold it down until the glue dries. But don't put so much weight on it that you break the glass blank, something we've done. Remember, if your wire is too stiff for the design, you can always anneal it to make it more pliable. However, don't anneal all your wires as a matter of course. Nichrome wire tends to become more rigid and quite brittle as it is heated.

Wire lamination is used for practical as well as artistic effects. Wire loops can be used as hangers. But when making a wire loop, don't get carried away and allow it to become the focus of the piece. Loops can be formed of fine nichrome wire glued to the blank and subsequently covered with a symmetrical or asymmetrical segment of glass only slightly larger than the size of the loop. This technique is a favorite one for jewelry and similar small suspensions, especially if you don't have the equipment for drilling holes in the glass.

A hint to shaping hanging loops of wire: No matter how effectively they are laminated, if they are straight, they have a distressing tendency to pull out of the glass space when cooled. This is especially so if these loops are made in a "U" shape. We curve each arm of the "U" into a hook paralleling the main arm, so that after laminating it becomes almost impossible for these wires to pull out. In this case, they will now be pulling against the glass, rather than just out of a tunnel in the glass. It takes more time and care, but it is worth it not to see the final project plummet to the floor after hanging it.

Glass Casting

So far, we have been speaking of laminating two surfaces of glass. However, glass casting allows many surfaces of glass to be laminated. Cast glass has rules and regulations of its own, and we will only touch upon the subject here.

Some simple forms of casting can be done with glass providing you take the time and have the patience to accomplish them. To begin, start with a simple shape, such as a flower. This is a fairly good three-dimensional

117

Fig. 7–4. The model can be released readily from the mold once the impression is made.

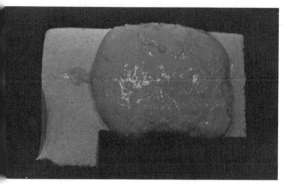

Fig. 7–5. The model covered with the mold material.

Fig. 7–6. Once the material hardens, the model can be pulled directly from the Styrofoam pocket. Any mold material that has slipped behind it can be cut away.

Fig. 7–7. The models, front and back.

Fig. 7–8. The mold is filled with small pieces of clear glass preparatory to casting. (Casting for this amount of material will occur at about 1700 degrees F.)

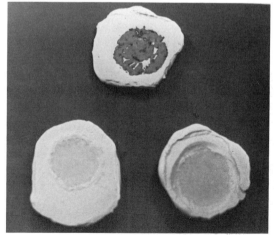

Fig. 7–9. The glass in the molds after being heated and removed from the kiln. Clear glass was used in the two lower molds; colored crushings were used in the top mold.

Fig. 7–10. Some of the results of glass casting. The objects must be treated further. In the case of the heavy casting of clear glass on the lower left, a mixture of sulfuric and hydrofluoric acid (in a mix of 1 to 3) will clear the surface and make the glass less opaque. The other items can be painted or outlined. The more marked the different levels of the mold, the more dramatic the cast results will be, as noted by the flower in the center.

Fig. 7–11. Some final results of glass casting, cleaned with an acid bath.

shape because it allows for a wide, open base. The casting model can be made of clay, wax, or even an organic matter such as a real flower. The model is encased in the mold material (we use the dental investment material Co-Sep) and burned out in the kiln. This burning-out process (also known as the *lost wax process*) provides two advantages. First, it takes care of getting rid of the model, leaving only its indentation in the mold. Second, it matures the mold, making it hard and able to withstand handling. The broad, open base behind the model is necessary as an entree for the molten glass.

Many forms of glass casting are possible using either colored glass or clear glass. We use a fairly fine measurement of glass particles for casting, one that is almost a powder. Hammering glass shards in a rag is a good start. Once the pieces have been reduced to a reasonable size, we place them on a palette and grind them further with a pestle. Then we place them in the mold and heat them until fusing (casting) occurs.

Using Ceramic Lusters

Most lusters are basically resinates, and as such they differ in a single wavelength of light and produce an entirely individualistic effect. Although most lusters become transparent when fired to their maturing temperature, they don't act upon glass in the same way as other transparent luminescents. In fact, they become more or less iridescent because of their metallic nature.

Lusters can be used either on the glass surface or within the laminate, depending on the effect you want. They are mainly low-firing materials, and their best effects are achieved at about 1080 degrees F. Lusters are used as overglazes in ceramics, and they have varying uses with glass. They are not as easy to work with as the glass paints and stains because they don't flow well. Basically they must be "plated" onto the glass surface, dipped on with a brush rather than brushed on. Be sure to use a good brush, one that will not shed bristles. Because lusters can be quite viscous, they attract dust particles, pieces of lint, and brush hairs. If these extraneous invaders aren't removed, they will leave marks after firing. Since lusters dry rapidly, they must be applied rapidly. We usually limit our work with lusters to small areas. Overall coverage is almost impossible.

Lusters should not be put on too heavily. Instead, you must float them on, dipping your brush in luster and touching it to the glass, rather than painting it on, trying to avoid a streaky look. One of the tricks is to keep the luster-water mix from becoming so sticky that it will cover only tiny portions of the glass surface. A thin coating usually works best. Don't expect irregular layers to smooth out in the firing. Any object going into the kiln should be as perfect as you can make it. Too many workers expect too much from the firing process in this regard.

Many ceramists who have begun working with glass try to transfer the techniques of one medium to the other. This is alright only to a degree. Because lusters are usually mixed with water, there is a more rapid drying time when used on porous clay rather than on nonporous glass. Allow the latter to dry for a good forty-five minutes before firing. This is especially true if you are using it in a laminate, where the water evaporation can become trapped between the glass blanks and cause hazing of the surfaces or misaligning of glass pieces used for laminating.

It's possible to blend two different lusters together to get a mixture of tones. Do this in the "wet" and allow the tones to blend into one another. If you do it after the lusters have dried, they will tend to smudge more than blend, forming an irregular, unsightly boundary line.

The rules of cleanliness, drying, and firing also apply to lusters. Remember that glass is transparent, so any smudges act as fingerprints against the enveloping haze of color that you are applying.

PART III
Sagging and Molding Glass

Chapter 8

Glass Sagging Techniques

Fig. 8–1. A sagger mold. This is the positive from which the saggers are made.

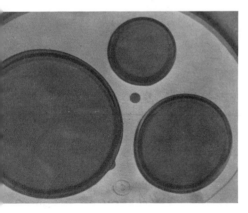

Fig. 8–2. Slip is poured into the mold and allowed to set until hard, when it will begin to separate from the side of the mold and leave a noticeable gap between the edge of the sagger and the mold. The saggers are simply lifted from the mold.

Glass sagging is mainly done to make decorative bowls and plates. To understand the technique, you must first understand the difference between a sagger and a mold.

Saggers and Molds

A mold is the "positive" from which a sagger is made. Commercial saggers are usually made of slip, a watery type of clay. Each supply house has its brand of slip, and hobbyists inevitably have a favorite slip that works best for them. Most glass hobbyists buy their saggers; some have never seen a mold. But it is a simple process to make your own saggers.

The slip is poured into the mold and allowed to set for a few minutes. Then the excess is poured off. This leaves a remainder of semihard slip attached to the bottom and sides of the mold surface. After being thoroughly air-dried, the slip will separate from the mold. At this point, it can be picked from the mold and placed upright on the table. It is quite fragile at this stage, so it should be handled carefully. We let our brand new saggers air-dry for several hours before firing, just to make sure all the water has evaporated. The sagger is fired to 1600 degrees C. and allowed to cool down in the kiln. When the kiln is cold, the sagger is ready for use. If you have a fairly large sagger or one with many convolutions, put a number of pinholes into it before firing, especially at those places where air is likely to be trapped by the sagging glass. These areas can form pockets; as the glass starts to sag, the air pressure may prevent the glass from sagging properly.

Remember that the sagger is the *negative*. What is raised in the sagger will be indented in the glass; what is indented in the sagger will be raised in the glass. Saggers can be either simple or complex, but the simpler they are, the easier it will be to sag the glass properly. A sagger full of curves, angles, and twists may look like a marvel, but the glass may not be able to match it in complexity from a simple gravity flow. Keep in mind, when choosing your sagger, that it is gravity that sags the glass. The force of gravity is limited, so you can see that there is a limit to how complex a sagger can get and still be workable. We have seen saggers with very thin lines and deep pockets that obviously the glass would not be able to conform to, considering the pressures and temperatures. Consider the limits of your material when you buy a sagger.

Preparing the Glass for Sagging

Any kind of glass can be sagged, but many workers use plate glass for two reasons: (1) it is a soft glass and sags well, and (2) the bulk and weight of plate glass makes a nice bowl or dish. Before you begin the sagging process, coat your sagger with separator. The classic separator is whiting mixed with water. Although the whiting works fairly well, we find it erratic at certain temperatures and on certain saggers. Also it can be lumpy if it isn't well mixed. We have used many commercial separators and find that Harper's Kum Klean works nicely. We suggest a liquid separator—a powder mixed with water—rather than the dry powder or kiln wash that is just sprinkled on the sagger. Liquid separator gets into the nooks and crannies of the sagger, and it spreads far more evenly than the dry powder sifted on. However, many workers continue to sift their separators with good results. Once the sagger is coated with separator, let it dry. Go over it and reopen any air holes that are clogged. We always stand our saggers on stilts to allow for maximum air flow beneath them, rather than flat on the kiln shelf or floor.

When the sagger is ready, place a piece of glass over it and draw the outline with a glass pencil. Cut the glass either freehand or with a circle cutter, and make sure all the edges are smooth. We use a Carborundum belt to smooth the edges. Many workers feel that the edges will smooth out in the firing, but we have found that just one slightly irregular edge can catch on the sagger and hang, preventing the glass from sagging properly in that area. It takes just one rocky bowl to appreciate this, so we always sand our glass carefully.

The glass should be cut to match the sagger as closely as possible. It can be a little smaller, but not much or you will lose some of the sagged design. If it is more than $\frac{1}{8}$ inch larger, it might hang up on the sagger and not flow properly.

The cleanliness of the glass is imperative. You can use glass cleaners, but many of them leave a film. Soap and water is better. Dry the glass with newspaper, and

Fig. 8–3. Some examples of saggers, the negative of the mold.

Fig. 8–4. Decorated glass on a small sagger ready to be fired. The sagger is coated with mold release or separator and left to air dry until the separator hardens.

Fig. 8–5. Glass prepared for sagging on a large sagger. The size of sagger you can use is limited only by the size of your kiln.

Fig. 8–6. A piece of sagged, undecorated glass.

Fig. 8–7. A sagged, decorated dish. The colors are Onida's and are food-safe.

Fig. 8–8. A sagged, decorative dish. The possibilities are limitless.

the glass should come out sparkling clean. Handle it only by the edges: Fingerprints and smudges can fuse into the surface.

If you are going to laminate two pieces of glass, try to cut them both from the same piece to avoid incompatibility of expansion coefficients. Lamination should have a purpose and not be done for the sake of novelty alone. You can laminate to strengthen a piece of glass that is too weak or too fragile for sagging. This will protect a design that otherwise would come off the surface, or to lock in colors that are not food-safe. Lamination will make a weightier dish. Instead of cutting and breaking out plate glass, you can prepare two thicknesses of double-strength window glass with far less difficulty than plate and still have a weighty dish. In general, the configuration of the mold does not have to be taken into account in laminating. If it will comfortably sag a single piece of glass, it should do the same for two. If it will give "hang-ups" (glass doesn't reach bottom of the mold), with one piece, sagging two pieces will not add enough weight to overcome them.

When the glass is prepared for sagging, you can fire it over the sagger immediately or take time and decorate it.

Decorating Glass

If you are going to decorate your glass at all, it should be done before you sag it. The sagging process and the paint maturation will take place at the same temperature, provided that the paint you are using will fire at that particular heat. Not all paints will, of course. Some are made to fire at approximately 1400 degrees C., the sagging temperature of most glass. We have occasionally gone to 1450 degrees to sag a complicated piece, and even to 1500 degrees, although the paint color begins to fade at that temperature.

The paints we use for sagging are Onita's Translucent Colors. They fire up well in the sagging range, are food-safe, and provide a luster and color range that will serve for all purposes. They are best used directly from the bottle; if necessary, a little water can be added. A small rod will suffice for stirring. Don't use this paint on a palette: The color will tend to run over the glass and thin out. Onita's colors achieve a fine sheen and mix when they are floated onto the glass from the brush, rather than being stroked on. If you want to stroke them, use the tip of a fine brush and go over the line or alongside it to get the maximum color. In this way, you will still be more or less "floating" the color on.

You will be floating the color on the design through the cloisonné approach. The outlines of the design are laid down in a thin, delicate border of ornate tracery or thin, straight lines. The best instrument we have found to do this is the Wrico pen.

Fig. 8–9. The Wrico pen. The plunger in the back allows paint to flow when it is up. The reservoir is just above the nose cone.

Fig. 8–10. The Wrico pen comes apart for cleaning. There are four sections: nosecone, reservoir, barrel, and plunger. The plunger comes apart into two pieces. The thin wire rod at the end, which goes through the small opening in the nose, is worked by the plunger. This wire bends easily, but it can be straightened delicately by hand. If the wire snaps off, the pen is useless.

Fig. 8–11. A medicine dropper is used to fill the Wrico pen. The plunger is pulled back to allow the reservoir to fill completely. Remember that the plunger must remain in this position in order to use the pen. To stop the flow of ink through the nose, the plunger should be pushed in.

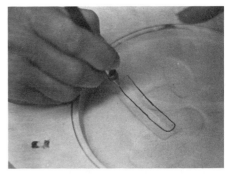

Fig. 8–12. Outlining with the Wrico pen. For best results, the pen is held straight up and down. If the ink doesn't flow steadily, push the plunger in and out.

The Wrico Pen

Essentially the Wrico pen is a fountain pen that writes with paint. There are three sizes, each of which provides a line of different thinness. None of these lines is obtainable with the usual brushstroke in a single flow. The pen is particularly good for making the thin veins on a leaf. In fact, it is altogether a handy little instrument. It is composed of a nosecone, reservoir, barrel, and plunger. Ink or thin paint is placed in the reservoir with a medicine dropper. The plunger is then worked up and down to prime the pen. Actually, the plunger pushes a thin rod back and forth through the tiny nosecone, keeping it clear. The pen is used with the plunger drawn back (removing the rod from the nose). The best way to hold the pen is straight up and down.

If the pen plugs up while you are using it, work the plunger up and down to free the nosecone. Don't forget to pull the plunger up again, the most common mistake made with the Wrico pen.

The Wrico Pen was initially introduced for gold work, and if you use gold, you should keep one pen for its use. Gold can be a difficult paint, and since it is expensive, you don't want to waste any. If you want to use gold as your decorating graphic, you must practice on a spare piece of glass to get the right consistency. Gold paint is usually thinned with Gold Essence from the Hanovia Company. Use this material sparingly so that you don't overthin the gold. When you are finished with the pen, clean it immediately. A good cleaner is Energine, which is available in cleaning supply stores. Save the Energine that you use to clean your gold Wrico and keep it in a bottle. You can use this for brush decorating as "shadow gold" or as background touches.

The Entrapment Technique

Gold and outlining inks are oil based, whereas decorating colorants such as Onita's are water based. Thus an outline drawn with gold or ink must contain the paint. The easiest way to draw an outline is to place the pattern directly under the glass and trace it. Then allow it to dry before flowing on the color. It's as simple as that. Removing a mistake on the outline is difficult because it smudges, and the more you try to fix it, the worse it gets. If you do make a mistake, start over. On the other hand, if you have only a weak or slightly misplaced line, you can thicken it or even go over it with gold or ink. Remember that any surface dirt will interfere with the flow of the outline and interrupt the color consistency. Gold should dry for at least an hour.

Sagging over a Single-Use Mold

Occasionally a design will call for a fairly wide curve of glass, particularly for lampshade panels. To make a single-use mold for this, we mix a pound of regular kiln wash with about half a pound of diatomaceous earth and about three-quarters of a pound of calcium carbonate (whiting). The consistency is determined by the whiting, which should be added to the other two items a little at a time. The consistency is adequate when the powder will retain an impression. For making a lamp panel or any large bend, mound the powder directly in the center of the kiln (a top-loader must be used) and impress the shape into it. We have used plastic shapes, but another material to use as a template for bending and curving is copper. We have made sails for ships, lamp panels, and even bowls and tableware by sagging over this impressed mound of powder. You cannot do the fine sagging that you can with a clay sagger, but as an additional technique, or used alone, it adds to the flexibility of things that can be done with a kiln. We've saved this project until last, just to show how simply and inexpensively glass can be molded into intricate shapes by the worker at home.

Chapter 9

Glass Molding Techniques

The difference between glass molds and glass molding is more than one of semantics. The process of glass molding literally produces a three-dimensional shape. The idea of molding glass is hardly new. But our approach is somewhat different from the usual one. The material for glass molds varies from moist sculpture clay to Kastolite, and all have their drawbacks. Clay is the classic mold material, but you have to be a sculptor to mold it into all but the simplest shapes. Other mold materials have to be mixed with compounds not readily available in local stores—and then they must sit for twenty-four hours or so to harden. Others are finicky when it comes to high temperatures: They will shrink, are too fragile, develop fine lines, need to be prefired, trap air bubbles, and need venting holes drilled in their sides and special containers for casting the wet mold materials. After a while the project becomes making the mold, rather than using it.

Liquid clay, or "slip," works well for making saggers because you are plating thin material over a porous surface (the commercial mold). This allows the slip water to evaporate in a reasonable length of time. Although it gives the impression of overall use, slip is extremely limited when it comes to making thick molds. Here it must sit for days to evaporate the water, and even then, because of irregular evaporation, the semihard slip can break apart when you remove it.

The Ideal Mold Material

A good molding material should have the following characteristics:

1. Inexpensive
2. Readily available
3. Able to mix with water
4. Uncomplicated, needing no exotic ingredients or even any ingredients other than the prepared mix

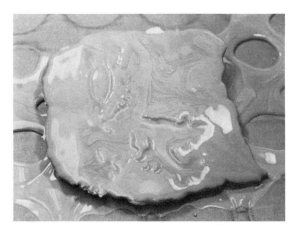

Fig. 9–1. Slip (liquid clay) applied over a mold. The material is still wet after several hours; the mold isn't porous enough to absorb the water.

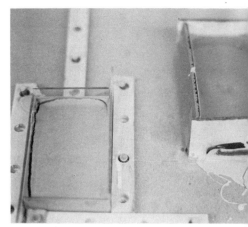

Fig. 9–2. Because it is watery, slip must be contained. On the right is a cardboard box we made for a slip mold; on the left a plastic one. Both are bottomless. The slip ran out the bottom, but it didn't harm the mold. These slip molds took three days to evaporate the water.

5. Easy to mix by hand
6. Quick setting (within minutes)
7. Able to place in the kiln immediately
8. Able to withstand temperatures up to 1800 degrees F. without cracking
9. Able to release the glass, even a painted surface
10. Able to transfer fine impressions
11. Permanence for storage and for reuse

This list is completely fulfilled by two items working in conjunction: They are materials used in the dental profession. We have experimented with most of these materials to take impressions and transfer them to a permanent working model. Some were not suited to glass. However, alginate and soldering investment seem to be the answer to everyone's mold-making dream.

Working with Alginate

Alginate is made under various trade names, but if you ask your local dental supplier for it under this general name, you will get the right stuff. Alginate is extracted from seaweed. It comes as a fluffy powder and can be mixed with water in a rubber bowl with a spatula. Both of these items can be purchased at your dental supply house. Alginate comes in a fast-set and a normal-set mix. For your first attempts, use the normal set; the fast set may well be too fast.

In mixing alginate for glass work, disregard the instructions on the can. Use approximately twice as much water as alginate. Measure the powder and mix it

Fig. 9–3. Casting directly into investment material. Standard containers can be used for investment molding, but we do not advise them. In one instance, seen in the container on the top, we had to cut into the back surface to pry out the mold.

Fig. 9–6. Fill the cavity with soldering investment.

Fig. 9–7. Take the impression of your model.

Fig. 9–4. A mold container made from a piece of Styrofoam. Square it off to the approximate size.

Fig. 9–8. The final impression. To make a raised impression, you would have to pour alginate into this. Soldering investment is brittle for direct casting; alginate is rubbery and far more flexible. It also picks up fine lines and transfers them with fidelity.

Fig. 9–5. Measure the surface area for scooping out for the mold.

Fig. 9–12. Select your model for the mold.

Fig. 9–9. Making a mold with alginate and investment material. The powdered alginate is put into a rubber bowl.

Fig. 9–13. The model is coated with alginate.

Fig. 9–10. Water is added. The material sets fast, so be alert.

Fig. 9–14. A perfect negative of the model after setting.

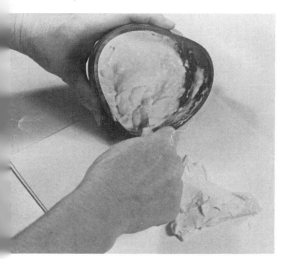

Fig. 9–11. Mix the alginate vigorously.

Fig. 9–15. Alginate applied to some deep indentations to get a better reading.

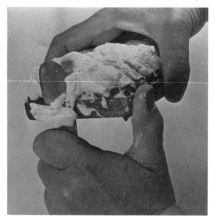

Fig. 9–16. Excess alginate is cut away with a spatula.

Fig. 9–17. A perfect impression.

vigorously in the bowl. Considering its fluffy nature, fold it into the water before stirring, but work fairly quickly or the alginate will begin to set. A good mix of alginate will be pasty and thick, and it may look lumpy. Once it has gotten to this point, pour it (more applicably, push it) over the model and pat it down with your hands. The alginate is slightly sticky, but your fingers will get it just right.

If the mix is too watery, it will flow off the sides of your model. However, this is a molasseslike flow, so you can easily scoop the excess back onto the main pile. Because alginate sets quickly, you don't have to make an enclosure for it. In fact, it sets faster if you don't, since all of it will be exposed to the air. If you want to use a container, use only a four-sided one; the tabletop is the fifth working surface. It is tempting to make things especially neat and make your alginate impression in a plastic container. However, it is difficult to remove the alginate mold from the container because the bottom surface will adhere. You can remove the alginate by running a spatula along the sides and tapping vigorously on the bottom, but the object is to make this procedure as simple and trouble free as possible.

To achieve a considerable thickness of alginate—for instance, when you are taking an impression of a particularly thick object—we make plastic "sides" into which we pour the material. This gives a nice flat-top surface, which, of course, becomes the bottom surface when the mold is turned over. Occasionally we want such a surface to make sure the object lies perfectly flat in the kiln, as with an indent for a sagger.

Alginate can trap air bubbles, so it is a good idea when pouring to tap the top surface of the material with the spatula as you go. This will bring the air bubbles to the surface and allow you a better control of the flow over the surface of the model. Pour a small amount of alginate from the bowl and arrange it with the spatula; then pour or scoop more from the bowl and arrange that. Make sure that all your separate scoops are melded together over the model surface so that there are no separation lines between them. Again, gentle tapping with the spatula as you go will get the alginate to meld.

The alginate sets in a minute or a minute and a half, but you should be able to cover the surface of almost any model in that time. Once the alginate sets, you cannot add more to it, for it will merely peel away. (This is an interesting phenomenon, and we will put it to good use shortly.) Once the alginate is set—it will feel firm to the touch—simply remove it from the model. Alginate that is set is rubbery. So long as the model has no undercut areas where the alginate can hang up, it will come loose easily. We have never had to use any separator on models for alginate impressions; indeed, when we did, it only interfered with the impression.

Once you have peeled the alginate from the model, you will have an exact negative. You now have two possibilities: You can remake the positive impression with casting material, which will be the firing mold, or you can make it with alginate so as to have a negative casting mold. It depends whether you want to cast the inside or the outside.

Since alginate, once set, does not adhere to itself, you can recast with it directly on the cast you have already made. There are distinct advantages to this, particularly if you want both sides of a particular model. This is especially handy when it comes to leaf making.

Alginate molds are an intermediate step; they are not meant to last. Shrinkage will occur gradually over a period of time. We have used alginate molds as long as a day and a half later, but, of course, our tolerances are considerably less demanding than those of dentists casting an inlay. Generally, we try to make final molds from our alginate impressions as soon as possible. However, if you cannot make them immediately, don't worry; there is time to do them the next day, provided you understand that a slight amount of shrinkage will have occurred. If you wait several days, however, you will find your alginate molds getting hard and somewhat distorted. Don't try to use them at this point; make new ones. The beauty of the process is that it's so easy to do.

Casting Stone

This is the material dentists use for models in orthodontia. It is strong and durable, and it comes out of the alginate impression with a smooth finish. It lasts

132

Fig. 9–18. Making a mold from the intermediate alginate. The two negative impressions are waiting. Water is added to the powdered soldering investment.

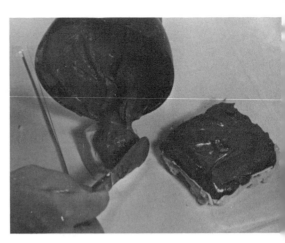

Fig. 9–21. Pouring the investment. No container is necessary, since the mix is thick enough to spread without running.

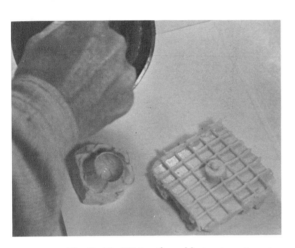

Fig. 9–19. Mixing the soldering investment.

Fig. 9–22. Tapping the unset material to relieve air bubbles and to get an even spread over the surface.

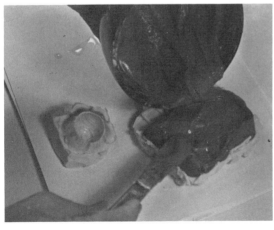

Fig. 9–20. Spreading the investment over the alginate surface.

Fig. 9–23. The final impression. The excess can be trimmed before it has fully dried.

just about indefinitely and will separate from glass, giving a clean form to the glass. In fact, there is only one thing wrong with it—it breaks apart under the heat of the kiln.

It bothers our sense of economy to use casting stone as a final mold material, even when we are casting on a one-time basis. Instead, we use it for permanent storage of molds. First, we make the mold from alginate; then, if it is a mold we want to keep, we make it from casting stone. Thus whenever we want to use the mold, we can recast the alginate over it, since it peels easily from its surface.

Casting stone also comes in a powder. The mix here is about three-quarters powder to one-quarter water. The consistency should be thick enough so that if you turn your bowl upside down the mixture just begins to flow out. If you use too much water, you must add powder until you get the right consistency. If the mix is too thin, the final mold will break apart easily.

Once you have the mix right, simply pour the casting stone over the alginate impression. Again, you really don't need a container; the mix is thick enough to sit right on top of the model. However, if you want to use plastic walls for neatness, do so. It is a good idea, however, to lift them off the impression as it just starts to harden. Otherwise you may have to pry and push to accomplish this task once the hardening process is completed.

Fig. 9–24. Some other impressions. Top: the alginate. Bottom: the investment molds made from the alginate impressions.

Casting Impression

Casting impression and the more effective soldering impression are high-heat materials. Casting impression comes in powdered form and is mixed with water. However, it is quite fragile in its unfired state—and often in its fired state as well. The thinner the mold, the more delicate it is, and we have had unfortunate instances of one of these molds breaking apart on its way to the kiln. This material is only so-so for glass, and it is a waste of time to fool with it when soldering investment is much more effective.

Soldering Investment

We use soldering investment to form our final mold. It is mixed in the same proportions of powder to water as casting stone, and it hardens within three to five minutes, depending on the amount of water and the humidity of the room. Soldering investment can be poured directly onto the alginate model with no separator; the alginate pulls away easily from the impression mix, having precisely transferred its negative impression to a positive one. Soldering investment, unlike stone, can be worked with a fine tool to make lines or to get rid of air bubbles. The mix must be absolutely dry before you attempt this. Soldering investment is by no means as strong as stone, so handle your final mold with care. We find it a good idea to make these molds thicker than the alginate model to give more substance to them; however, we have fired extremely thin soldering impression molds and found them to hold up just as well as the thick ones under heat. It is a question of convenience in handling the final mold that determines how thick one thinks it should be.

Soldering-investment molds cannot be used conveniently to remake others, so we do not store them. Using this mold, instead of casting stone, to pour alginate upon leads to a mess rather than to a precise impression. The soldering investment does not reimpress well, nor does it release from the alginate readily. Clumps of it come away with the alginate. Casting stone is still your best bet if you have a mold that you want to keep for further impressions.

Other than this, soldering investment answers just about all the problems inherent in mold making for glass. It gets hard after the initial firing, yet it will break apart easily when it is necessary to release entrapped materials, as in tunnel molds.

An Efficient Liquid Separator

The most efficient separator for small high-heat objects on molds is the dental material Co-Sep. This is applied with a brush, and it dries readily, although we have fired over it wet and had no problems. It is efficient because it's easy to apply and comes in a liquid form so that you don't have to mix it. We have used Co-Sep in firing painted surfaces down against the mold even for a primary firing without the glass sticking to the mold. It can be used as well over large surfaces, such as saggers, with no sticking problems. However, with saggers, it is probably more economical to use one of the standard ceramic separators.

Co-Sep is not inexpensive, but a small bottle goes a long way when you are firing small objects such as leaves. It will flow nicely into small crevices in the mold surface. Of course, standard ceramic separators can be used on soldering-investment molds. However, we have had some plugging of fine lines with them. With Co-Sep, you will not have this problem.

Slip Molds

We have made slip molds (as opposed to slip saggers) with good success, but our objection to slip as a mold material is threefold. First, it takes a long time to dry out. Second, slip will not release from alginate impressions. Third, the watery slip runs, so you must make a container for it. The best container is one of fired clay since this is porous; a bisque-ware saucer will do the trick, but you must get the right size. A considerable amount of ad-libbing is necessary—and then you have to go through it again when you change sizes. Of course, you can prepare different hollows out of clay and bisque-fire them. Even here, you will be faced with two problems: the negative mold upon which to cast the slip, and the need to prefire the slip once it is cast. You can make a negative mold out of casting stone, but if you've gone this far, you might as well use soldering investment. Soldering investment doesn't require prefiring, so, again, you are ahead of the game in time and money. Slip is inexpensive of itself, yet by the time you go through all the shenanigans, you have added considerably to the price you've paid.

In short, slip is a fine material for making saggers. Here it is already placed in a mold made to accommodate it and to allow it to release properly. When it is used in other states and with other materials, it tends to be stubborn.

Transferring a Raised Impression to a Sagger

Our model for transferring to a sagger is a bas relief from a decorative mural, as shown in Fig. 9–25. The design could be dramatic as an indent for either a shield or a sagged bowl. The technique can also be used with glass cut to a shield pattern if you don't have any saggers. The complete process is shown in Figs. 9–27—9–38.

After you have chosen your model, the first step is to lay the model flat on the table. No separator is necessary. Mix the alginate and pour it over the model. Remove it after it has set. Next, mix soldering investment and pour it into the alginate. Since the top surface of the soldering investment is to be used as the bottom of the relief mold, it should be as flat as possible. Once the investment is set, remove the alginate. Select a sagger of the approximate size and place the relief mold within it. To prevent the glass from sagging around the mold, use modeling clay as a border around it. Paint the mold and the clay border with Co-Sep.

The glass should be cut in a circle calculated to fit the sagger. We use the large circle cutter made by Stanford Engineering. The sagger should be coated with standard ceramic separator and let dry overnight. Now, with everything ready, place the sagger and glass

136

Fig. 9–25. The model for transferring a raised impression to a sagger.

Fig. 9–28. The mold made from the alginate impression.

Fig. 9–26. Alginate impression of the original model.

Fig. 9–29. The alginate impression above, the investment mold below.

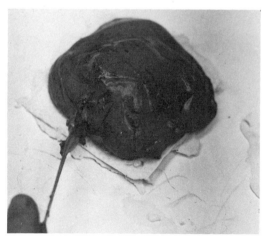

Fig. 9–27. Making the mold from the alginate impression.

Fig. 9–30. The selected sagger.

Fig. 9–31. The mold placed within the sagger.

Fig. 9–32. Modeling clay fills in the space around the mold to allow the glass to sit evenly.

Fig. 9–33. The sagged glass with the mold impression outlined.

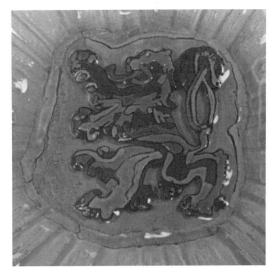

Fig. 9–34. The painted central impression; the project completed.

Fig. 9–35. Right: two alginate molds, one made from the other. Left: the investment mold, from which more alginate molds can be made.

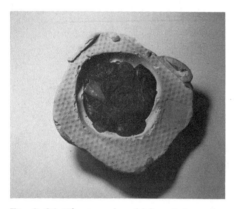

Fig. 9–36. The tunnel mold from below after firing. Fusing of the different chunks has taken place.

Fig. 9–37. The tunnel mold broken apart to release the rose from within.

in the kiln and heat to 1350 degrees F. This heat is arbitrary: For hard single-strength glass we used for this project, and for our Stuart clay kiln, it was the correct temperature for sagging. Finally, the piece can be painted (we used Onita's Translucent Colorants) and refired to approximately 1350 degrees once again. Fig. 9–34 is the result.

Tunnel Molds

To prove that investment material can take extremely high temperatures in the kiln, we decided to fuse glass in the shape of a rose, as shown in Fig. 9–35. First, we mixed alginate and poured it into a deep pocket. It separated out readily when it set, even though no separator was used. Since we couldn't cast into this, we mixed more alginate and poured it over this negative impression to make an exact duplicate of the primary model—what we call a tunnel mold.

We made soldering investment molds of both alginate molds—the tunnel mold (made from the upright alginate mold) and the reverse of it. Once the soldering investment was set, we placed into it various bits and pieces of chunk glass, breakage pieces from dalles. We placed this mass of chunk glass in our small Huppert enameling kiln, which has given us very good service over the years, and turned the temperature on. We vented the kiln for only five minutes or so, then closed the door and turned the temperature to medium. At 500 degrees, we go right to high. The firing of the rose was accomplished at 1800 degrees C. The kiln was allowed to cool to cold. With such a substantial amount of glass, we were afraid of cracking. The result is shown in Fig. 9–36. In Fig. 9–37, the mold was broken to release the rose. To differentiate the folds of the petals more clearly, Hancock's Tracing Black paint was used. This was fired at 1175 C. The lines of the petals are delineated nicely.

A Casting Crucible for Fusing

Because it can take high heat without cracking, soldering investment can be used even in small amounts to hold glass crushings for fusing. For the fused flowers in Fig. 9–38, we used both a torch and a kiln. The mold "crucible" was made by impressing a small pocket into the wet material. Either a spoon or the bottom of a small plastic container can be used to make this. The impression material is then allowed to dry. No preheating is necessary. Glass crushings were placed in the well and a torch applied. Fusing was accomplished with a minimum of fuss; piece of ni-chrome wire placed into the glass crushings provided stem for the flower. The same process can be accomplished in the kiln with even greater ease if you want to make many flowers at the same time.

Mold making is an endeavor which is usually considered as background to the final product. Yet, whether the mold is fruitwood (as in many glass-blowing endeavors) or, as described in this chapter, a material primarily used in dentistry, as much time and effort—sometimes more—are required for the mold as for the final product. Too often students hurry through this part of the glasscrafting technique simply because making a mold is not considered a particularly aesthetic experience; there's little to show off that will represent the amount of time you put into it.

But wait. The better, the more developed the mold to account for the exigencies of the casting experience, the finer, the more precise, the more beautiful will be your end result. What is more, the final product can be readily duplicated from the mold.

Obviously, we have not exhausted all the possibilities of the wonderful mold material described in this chapter. You may find more and better uses for it. Don't be afraid to make experiments on your own. It is not only fun, it is the best way to become adept at using the material.

Fig. 9–38. A mold crucible in which the flower, resting in it, was formed. A vase of fused flowers sits in the background.

PART IV

Projects: Putting It All Together

Chapter 10

Leaf Making

To duplicate leaves and flowers as closely as possible— and to do this in glass *and* by hand—is a fine craft. Here we will cover the basics of leaf making as they apply to shaping, veining, and coloring. The object is to have the result come out almost true to life.

Preserving Leaf Models

Since we work directly from natural models, we are always on the lookout for unusual shapes. When we find one, we can't always take a mold of it, and in several days the leaf will be shriveled and of no use. To preserve our specimens, we spray them with Bond spray adhesive. We lay the leaves on wax paper and spray one side, then the other. If you wave the leaf in the air by the stem, the adhesive will set. We have kept models for weeks, and they haven't lost any of their shape and color.

Making the Mold

The leaf mold is made in the same way as described in Chapter 9. The leaf, stiffened by the adhesive, is placed on the bed of alginate. The alginate is then allowed to set. Another mix of alginate is poured on the first, trapping the leaf between the two. Since alginate will not bind to itself, when this second pour is set, the two pieces may be easily pulled apart. You now have a cast of the leaf, front and back.

A word of caution: When you first press the leaf into the alginate, make sure the stiffness of the alginate doesn't flatten the leaf. Maintain its natural curl with your fingers until the alginate has set. This will give a more natural look to your leaf.

Set aside the two alginate models while you mix the soldering investment. Unlike alginate, soldering investment at first seems to be too thick, and then

Fig. 10–1. Making the alginate impression from leaves.

Fig. 10–2. The alginate leaf impressions.

Fig. 10–3. Leaf molds being made over the alginate model.

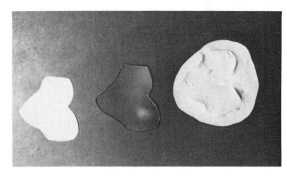

Fig. 10–4. Leaf pattern in paper, glass, and the mold.

Fig. 10–5. Leaf impressions and their models.

Fig. 10–6. A raised leaf mold.

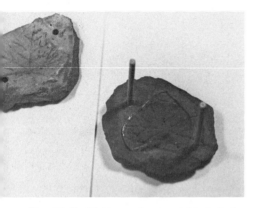

Fig. 10–7. Making a plunger mold. Left: the mold with holes for the porcelain rods. Right: the glass blank rests on the lower mold with the rods in place.

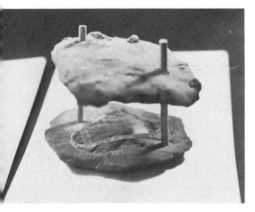

Fig. 10–8. The plunger mold in place, about to be lowered against the glass.

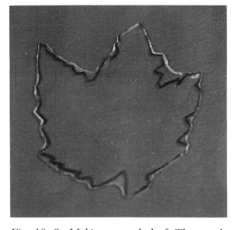

Fig. 10–9. Making a maple leaf. The rough is cut out of glass and the blank sketched with a glass marking pencil. All cutting was done by hand because of the angularities of the cuts.

suddenly it thins out with just a small amount of water. If your mix is too thin, the mold will be fragile, probably breaking on the way to the kiln. It is better to add more soldering investment to the mix than to wait for the excess water to evaporate. A thick mix is best. When you have this, pour it over the alginate models.

As the investment hardens, it becomes warm to the touch. When it has hardened completely, it will cool. Now you can pull the alginate away. Don't wait too long to do this because soldering investment can become quite hard, and if there is excess, you will want to cut it away while the material is still warm.

Using a Plunger Mold

In Chapter 9, when we made the alginate model, we took a cast of the front and back of the leaf for two reasons. First, you can save time by making two molds: one for sagging the leaf into the mold, and the other to sag the leaf over. The leaf comes out the same whichever mold you use. However, if you want to make an exact casting of a particular single leaf, you must use both parts of the mold.

To make a plunger mold for a particular leaf, pour enough alginate to extend beyond the borders of the leaf. Insert two porcelain rods into the soft alginate, as shown in Fig. 10–7. As the alginate hardens, twist these rods so that they are fairly free. When the alginate is hard, remove the rods. When you pour the investment material, insert the rods. The holes are thus transferred to both halves of the investment and hold both halves of the mold together, one on top of the other. When you put the glass blank between them, the rods will position the top and bottom of the mold precisely. As the glass melts and starts to sag, the top mold will slide down the rods and press on the softened glass to form a perfect fit into the bottom half of the mold. It literally *plunges* into the bottom mold.

Shaping the Leaf

You can shape a leaf in one of two ways. The easiest is to hold a piece of glass over the mold and follow the curvatures with a glass marking pencil. If you don't trust your eye, put the leaf under a piece of paper and take a rubbing of it with a pencil. Cut this out and use it for your pattern for cutting the leaf from window glass. Any tricky curves can be achieved by using a glass grinder. If the leaf is particularly complex, grinding is the only way to approximate its natural shape. Make your shape as exact as possible. Do all of the shaping at this stage rather than after the leaf has been sagged onto the mold.

Making the Stem

Stemming leaves is tricky. The easiest way to do it is to use glass tubing around the wire, almost as an insulation. Use 4 mm. clear soda-glass tubing and run 22-gauge nichrome wire through it, as shown in Fig. 10–12. Cut off a length of tubing by nicking it with a triangular file and push the wire through it so that some wire sticks out either end. Light your torch and heat the tubing. To save material, heat the tubing as close to one end as you can conveniently hold it. As the tubing begins to sag from the heat, you will be able to pull it apart. Pull the longer end away from the shorter end. As you do this, the glass will begin to melt around the wire. If you pull too fast, you will separate the glass from the melting portion and leave yourself with bare wire. If you pull too slowly, you will get globs of glass on the wire. However, it is easy to "feel" for the correct amount of pull. Once you do, you will find the tubing running happily along the wire until the wire gives out. At this point, the tubing will separate. In one hand, you will have the thin wire surrounded by an insulation of thin glass and, in the other, a piece of unused tubing. The wire, now insulated with glass, becomes your stem.

Cutting the Stems

After you have insulated your wire and it has cooled, you can cut it into lengths for stems. Decide how long you want the stems to be and whether you want them straight or curved. Your wire is already straight within its glass tunnel, so straight stems are no problem. A warning: You may find it difficult to believe that the wire is there, even with a magnifying glass. But it is, if you have torch-fired correctly. Many students try to bend the wire into a curve and get the glass in their fingers.

To curve a stem, you must heat it in the coolest part of the torch flame so as not to melt the glass. As soon as the wire bends, take it immediately out of the flame.

We cut our stems with a wire-cutting pliers. Use sharp cutters to minimize the amount of glass you will lose. Don't try to saw the stems into lengths with a file, and by no means should you use pliers and twist the wire back and forth. You won't have much glass left on the stem. Cut them longer than you want, since you will end up with some bare wire at point of the cut. The excess can be trimmed later.

Fashioning the Stems to the Leaves

Although in the past we have torch-fired stems onto leaves, it is more trouble than it is worth and we do not advise it. A better method is to glue them onto the

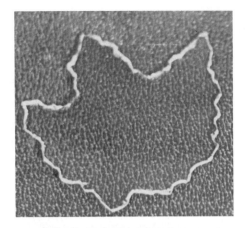

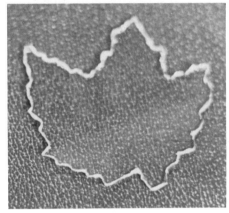

Fig. 10–10. The glass blanks (two separate leaves) showing the final cutting.

Fig. 10–11. The glass blanks are stemmed and molded in the kiln into the "natural" leaf shape.

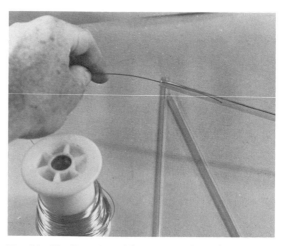

Fig. 10–12. Stringing nichrome wire through a glass rod to make stems. The wire goes through the entire length of the rod.

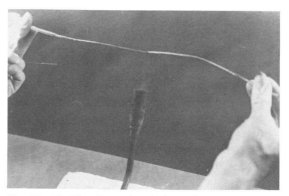

Fig. 10–13. The glass rod with the nichrome wire within is drawn into the flame to make leaf stems. You learn quickly how much to pull.

leaves. The stem becomes the central rib of the leaf traveling all the way to the leaf's tip. Make sure your glass stem is in the center of the leaf. Then glue it to the back of the leaf with Elmer's glue. It takes a while for this to harden and hold, but it is reliable once it does. Place the leaf back on the mold with the stem down against it. This is very important. If you place the stem uppermost, it will not sag with the leaf even if it has been well glued. For the stem to take the shape of the sagged leaf, it has to be borne downward by the weight of the sagging glass. This will make the stem an actual part of the leaf, rather than being merely tacked on.

Sagging the Leaves

Coat all molds thoroughly with Co-Sep or with a similar separator. Place the leaves with their attached stems on the molds. Obviously it isn't a good idea to fire a single leaf, so stack your kiln with all sizes and all shapes, or all of the same shape if you want a branchful. You can easily fuse the wire/glass stems to the glass branch with a pinpoint torch heating. Remember to keep your stems against the molds, not atop the leaves. If you want, you can add texture to your molds by carving in veins or, conversely, using a mold that has the veins sticking up. For a truly realistic leaf, we use a plunger mold.

Heating the Kiln

Whether you use a regular mold or a plunger mold, you still have to sag your glass against a bottom mold. Fully shaped leaves of single- or double-strength window glass (single strength makes a more natural leaf) requires a temperature of 1750 degrees F. You will see strain patterns which begin to look like tiny little veins. In the cooled glass, these markings add texture to the leaves. Once the kiln reaches firing temperature, turn it off and let it cool down by itself. No annealing is necessary because you are working with fairly small pieces of glass. When the kiln is cold, remove the leaves from the molds—they should release with no difficulty—and stack them on the work table. You are now ready to vein the leaves.

Fig. 10–15. Some leaf blanks, shaped, fired, and stemmed.

Fig. 10–16. Some finished leaves.

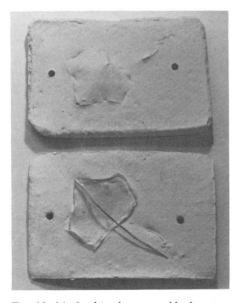
Fig. 10–14. In this plunger mold, the stem on the leaf blank is wrong side up.

Fig. 10–17. Glass leaves on a glass (torch-fired) branch. The branch was not painted prior to fusing the stemmed leaves to it.

Veining the Leaves

The process of veining is a tedious one, and it helps if you have good eyes or a pair of magnifying glasses. The veins should be unobtrusive but eye-catching, giving verisimilitude to the leaf without overpowering it. Observe the vein structure of a real leaf. Don't confuse the veins with the ribs. The main rib is a continuation of the leaf stem. Many leaves have side ribs branching off from the main one, and these diminish into the vein structure, which covers the leaf surface. The main ribs and some of the larger branches are somewhat raised from the leaf surface. To reproduce this, use a very fine rigger brush and Onida's paint. This paint tends to raise from the surface when the consistency is thick enough, and it maintains this even when fired. This is precisely the kind of standing line you want to produce. To keep the paint from slumping, especially where the line is extremely fine, we oil the leaves as a preparatory step.

Oiling the Leaves for Veining

We have tested several of the oil media to determine which best maintains a raised line in a water-base paint. Pine oil, lavender oil, and oil of copaiba work equally well. Since Onida's paint is the best for maintaining a standing line, and since it's a high-fire paint, maturing at 1400 degrees F., there's no reason to color the leaf and fire for veins at the same time. The color simply burns out at the temperature necessary to achieve veining. Instead, we use Reusche low-fire enamels for color in a second or even third firing, preferring to treat veining as a separate process.

The first step is to oil the leaf blanks. We use oil of copaiba, since it is thick and sticky and furnishes a good "ground" for the paint. It also provides a nice drag to the veining brush. All oils take a long time to dry, so we smear the oil over the surface of the leaf and then wipe most of it away with a paper towel. This leaves enough stickiness behind to keep the water-base paint in line, but not so much that it interferes with the veining process. In this manner, you can start veining immediately.

The Standing Line

In choosing a color for the veins, pick a fairly neutral one by Onita, since you will cover it up later with the leaf color. Use the veining paint sparingly. It's impossible to put in a rib or a vein at a single swoop; you will have to go back and pick up the line. If you have the right amount of oil on the glass, you will see the thin lines begin to form themselves almost into edges. If you

Fig. 10–18. Unstemmed leaf: practice in veining and coloration.

Fig. 10–19. Practice in raised lines. The shadowing below gives an indication as to the raising of even the thinnest paint lines.

have too much oil, it will prevent the line from forming, and you will see it breaking up. In this case, wipe off the excess oil and start again. With the right amount of oil on the surface, the right consistency of veining paint, a good rigger brush, a steady hand, and good eyes and light, you will be able to make realistic veins.

The rigger brush is particularly sensitive to the pressure from your hand. It is easy to control and its bristles are long enough to maintain a reasonable reservoir of paint without leading to smudging these delicate lines. Always work with the point of the brush, and take your time. You should be able to get the thinnest line to stand up; if a line begins to slump, check the consistency of your veining paint.

Since the veining paint takes a high fire, once you have the veins in place, put the leaf or leaves back on the molds. Otherwise they will flatten out. Don't try to skimp on this firing; if you don't go to 1400 degrees F., the veining paint will chip off the glass. You can save time by opening the kiln at about 1000 degrees. These small objects usually don't fracture. However, this does violate all the rules—and you might be the sadder for it.

Coloring the Leaves

Once you have the veins in place, don't be alarmed at how overwhelming they seem. Remember, you are looking at a skeleton against a wall of blank glass. What you have to do now is make the leaf *look* like a leaf by coloring it. The color will diminish the effect of these straight line angulations.

Using Matt Paint

To make the leaf realistic, you have to relieve much of the glassy effect of the glass. You can do this with matt paint, in this case Reusche's leaf-green matt. Matt paint diminishes light on the glass; it modifies the light coming through but doesn't block it out. It also adds depth to the glass, and depth is exactly what you want. The leaf-green matt appears light green on the back of the leaf after it is fired, and it is quite realistic. The matt can be fired down against the mold if the mold is coated with Co-Sep. We have had no problems with any of these molds sticking.

Apply the matt to the back of the glass and brush it out with a Badger blender or any small soft-haired brush. This will allow the matt to spread evenly; otherwise you may get blotches. We either fire the matt separately or together with the surface paint. However, depending on the effect and depth of color you want, a matt backing may not be enough to give the proper depth. In fact, this is often the case. In these instances, we turn to Obscuring White.

Fig. 10–20. The veining process, done over the clear glass.

Fig. 10–21. The back view of the leaves after being fired with Obscuring White to add depth to the glass.

Fig. 10–22. The front view of the leaves after firing with Obscuring White.

148

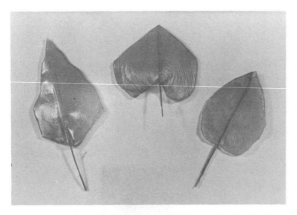

Fig. 10–23. Stemmed leaves, the backs fired with leaf-green matt.

Fig. 10–25. Two completed maple leaves.

Fig. 10–24. Stemmed leaves. The top leaf is clear; the two bottom ones have been fired with Obscuring White.

Fig. 10–26. The leafed rose. The rose we made in Chapter 15 looked rather forlorn, so we added some leaves.

Using Obscuring White

The enamel Obscuring White is an intriguing paint. It does exactly what its name implies—it obscures light. If you pack it on, it will effectively block out the light. However, we use it in a medium wash to add depth to the glass, usually applying it on the back of the leaf. We either fire it separately, or with the veining, which can be risky. Obscuring White takes a fairly high fire, about 1400 degrees F. Although much of it burns out at this temperature, a surprisingly large amount remains. Probably it is best to put it on directly after the firing for veins. Depending on how much you use, how thick you make it, how well you blend it, and to what temperature you fire it, you will get a greater or lesser obscuring of the light through the glass. When the leaf-green matt is fired on top of it, it will easily give the depth you want. You cannot get this effect if you mix the matt with Obscuring White and fire it. It seems to be the layering effect that gives the essential depth.

The Basic Coloring

Coloring the leaf is the final stage in leaf making. Choose the color or colors according to the kind of leaf you are copying. For our project here, we have stuck to a single color and have not shown any of the interesting variations furnished by nature. We chose a combination of two low-fire enamels in leaf green and bright green in order to get a deep green leaflike color. The paint can be spread over the entire surface of the leaf, including the veins, and blended with a fine-hair brush. You can work with scrubs to give small veiny lines, or mottle it for an effect of sunlight falling on the surface. If you have painted your veins with a deep yellow, you will get a different-hued green from the surrounding leaf. Veins and ribs are not always the same color as the surrounding leaf, so this would be a natural variation. In the beginning, though, you may be happy just to get veins that stand out from the leaf and a natural leaf color. That is what we have settled for in the illustrations. However, the opportunity remains for you to experiment on your own. Any number of things can be done with leaves. Why not try tomorrow to turn over a new one for yourself.

Chapter 11

The Leaded-Glass Flower Cart

Everyone is familiar with leaded glass from church windows and from Tiffany lamps, made by Louis Comfort Tiffany in the early twentieth century and widely reproduced since then.

Leaded glass is a fine art, and it is one that is now available to the hobbyist and craftsperson. For our leaded-glass project, we have chosen a unique flower cart designed by Kay Kinney, one of the leading glass artists. The project is reprinted with permission of *Popular Ceramics* magazine. It originally appeared in the May 1969 issue.

The Materials

The Glass. Any type of sheet glass will do, including stained glass and plate. We use double-strength window glass, coloring it with glass lucents, stains, and paints.

The Came. Came is made from lead, which accounts for the terms *leading* or *leading up*. Lead is flexible and allows sections of glass to be joined together.

Nailing Board. Use any soft, flat board. We recommend particle board (available at lumberyards) since nail holes have a tendency to close partially. You may find a very good use here for the portable glass-crafter's unit described in Chapter 3.

Nails. When fitting the came, glass sections must be held securely in place. Use ordinary slim nails, brads, or horseshoe nails.

The Leading Knife. There is no substitute for this. Other knives dull quickly and often produce ragged edges.

The Lathkin. This is a tool for opening twisted or damaged came. Lathkins can be metal or wood. Many professionals make their own from flat hardwood, often from a chair slat or rung.

Soldering Iron. Use a 100-watt iron. Lightweight irons usually cannot cover a $\frac{1}{4}$-inch joint neatly.

Solder. In general, 60/40 solder is preferred.

Flux. There are many good ones on the market. Use solid-core solder rather than one with flux in it.

In addition to these tools, you will need your glass cutter and grozzing pliers.

Designing the Pattern

Before leading any glass, the various shapes must be cut accurately and allowance made for the space that will be taken up by the lead came. The patterns must be precise, and the best way to accommodate the lead is to sketch a full-size design; then duplicate it by redrawing over the outlines on two pieces of paper with two sheets of carbon paper between. On one copy reduce all outlines, except the outer edges of the complete panel.

There are three ways to do this:

1. Go over the pattern lines with a felt-tipped pen that will produce a $\frac{1}{8}$-inch broad mark. This is difficult to maintain on curves because the pen will turn, making some of the strokes thicker.
2. Use pattern shears. These have three blades instead of the usual two, the top blade cutting between the two lower ones, and strip narrow slices of paper away automatically. They are indispensable for leaded-glass work and foil work.
3. Improvise a tool by placing a piece of cardboard $\frac{1}{16}$ inch thick between two single-edge razor blades. Tape them at the top. The cardboard spaces the razor blades equally. Keeping the pattern lines in the center of the space, the razor blades will remove a sliver of paper almost as well as the professional pattern shears. However, it can be a tiring and awkward process.

Step 1. Using double-strength glass, cut each section and number the pieces on the undersides of the glass. Be sure that each piece corresponds with the paper patterns.

Step 2. Repeat Step 1 until you have enough pieces for all four sides of the cart.

Step 3. Cut a rectangle of glass to form the bottom, with an allowance of $\frac{1}{16}$ inch all around.

Step 4. Cut two disks $4\frac{3}{4}$ inches in diameter for the two wheels. Each wheel is divided into four curving sections. These sections don't have to be reduced since they will be the same size when separated by the came.

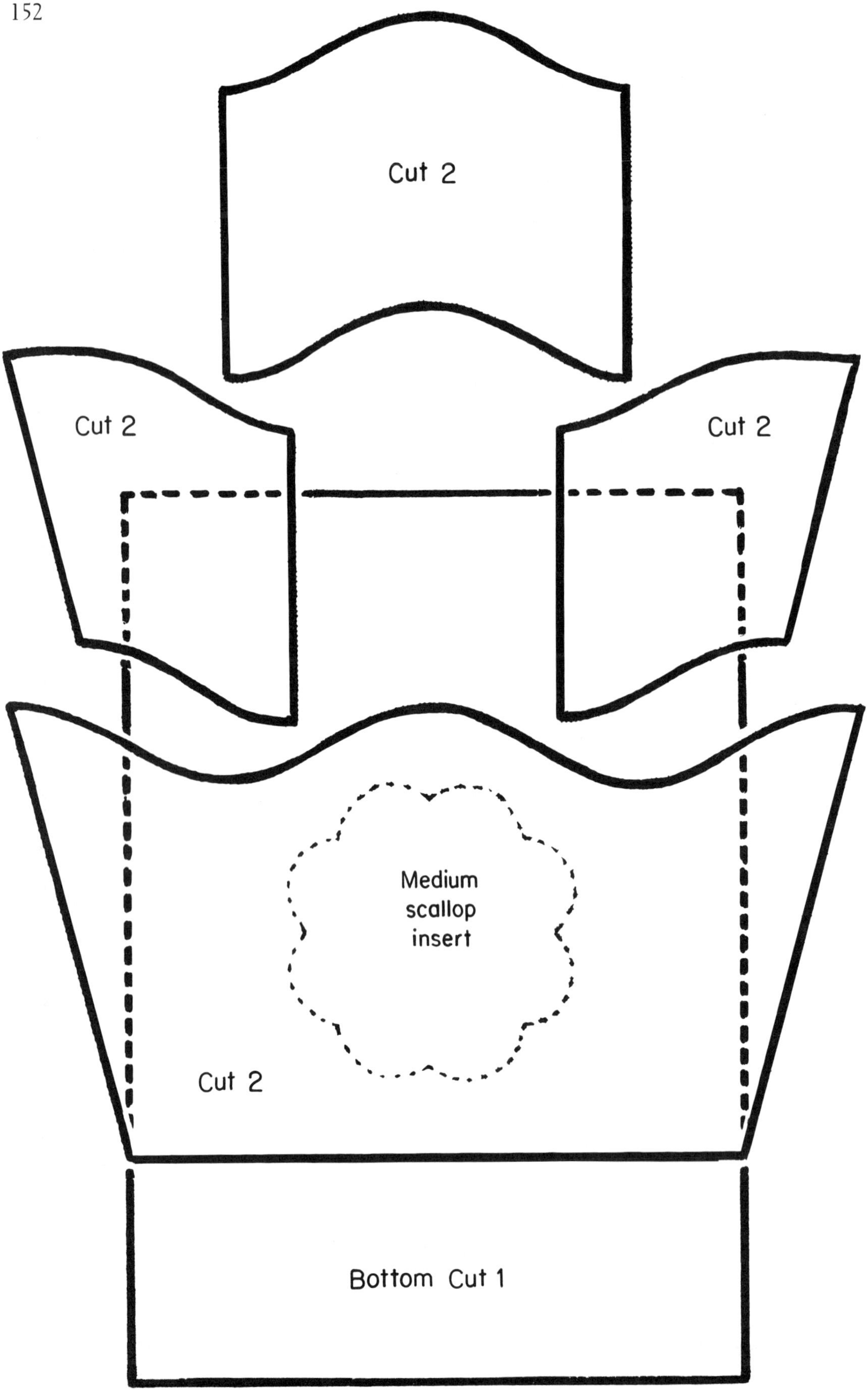

Cut 2

Cut 2

Cut 2

Medium
scallop
insert

Cut 2

Bottom Cut 1

153

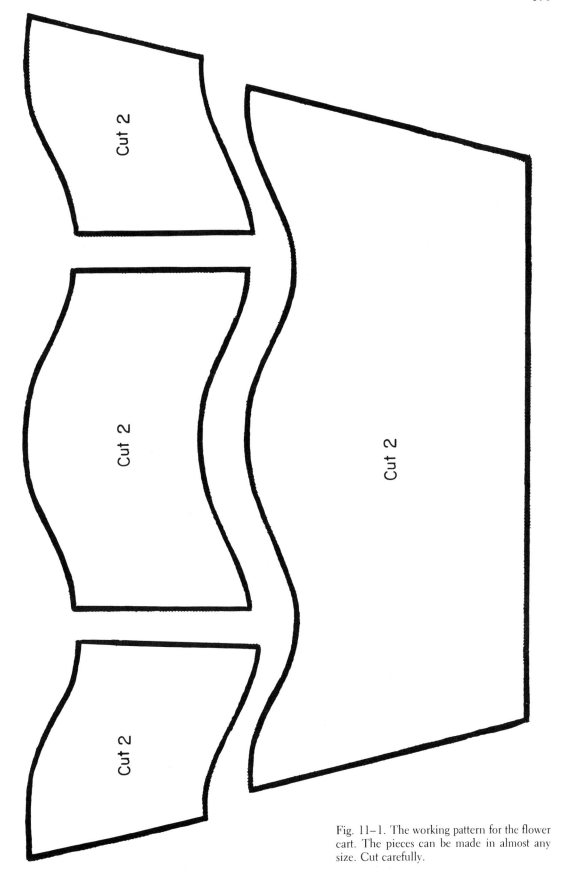

Fig. 11-1. The working pattern for the flower cart. The pieces can be made in almost any size. Cut carefully.

Fig. 11–2. Cutting lead to length with the Anderson lead chopper, a fast, precise tool just made to order for this project.

Fig. 11–3. To stretch the lead, we are using the Anderson lead stretcher. This intriguing device clamps to the table and, because of a swivel arrangement, can be pulled in any direction.

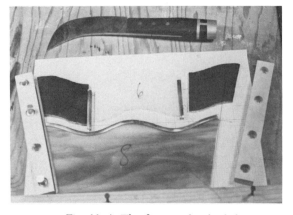

Fig. 11–4. The first panel is leaded up. We also use a standard lead knife. Note the angle of the side pieces, as well as the predrilled holes to hold pushpins. The pushpin idea is from Morton Glass Works, the maker of the glass-crafting unit discussed in Chapter 3.

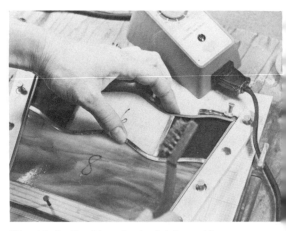

Fig. 11–5. Brushing the lead joints with a stiff brush will remove any oxidation. Above is the Glastar rheostat.

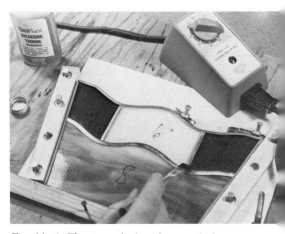

Fig. 11–6. Flux is applied to the joint before soldering. Tara-Flux works well.

The wheels thus become a little larger than diagram measurements, but they are planned with this in mind so that the cutting patterns can be used as they are.

Coloring the Glass

For this phase of the project you will need a #5 pointed sable brush, glass paints, and glass lucents. Choose your own colors. If you are using stained glass, your color choices are varied according to the glass. You can use opalescent, reamies, or streakies. English streakies are especially effective, but they are difficult to lead because of their irregular thicknesses.

Step 1. Line up the three sections composing the tops of the side pieces. The glass can be made secure by applying a little rubber cement to the work table or paper on which the glass is placed. Now paint sweeping thin lines of color in a more or less continuing manner across all three panels. Break the lines when the color is exhausted and pick up the line again about a half inch beyond this break. In this way you will be maintaining a continuous but irregular pattern.

Step 2. On either side of this first color line, paint a broader band of a second color, leaving a bare space of at least $\frac{1}{2}$ inch from the first color. Fill in the remaining spaces generously with a third color, feathering it into the other colors. This method produces a marblized effect reminiscent of Tiffany opalescent glass.

Step 3. Decorate the wheel sections in the same manner, carrying the brushstrokes from the center of the wheel to the outer perimeter of these glass pieces. The wheels can be in two or three colors matching the colors of the panels, or different from them.

Embossing

This process is also called *indenting*, which we discussed in Chapter 8.

Embossing the front and back lower panels is easy to do, and it provides a further design to the cart. Cover the insert with separator (we are using a clay mold) to keep the glass from sticking. Then place the glass over it and dab some rubber cement on several of the highest areas to keep the glass from moving in the kiln. Attach the corresponding glass panel on top of the indent (we use a scallop design) and align it carefully with the outlines of the cutting pattern. Let this set overnight so that it cannot shift off center.

You will need an identical panel for the other end of the cart, so repeat the procedure. We use two inserts; you may do that or fire the second glass panel after the first is finished.

Color these plain lower panels (if you are not using stained glass) with a $\frac{1}{2}$-inch soft, flat, square brush.

Puddle an adequate amount of paint, about the size of a half-dollar, approximately in the center of the panel. From this puddle, pull generous strokes outward to the edge of the glass. Be sure to keep the brush well loaded with color at all times to ensure even coverage. Overlap each brushstroke about $\frac{1}{4}$ inch and keep the brush as nearly horizontal as possible. Use very little pressure. After drying, clean the glass edges of any excess color.

Fire the panel on a kiln shelf that has been protected with separator until the edges are well blunted but not rounded. Repeat with the other three panels and the cart bottom.

Leading Up

Step 1. Lead came usually comes in six-foot lengths, but we need only three feet here. Mark off three feet with a pencil or nick it with the cutting knife. Push a block of glass into the came channel on both sides at the nick and rock the knife back and forth over the mark until it cuts through the came to the glass level. This prevents squashing the two sides of the came together. Remove the blocks and cut straight down through the rib and bottom width of the came. (Or you can use any of the quick lead-cutting devices mentioned in Chapter 3.)

Came must be stretched before it can be used. Being flexible, it can stretch from the weight of the encased glass, but prior stretching stiffens the came enough to ensure a snug fit around the glass. Pinch the came together with pliers for approximately $\frac{1}{2}$ inch at one end. Place the flattened came in a vise and grasp the other end with pliers. Pull slowly until you feel the came "give." Lay the came on a flat table, channel side up, and run your lathkin from one end to the other. This removes any kinks and curves. Turn the came over and repeat.

Step 2. Nail a wooden strip to the nailing board. Two nails should be enough. Place the embossed panel firmly against the strip and tap a nail to either side.

Step 3. Lifting one upper end of the panel slightly with the flat of the knife, sleeve the glass with the came, both over and under, starting about $\frac{1}{8}$ inch from the edge. Gently shape the came to the curve by running the heel of the lathkin in and out of the curve.

Step 4. Place the glass pieces, or a glass piece, at the first inner curve and nail it tightly. Repeat on the center up curve. This will hold the came and glass securely in place. Nailing directly against the came produces nicks and ragged edges. Using this scrap glass piece to hold the came while you are working does away with this problem.

Step 5. Place one end section of the border into the upper, open came channel and nail the section securely. Cut the came $\frac{1}{8}$ inch short of the glass edge, using the method described in Step 1. Remove the border section after the rib has been reached and swing out the came, insert a scrap glass piece to hold it and cut all the way through the came. Replace the came and renail the border section.

Soldering

When the came has been fitted to the sides of the cart, the joints are ready to be soldered. The panel is still against the wooden strip, and the scrap glass pieces are holding the other three sides securely. The soldering is done directly against the joints; use a rheostat for your soldering iron so that you don't burn holes in the lead with an overheated iron. Each joint to be soldered should be wire-brushed to remove oxidation from the lead surface. The iron should be hot enough to cause the solder to flow freely over the entire diameter of the joint. When one side is soldered, turn the panel over and solder all of those joints as well. It is not necessary to nail the piece in place at this point. Do all sides as described and then solder the bottom of the cart to the sides; it should fit evenly all around. If it doesn't, you will have to do some maneuvering, but this is easily accomplished.

Assembling the Cart

Step 1. Here we're going to be using a double-channel lead, H came. Working from the underside, press or rub the top edge of the H came down to meet the parallel edge binding each side and the bottom of the cart. Place one wide panel face down on the table and hold one cart end against it at right angles. Wire-brush the entire seam and solder after applying flux.

Step 2. Repeat with the other two side panels.

Step 3. Position one unit on the binding of the cart bottom and solder together at the corner of the bottom. Repeat with the second unit, soldering also the vertical seams of both units.

Step 4. Wire-brush the outer edges of each unit and apply flux.

Step 5. Add the second unit to the first, lining it up with the bottom; solder the floor corners, and then straight up the alternate side seams, formerly the outer ends of the units.

Step 6. Spot solder the outside corners and the border joinings.

The Wheels and Axle

Step 1. Bind and solder two large round, domed jewels with lead came or foil. Then fit came between each wheel section. Cutting the came $\frac{1}{16}$ inch short of

158

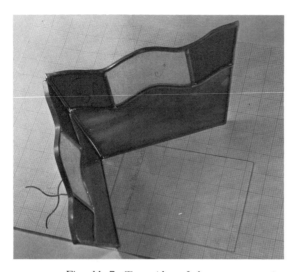

Fig. 11–7. Two sides of the cart are tack-soldered together. To make sure they fit properly, fit them back onto the pattern, shown below on graph paper.

Fig. 11–8. A securely cut bottom is important to keep all sides exactly parallel. Each side should not take up any more room against the bottom than you have calculated for. If it does, you will be in trouble with the next side.

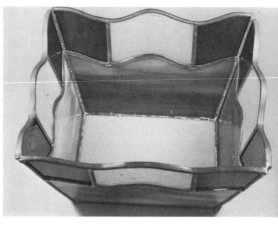

Fig. 11–9. The completed soldering of the cart walls and the bottom.

Fig. 11–10. The cart and its underpinnings. Note how the axle goes across to support the wheels and the brackets to either side to keep the cart upright. We use contact paper to protect the surface of the bottom; on this model, we used a mirror as the bottom.

the outer perimeter of the wheels, fit the came in place between the glass pieces. Bind the perimeter of the wheels with came, fitting and cutting the came at one of the section joinings so that you do not have odd soldering spots over the perimeter. Solder all joinings, front and back. Solder your lead- or foil-bound jewels to the center of each wheel, using the existing lead lines to bind them.

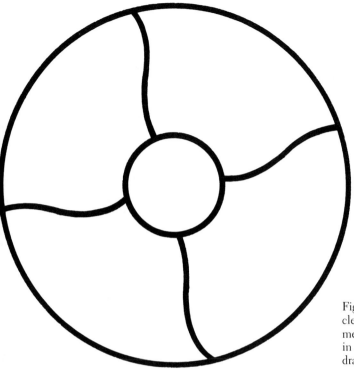

Fig. 11–11. The cart wheel. The center circle represents the jewel, which will be rimmed with lead came. The lead lines are drawn in slight curves for design. The diagram is drawn to size.

Step 2. The axle can be made from a copper-clad rod. Measure across the cart and allow enough extra to set the wheels out on both sides, plus ½ inch at either end. Mark the cart width on the rod.

Step 3. The rod can be "tinned" with solder if it is solderable. Otherwise, it can be wrapped with copper foil and then tinner. Or a brass rod can be used, which is solderable. Solder the rod to the edges of the cart floor and to the came opening in the center of the wheels on the inside.

Step 4. Solder the glass hubs to the outside openings in each wheel.

Step 5. Bend a fairly heavy-gauge copper wire length into a "V" for support at the front of the cart to keep it from falling over. Solder the "V" into the channel of the bottom came.

Making the Glass Flowers

To make the glass flowers, you can use either window glass that you have stained or painted or stained glass. (We used stained glass.) You will need six glass petals cut to pattern. If you want to paint the petals, use a No. 3 and No. 5 pointed sable brush. You will also need some rubber cement and two 1-inch pieces of 12-gauge copper wire, as well as one 11-inch length of 12-gauge copper wire.

Fig. 11–12. Diagramming the petals of the glass flowers.

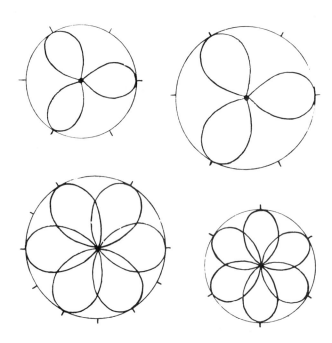

Fig. 11–13. Diagram showing how the petals will fit in the mold.

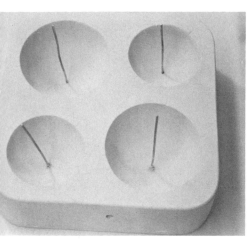

Fig. 11–14. The mold coated with separator and the wires in place.

Step 1. After cleaning the petals with a silicone-free glass cleaner, turn them over. Place each on the design pattern and sketch the lines with a fine felt-tip pen. Mark the bisecting center line on the vertical glass edge so that later you can align the petals on the mold.

Step 2. With the No. 3 brush, without stirring your paint, get the thickest portion onto the brush. This is usually the heavier sediment at the bottom of the jar or from the pile on the palette. Fill in the areas of the sketched slashes, working from the thin line to the wider arcs at the top of the petals, concentrating thicker application high on the petal. Note that the slashes begin well above the petal points. (If you are using stained glass, you may still paint for graphic delineation.)

Step 3. Clear glass only. With the lines still wet, fill in the background with color, starting at the curve above the point and working toward the upper edge. Work the point of your brush back and forth between the two colors, feathering them together.

Step 4. Clean any traces of color from the vertical edges of the petals and dry thoroughly.

Step 5. Coat the mold with separator evenly and place the 1-inch pieces of copper wire into the holes at the bottom of the well of each mold. Be sure that the wires are perfectly straight.

Step 6. Put a dab of rubber cement on the tip of a petal and at the upper curved top. Prop the petal tip

Fig. 11–15. The petals are placed in the mold, now ready for firing.

Fig. 11–17. Two groups of petals are placed in the same mold. Both will be fired together.

Fig. 11–16. The petals after firing.

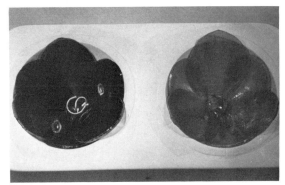

Fig. 11–18. The petals are placed and ready for firing. Left: a copper spiral has been placed in the "heart" of the flower. Right: a jewel has been rubber cemented to this spiral. When the kiln is fired, the jewel will fuse to the copper, thus forming the center of the flower.

against the wire "post" and line up the center mark with one indented mark at the top of the mold. Add two more petals in the same way at every other mold mark.

Step 7. Repeat in the second mold well of the same size. Fig. 11–15 shows placement of petals. The mold has space for two sizes, but this project concerns only the medium-size flower. Both sizes are done in the same manner.

Step 8. Fire to 1200 degrees F. or a cone 0-19. If possible, try to keep a close watch on the firing; the edges of the petals should be blunted but not rounded, and the petals should have barely assumed the contour of the mold well. This prefiring is necessary because it is impossible to fit all six petals into the well while the glass is flat.

162

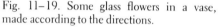

Fig. 11–19. Some glass flowers in a vase, made according to the directions.

Fig. 11–20. The completed cart with flowers.

Step 9. After cooling, arrange all petals into one well as shown in Fig. 11–17. Attach petals at points of contact with each other with rubber cement, but omit the cement on the points against the wire post. The inner petals are somewhat upright and will not conform to the mold shape until fully fired. The colors are fused to the glass, but they will not be fully developed until the second firing.

Step 10. Make a spiral at the end of the 11-inch copper wire. To keep this "stem" in the center of the flower, bend the wire over at right angles about $1\frac{1}{4}$ inches from the end, then curve this short end around with needle-nose or round-jaw pliers. This can be done easily by using two pairs of pliers, or by inserting the long end of the wire into a vise before shaping with the pliers.

Step 11. Remove the 1-inch post gently and replace it with the "stem." Pull the wire all the way through the mold hole until the spiral rests on top of all petals. Holding the spiral with the left-hand thumb, reach under the mold and bend the stem up underneath the mold. Attach a jumbo jewel to the spiral with rubber cement.

Step 12. Fire the flower to the temperature required

for window glass in your kiln. (Stained glass will usually fire at a lower temperature; do a test firing first.) The petals should be well fused and the jewel firmly fused to the petals, thus laminating the wire spiral in place.

For the fired flower, leaves can be made according to the methods discussed in Chapter 10.

Chapter 12

The Scarecrow and the Wheelbarrow

Fig. 12–1. The completed pattern for the scarecrow. The colors are your choice.

The scarecrow and the wheelbarrow utilize many of the techniques we have described. You can use lead or foil or a combination of the two, with window glass or stained glass or a combination. If you use window glass, you will decorate the clear blanks with colorants; with stained glass, you can use either painted graphic detail or matting to modify the light through the glass.

The Scarecrow

The pattern shown is full size but can be made in any size you choose. The patches are, of course, overlying pieces of glass, which are fused to the lower sections. If you are using stained glass, make sure you use a similar type of underlying glass, as far as possible, in texture, thickness, and manufacture. The features are painted on and fired. You can add as much to the decor of the hat—or, indeed, to the entire figure—as you wish. Loops for hanging are soldered in back of the hat.

A word about the "straw." We have found window screening somewhat difficult to manipulate and solder. If you use screening, you must clean it thoroughly. Acetic acid (vinegar) is good for this, scrubbed on with a wire brush, although a lot of brushing of the acid onto the screening must take place. Because of the work involved, we prefer to use copper wire, which comes in different thicknesses. Or you can use the wire from inside a lamp cord. This gauge wire is just about the right thickness to simulate straw and it is easily solderable. You should have straw coming out of the hat, over the face, and out of the sleeves and pantlegs, but you can also have it bursting out of every seam if you want.

Soldering the straw is best done in bunches. Remember that copper conducts heat very well, so when soldering the bunches of straw together, hold them with

Fig. 12-2. The cutting pattern for the scarecrow

a pliers. Flux the ends of each straw bunch and solder all wires together. Allow the wires to cool, then solder the units of straw into place.

If you are using foil to make the scarecrow, you should foil all the pieces before soldering them together. When they are foiled, put them back onto the pattern to make sure they all fit correctly. Don't assume your cutting is that accurate. The slightest irregularity can be emphasized by the foil, and if this is added to another slightly miscut portion that it butts against, an entire section can be off and your scarecrow will be deformed. It is always easier to fix pieces *before* they are soldered rather than afterward.

If you are using lead to make the scarecrow, you don't have to reduce the pattern to make up for the width of the lead. The piece will come out slightly larger than given, but that is okay. Use H came inside the piece, U came for the border. We do not recommend using U came throughout; the end result will be unaesthetically bulky.

The Wheelbarrow

The wheelbarrow is an offshoot of the flower cart design in Chapter 11. In essence, it is a foiled box that you can put other glass items in. We filled our wheelbarrow with small indoor-gardening tools, some glass flowers, and a glass umbrella. These can be changed as you make other glass items, so your wheelbarrow can become an ever-changing display. Figs. 12–3 to 12–8 take you through the project step by step.

Fig. 12–3. Two views of the scarecrow. Right: the pieces atop the pattern. Left: an exploded view of the pieces.

Fig. 12–4. Part of the basic wheelbarrow pattern.

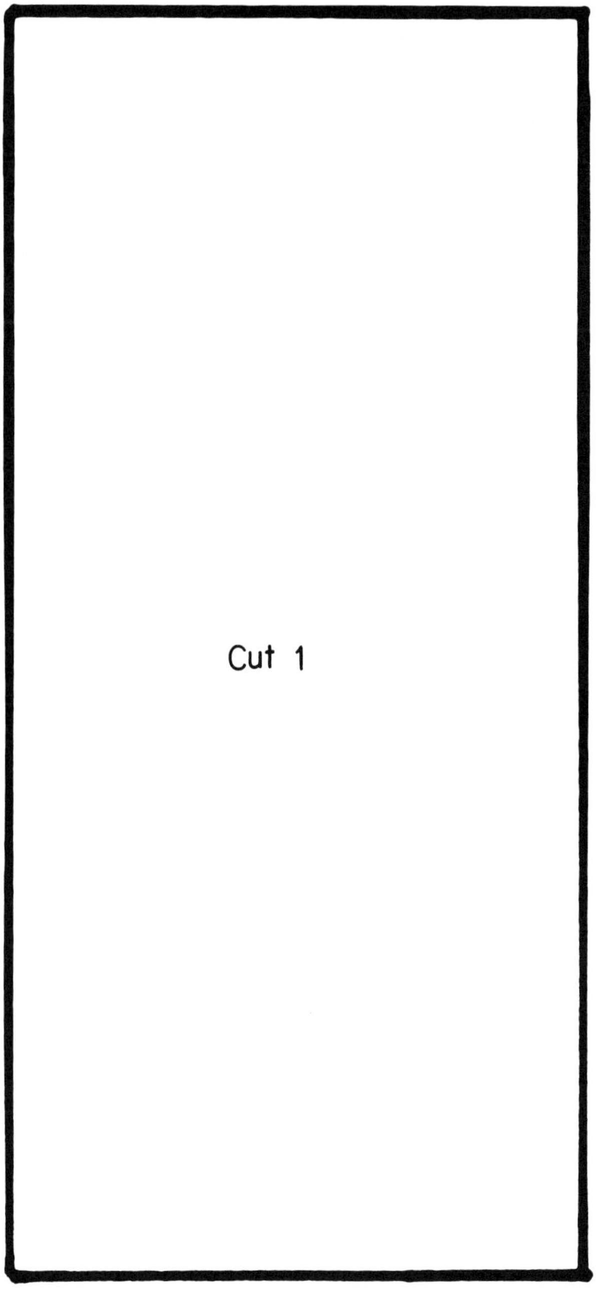

Cut 1

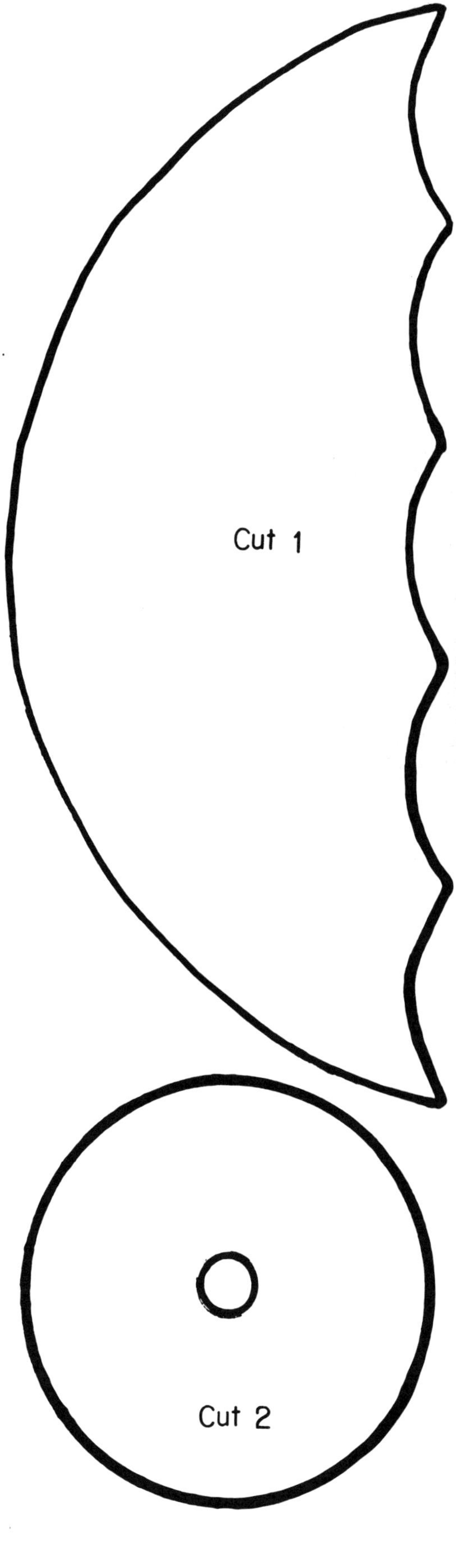

Cut 1

Cut 2

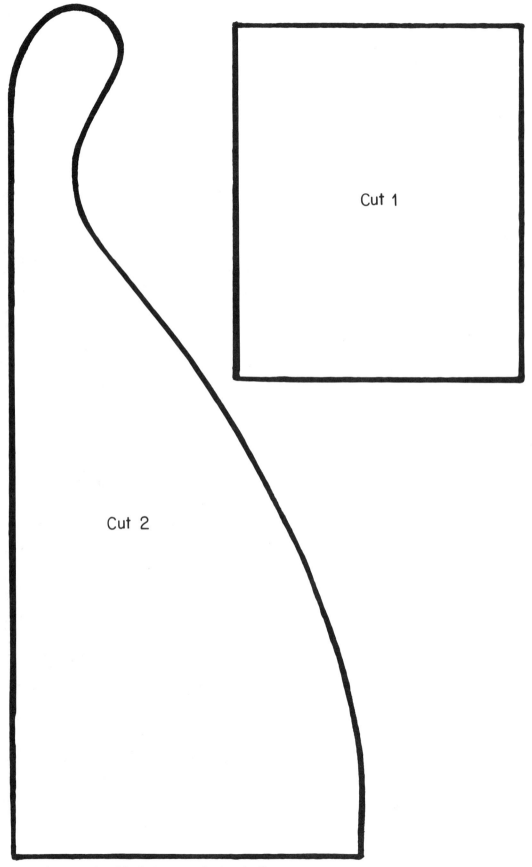

Cut 1

Cut 2

Fig. 12–5. Remainder of the basic pattern for the wheelbarrow.

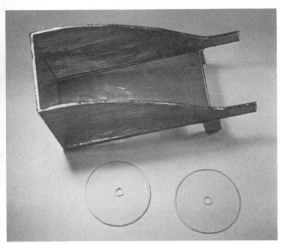

Fig. 12–6A.

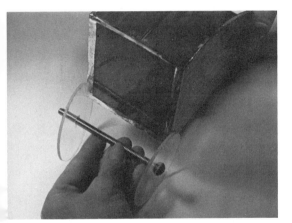

Fig. 12–6B.

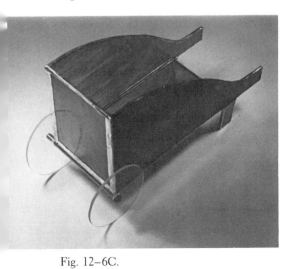

Fig. 12–6C.

Fig. 12–6A, B, and C. Assembling the wheelbarrow.

Fig. 12–7. The hole is drilled in the wheelbarrow wheel using Inland Products WIZARD router.

Fig. 12–8. The second hole being drilled.

170

Fig. 12–9. The wheelbarrow with umbrella and garden tools.

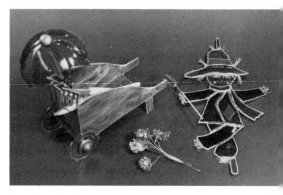

Fig. 12–10. The scarecrow and the wheelbarrow. The flowers will go inside the cart.

Fig. 12–11. Fused medallion with a clear window-glass base and painted pieces of window glass.

Chapter 13

Glass Portraits

At what point does a craft become an art? People have argued about this transition zone for ages. In the end, most agree that the choice is strictly a subjective one. Here and in Chapter 14, we let the glass artists speak for themselves. You will have the rare experience of hearing them go step by step through a creative process. In both instances are demonstrated technique, integrity, and a personal statement. Communication is immediate and provocative. The enthusiasm of the worker sparkles in the work and conveys to the viewer a sense of accomplishment. In each case, the worker is not only the designer but the craftsperson as well, totally involved with the medium. It should be stimulating and instructive for the beginner and the advanced craftsperson alike.

Marie Snell's Techniques

People ask me why I started doing portraits—I really don't know. Initially, I thought that a T-shirt design I had done from a Mucha poster of Sarah Bernhardt would look neat as a stained glass panel, so I did it as a birthday present for myself. One thing led to another—Nefertiti and then King Tut for my archaeology student daughter, and here I am. I do them because I like to! Most of my designs are inspired by pictures. A large book of Edward Curtis's Indian portraits struck a tremendous emotional response and itchy fingers. I especially like noncolor pictures because the planes are clear in a good photo and one has the freedom to make color choices without being influenced.

I usually make my drawings full-size to save a step. Since my panels are relatively small, there is then no need to make an enlargement. I sketch on tracing paper, first for likeness, giving special care to whatever quality of line or expression that drew me to the face

172

Fig. 13–1. "Lummi Madonna" by Marie Snell, copyright © 1980.
Reprinted by permission.

Fig. 13–2. "Porcupine Cheyenne" by Marie Snell, copyright © 1980.
Reprinted by permission.

initially. It seems to me that the faces I am attracted to are those that reflect human dignity, and I am always careful to preserve that feeling in my drawings.

As I go along, I break up the faces into areas that can be cut, but always keeping in mind the underlying bone structure. To work as I do, it is necessary to have some knowledge of anatomy so that the heads are solid. A child's face has fewer pieces because the planes are less sharply defined; however, these pieces must still reflect the fact that there is a skull under the surface.

In my overall design I avoid what I call "dumb lines," the arbitrary lines one finds in so much stained glass, whose only function is to provide the cuts necessary to get from the central design to the edge. In a good design, one should always have the feeling that all lines have meaning, that the design would be less successful without any one of them. For that reason, because of the nature of working in glass, I carry the designs right to the borders.

When I am satisfied that my pencil drawing is as good as I can make it, I place it under a sheet of tracing paper and go over the drawing with a black "Sharpie" (because it is waterproof, and sometimes pieces that have been ground are a little wet) blunt marker, which approximates the foil line. This drawing serves as my cartoon and is used for cutting, foiling, and leading. Since I do all my work on a light table, cutting freehand, there is no need for patterns, except on very rare occasions when the glass is too dense to see through. Then I can trace the piece on some scratch paper and use it for a pattern.

The light table is one my husband made for me, a piece of $\frac{1}{2}$-inch plate glass 18 by 22 inches (an arbitrary figure, the size available at the price I could afford to pay when I bought it), set into a table made of $\frac{3}{4}$-inch plywood with 2-×-2 legs. The glass in the table can be sandblasted to diffuse the light, but I just used Contact paper (again because of the cost), and it works fine, especially with the addition of the tracing-paper cartoon. The light box is about 3 inches deep and contains seven (as many as could be fitted in) 18-inch 15-watt Deluxe Cool White (they give the least distortion) fluorescent tubes. The table has switches built in to turn it and my overhead shop-light fixture on and off, and a plug for my soldering iron. The overhead fixture has regular cool fluorescent tubes. In addition, I use the ceiling light with a 100-watt incandescent bulb and the light from the north-facing windows, so I can check glass colors and their differing relationships.

Before I start to cut, I try to establish a light source for the portrait itself, and then keep lights and darks and shadows consistent with that source. One can learn certain rules about color, but ultimately there has to be a built-in monitor that says, "Warm, cool, relative warm, relative cool." The values, light, dark, and middle tones must be established just as they would be in a drawing or painting. Then it's a matter of going from bin to bin, trying different kinds of glass that will give the effect I'm seeking. I work around the panel as I would in a painting, testing color and value relationships. In other words, I don't start in one corner, for instance, and work up or down. My approach changes and grows the longer I work in glass, so I can't give a specific formula that works in each piece. I find myself setting different problems to solve in each, based on my feeling about the subject, what aspect I want to emphasize, and in what way. I have heard people say they use only antique glass, or only one thing or another. I use whatever works best for the effect I want to achieve.

Since the pieces of glass I use are usually quite small, I am able to keep an extensive selection of glass on hand. My studio is 11 by 12 feet, what used to be our daughter's bedroom. We have taken the doors off the closet and built in bins to hold the glass. With shelves all around, a small drawing board, and space savers wherever possible, I am able to manage very nicely in that size space—so long as I don't have any visitors! It also keeps me from accepting commissions larger than I really want to do. I find that it helps to have my books, materials, and tools placed conveniently so that I don't have to waste time looking for what I need. And while a loft might be nice, at least here I don't need roller skates!

As to tools, I use what I find best for me. I have a Supercutter, a MacInnes carbide, and one of Al Magewick's new carbide cutters (see Fig. 3–14), which I like very much. Since, other than the diamond grinder, stained-glass tools are inexpensive (it's glass and solder that get us into trouble), I prefer good ones, such as the soft Knipex grozzers rather than the cheaper ones. I *do* love my Glastar grinder. But I haven't tried the others, so I can't speak authoritatively. When asked, I do recommend an American Beauty soldering iron. Mine is a 75-watt with a Paragon No. 166 ironclad tip. I find that size more than ample for my needs (using it with a rheostat that my husband made from a dimmer switch). However, that size might not be suitable for everyone. Other than those, we all have our favorites—whatever we pick up as we go along.

In cutting glass, I'm willing to try other people's methods, but I prefer to push the cutter away from me because I find it easier and because I can better see the pattern line. Generally, I'm most comfortable tapping the intricate curves I use. However, I also grozze, push,

Fig. 13–3. Marie Snell at work in her studio.

Fig. 13–4. Fitting the pieces of a panel.

pull—and jump up and down if necessary! Actually, after working in glass for a while, one begins to feel the varying tensions in different kinds of glass and one adjusts the method of cutting accordingly. My advice is to try different methods and tools and then use those that you are most comfortable with.

As I cut the glass, I fit the pieces together almost like a jigsaw puzzle, using my grinder to clean and seal the edges of each piece, making it fit well, since the line is very important in my work. Working on a light table makes it possible to check constantly on the relationships. Sometimes a piece of glass just doesn't seem to make it and has to be recut, but there are no major goofs that show up only after the panel is placed in front of a window. Natural light will cause changes, but the overall relationships should still hold. In addition, when the piece actually starts to go together, sometimes a line just doesn't seem to work as well as I thought. Or the absolutcly perfect piece of glass doesn't break quite right. With the light coming through the cartoon, I can easily take my trusty Sharpie and make a slight alteration.

When the panel is cut, I square it (if it is square or oblong) with two large carpenter's squares, still on the light table. Since few of my pieces are meant to go into specific openings, keeping the panels to a preset size isn't really important, but I consider it good discipline to do so. Especially since I'm the sort of person who tends to cut two left sleeves when I'm making a dress! I try to have the border pieces meet the edges as squarely as possible. Then I start to foil, grinding a little more as necessary to fit as closely as I can, although in some instances I will purposely leave wider lines as emphasis or to act as shadows.

I use 1-mil foil because I find it easier to work with (although I have been told that people have trouble with it tearing), and the fit is closer. The only trick in using it is to keep it taut without pulling, especially going around sharp corners. I press it around with my fingers, making sure the foil doesn't show through from the back side. Most people have their own favorite foiling tools. I started with popsicle sticks and eventually evolved my present system, using something a friend made me from a lovely piece of tulip wood. I use this to press in folds and make hospital corners with the foil. Then I go over all edges with a burnisher from a wood-cutting set. The closer the foil fits, the tighter the whole piece when finished. I have never used any of the foiling machines, so I can't comment on them. Then I trim with an X-Acto knife, making sure all lines are clean with no ragged overlaps, and so no foil shows through from the back.

Although $\frac{3}{16}$-inch and $\frac{7}{32}$-inch foil are the sizes I use most, I have all widths, from $\frac{1}{8}$ inch to $\frac{1}{4}$ inch, which I ordered directly from Edco in Brooklyn. Careful foiling is most important, since it is the medium for the solder and determines fit and line quality.

I do *all* the work on my panels because I consider all steps important. I have heard "artists" say the design is the most important element, and the rest can be done by others. Maybe, if one doesn't want to be the very best.

Most of us develop work methods, usually through experimentation, that we consider best for ourselves. Using my American Beauty iron, and with a combination of 50/60 and 60/40 solder, I tack the panel together. Then with 50/50 solder, I run through from front to back, forming a heart as with came. I turn the piece over and fill in any gaps and finish by beading both sides with 60/40. This works well because the 60/40 has a lower melting point and narrower paste range than 50/50 solder. And I think it makes a stronger panel because of the extra tin. There should be little trouble with pop holes and not much waste of solder if the iron is not too hot. Using my rheostat, I have never found it necessary to use the iron wide open.

I've tried all kinds of fluxes and have not yet formed a definitive opinion as to the best (although I don't like the "greasy kid stuff" oleic acid and the like). Superior Red Lightning No. 72, a zinc chloride flux, works well and is fast, although I sometimes gag on the fumes. The No. 30, on the other hand, contains no zinc chloride and is slower. Laco flux is probably one of the best. Whatever flux I use, I put it on with a Q-Tip.

After soldering, I scrub the piece in the sink with a toothbrush and a solution of Shakley's Basic H, a tip I got from a friend, which cleans off the crud and seems to leach out the flux residues. Then I color the solder lines with copper sulfate. I have concocted various solutions myself, but so far, for a nice copper color, I like Allnova Super Brite (see Fig. 5–6), also applied with a trusty Q-Tip—or five or six. The copper burnishes nicely with glass wax.

Usually, I finish the panels with brass came, soldering front and back to the brass wherever a seam line joins it. I heat the came with my iron and sweat the seam to it. The brass gives a nice finish and serves to strengthen the panel, acting as a sort of girdle. I smooth the joins and shine the brass by going over the whole frame with very fine steel wool (no soap) and then touch up the solder with copper sulfate. I wipe the brass so it doesn't discolor. For hangers, I buy solid brass hooks and staples in the hardware store. Each set of two can be separated to make hangers for three panels. I tin (heat the brass until it accepts a wash of solder) the came and the eye to be soldered to it, hold the eye in place with a hemostat (as good a tool for artists and craftspeople as for doctors), take a blob of solder on my iron and hold it against both pieces of brass until the solder runs the length of the join, "sweating" the two pieces together. Then I take the iron away and hold the eye in place until the solder sets.

About cleaning: this, I think, is an extremely important step because dirty glass and fuzzy lines tend to undo all the hard work. After spending as many as seventy or more hours designing and constructing a panel, it is foolish to skimp on the hour or so necessary to clean it. The special beauty of glass is its interaction with light, much of which is lost if the glass is not clean. So I usually finish with Johnson's Klean 'n Shine, which polishes nicely, using those omnipresent Q-Tips and a secondhand dental tool to get into the corners.

I don't know if there are difficulties in my way of working—for me, it is the only way. Others might find it difficult. It helps to have lots of patience (remember, much of this is picky work), and be a perfectionist fussbudget. For one who is not, it might not only seem difficult to do this work, but impossible. Having a solid background in art, drawing, design, and color also helped me move fast once I mastered the technical aspects of working in stained glass, using the copper foil method. I prefer foil for the intricate work. I have not tried painting on glass, slumping, fusing (which I might experiment with one day), or dalles glass because I am more interested in creating glass painting than in experimenting with the various possibilities of glass. Maybe one day I'll feel differently.

At first, before I could cut glass, I took little scraps and put them together in tiny glass sculptures. I was very excited about the idea that glass could be more than just a single-plane medium. Actually, I still like that possibility, and in the piece illustrated, I have used Uroboros glass that drapes, overlapping pieces to suggest the quality of leafiness. I also like wavy end pieces and globs and jewels, but only where they work. It is easy to get carried away by all the possibilities and goodies, but the design concept itself should always be paramount. A little goes a long way, and a piece using every technique usually looks like just that to me—a bunch of techniques trying to become a happening.

Chapter 14

"Lilies of the Field": A Stained-Glass Panel

Barbara Saull works through her studio, Creative
Stained Glass, in Lakewood, Colorado. She has actively
worked as a professional artist (mostly in the field of
painting) for almost twenty years. She says she has been
very fortunate in having had the opportunity to study
under some of the Rocky Mountain area's finest artists.
As her painting skills evolved, she found the uses and
the tones of color becoming more and more important,
and eventually she became involved with painting light.
It was at this stage in her career that she became
involved with stained glass.

Barbara Saull's Techniques

Barbara Saull re-creates the story of how the panel
"Lilies of the Field" came about.

I've always been fascinated with the ladies of the turn
of the century. The way they dressed, the way they
lived, their values—everything. They represented a
constantly lovely, changing scene of grace and fantasy.
One day, several years ago, I ran across a rough
thumbnail sketch in our source file. This is a file of
sketches, pictures, cards, newspaper clippings—anything we happen to find that we perhaps somehow can
relate to glass. In our "morgue" are such headings as
Figures, Animals, Birds, Butterflies, Casting, Children,
Christmas, Circles, Designs, Flowers, Fruit, Landscapes,
Music. We have saved just about anything that could
provide a stimulus for an idea.

Somewhere in all this I found this small sketch that
had evidently been living in the file for years—since it
obviously lent itself far more to painting on canvas
rather than glass. However, it transmitted a potential to
me, and, perhaps even subconsciously, I began to
develop the design for stained glass, thinking up techniques that would achieve the effects I visualized. Of

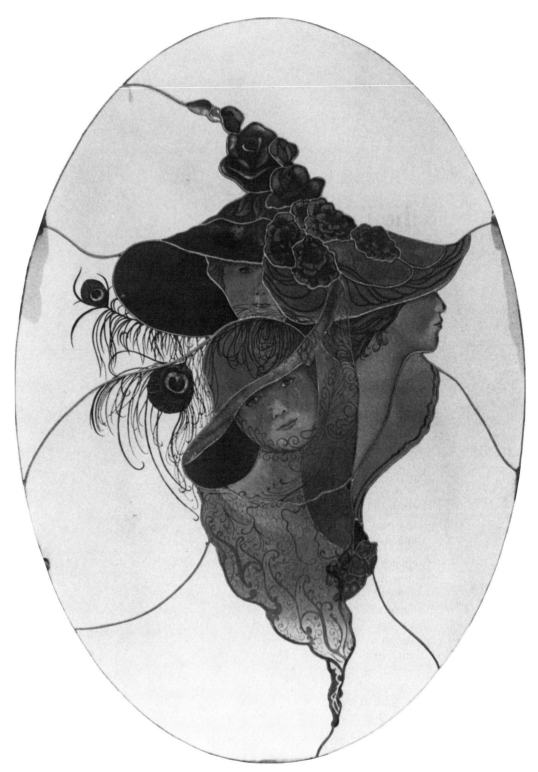

Fig. 14–1. "Lilies of the Field," the completed panel.

course, this was with the sketch in my mind's eye. Then I'd look at the real sketch and become completely puzzled as to how to work out the obvious problems. I'd already achieved a sort of ideal result in my mind. It's always easier to do it in your mind. However, I figured if you can conceive it, you can also find a way to do it. So last November we began—the studio and myself.

The first step was the easiest: the drawing. I did quite a detailed pencil drawing. Once that was complete, I did a simple line drawing in ink, defining the cut lines, and it was at this time that we decided to sit the ladies into an oval. We felt the oval shape of the panel would add to the feeling of elegance.

The next step was to select the color palette and the glass. We insisted on keeping in mind that all decisions from now on were to be made from the standpoint of contributing to that same feeling of softness, of charm, of wistfulness. Indeed, I believe had we not had this idea from the very beginning it would have been quite a wrenching sort of act to attempt to graft it on later and would have made the effect artificial. I think it's important to decide right at the outset what you want your effect to be and then bend every technique to it.

The panel, as completed, has fifty-five pieces of glass in it. There are different glasses, and different things were done to many of them. For example, the background glass is German opal. The purple flowers are controlled acid-etched flashed red on blue antique glass laminated to German gold-pink glass. The rose flowers are controlled acid-etched antique flashed red on amber. The veil is sandblasted, painted, and fired on French colonial white glass, which was then satin etched and laminated.

The ostrich feathers are painted and fired using Reusche low-fire paints. We had to use the low-fire paints because when the opal glass is taken up to high-fire temperatures in the kiln, the glass loses its translucency. Needless to say, by this time we were well into the experimental stages of the panel, literally learning by trial and error.

With the ostrich feathers I wanted to get the effect of real feathers—not an easy task, but none of this was—with the hints of green and brown that appear on the whispy edge of the feather. Also I wanted to achieve the turquoise and yellow-green color that is in the center. There was a lot of experimenting with different colors and mixtures and all sorts of media. One tends to realize what Dr. Jekyll went through trying to become Mr. Hyde. Or vice versa. At any rate, I finally found that to get the effect I wanted, I first had to trace all the brown lines of the feathers and then fire the glass. Then I took two different greens and two different browns and

Fig. 14–2. The initial drawing.

Fig. 14–3. The line drawing.

stippled the soft feather edges of the brown lines. At this time, I also added the areas of turquoise and yellow-green in the center of the feather. The glass was then fired again.

I should mention that up to the very start of this project none of us had very much experience with painting on glass or with acid etching. So when we began work in earnest, I read, studied, and practically memorized what I consider the best book on the subject, *Stained Glass Painting* by Anita and Seymour Isenberg and Richard Millard (also published by Chilton). With this book as my bible, I practiced and practiced and practiced and practiced all the techniques described.

Although I had done pretty well with the feather and other smaller areas, getting the effect I wanted in the faces of the ladies was quite another matter. The authorities I read advised that when painting a face, it was best not to try to change the color of the glass, Tiffany faces notwithstanding. Well, the ladies at the turn of the century had very rosy cheeks and fair skin. At least that was the way I wanted to remember them. I began to experiment with all the different colors and media that would give me the soft-rosy-cheek effect I wanted. I finally settled on one of the transparent carmines.

I did the faces this way: First, I traced the lines in brown, using the brown tone as a sort of trace paint. I did the lines of the hair, the eyes, the center line of the mouth. Then I fired the glass. Second, I stippled on the shadow areas, such as those under the hat, around the nose, under the chin, around the edge of the face. Then I fired that. Third, I stippled in the rosy blush. This was the most difficult part, since I wanted just a hint of the color to be seen, yet enough to make the emphasis over the shadow area. I really worked for that blush, it being a focus of the tonality I'd had in mind from the beginning.

At this time, I also did the stipple work on the hair. So there were three firings on each face, except the face with the red hat. That one had four firings because I had to trace in the lines of the feather. We really used a tack fire on each firing except for the first and, of course, the last. The first firing was always high fire, to the maturing temperature of the paint, but high compared to the tack fires in between. The back side of each face was satin etched to give a smoother skin effect.

The painting techniques used on the faces were arrived at finally after many trial-and-error experiments. The entire studio was particularly helpful with the rosy effect on the faces and pitched in to help. One of our employees, Char Johnson, a former cosmetologist, pointed out that applying the blush to the faces was

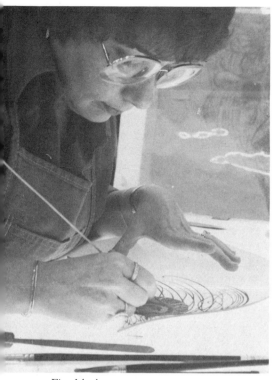

Fig. 14–4.

Fig. 14–6.

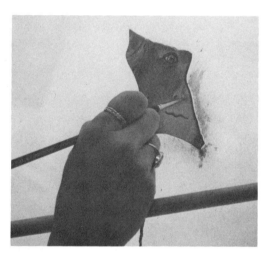

Fig. 14–7.

Fig. 14–5.

Figs. 14–4 through 14–8. Creative Stained Glass Studio at work on the panel.

Fig. 14–8.

similar to applying powder blush in makeup. I was extremely fortunate to have Char's help, as well as the help of everyone around. Char and I found that using her makeup brushes to achieve some of the effect of the eyes proved preferable to just about any other brushes I'd tried.

As for the eyes, I first did the traditional line tracing of these areas, but this didn't provide a soft enough expression. I wanted the eyes to be, if such a phrase exists, sensuously innocent. So I began experimenting with black and brown paint and kept trying different ways to get the eyelash effect and also the blue color. All in all, we had at least eight test eyes, as well as several sets of test faces, so this project was hardly an ongoing process in the instantaneous heat of creation. There was a lot of backing and filling. In addition, we had run at least three tests on the feather and three or four tests on color for the pink dress and the flowers on the dress.

The most incredible thing about the entire project was the team work that went into the making of the panel from its inception. From the standpoint of suggestions, creative criticism, and actual hard labor, everyone contributed. We all worked together as one creative unit with one purpose in mind.

Bill Barker on Acid-Etching a Panel

Even before the work got started on cutting the flower areas of the panel, I knew we were going to be etching them. I had to get over my fear of hydrofluoric acid and get used to working with it. I've known workers who have had problems with this material, one having lost the tip of a finger to an acid burn. I wasn't deeply enthralled with the prospect of keeping company with such a grouchy companion. But it had to be done.

I knew several things about hydrofluoric acid. I knew it can be resisted by anything plastic, wax, or, for short periods of time, rubber. When it comes in contact with human skin at the commercial strength, it burns, but the burn is not immediately felt. Unfortunately, the acid continues to burn through tissue right to the bone, and, if not treated, into bone. Treatment consists of injection below the skin to neutralize the acid.

I also knew that many, many people work with hydrofluoric acid without ever having any problems. I was determined to be one of them. My first action was to buy two new pairs of Playtex Living Gloves. To avoid fumes from the acid, now that my fingers were protected, I needed a good suction fan and a good light.

I started the experiments using Contact paper for a plastic resist. This works for what I will call gravity etching. This is where the surface to be etched is placed

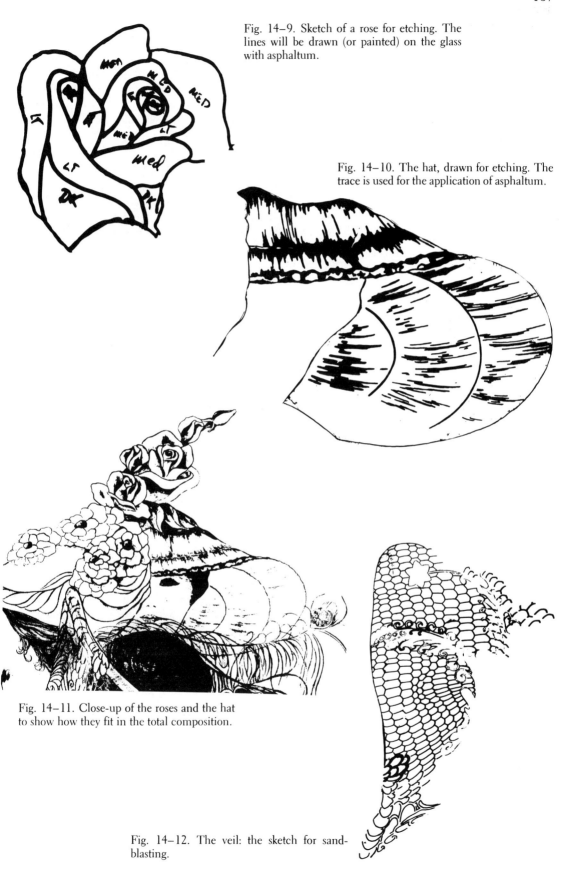

Fig. 14–9. Sketch of a rose for etching. The lines will be drawn (or painted) on the glass with asphaltum.

Fig. 14–10. The hat, drawn for etching. The trace is used for the application of asphaltum.

Fig. 14–11. Close-up of the roses and the hat to show how they fit in the total composition.

Fig. 14–12. The veil: the sketch for sand-blasting.

face down in an acid bath with the piece slightly elevated in the bath. As the acid eats away the flashed glass surface, the particles fall to the bottom of the bath. However, I was unable to control the extent of etching, since I couldn't see what was going on. I had to keep taking the piece out of the bath and that would stop the process. But it was the only way to have a look. It worked but was erratic.

However, it was a start. I began with the rosebud at the top of the panel. Using the Contact-paper resist, I cut out the areas to be etched with an X-Acto knife. On this piece, only two separate sections had to be etched, so the Contact paper worked fairly well. I was able to etch the area by dropping the acid directly on the glass and keeping it in motion with an acid brush. I could leave the acid on only for a short time, and then, when the piece was almost completed, I noticed that some acid had gotten under and behind the glass, giving a frosted effect on the back. This was frustrating to say the least, so I had to scrub that process. At this point, someone suggested that I use asphaltum. I did and began to learn more and more about etching as I progressed. I learned with every new piece of glass cut—and we went through a lot of French antique. (This is a flashed red on amber supplied by Bienenfeld.) Each try brought me closer to the final result, which was an acceptable rose for the design. Each piece had to pass Barbara's critique as to amount of shading and shadowing. Several times when we were very close to the proper amount of etching, just that little extra attempt would take off too much red and we would have to add that piece to the growing scrap heap.

The thickness of the flash was a constant problem. As each separate rose was finished, we learned, on each, to do the proper etching. The time consumed seemed endless. The largest rose piece took three full days to get a piece that was acceptable. Then I dropped it while foiling it. So I cut a new piece, which broke while I was grozzing an inside cut. So I cut another, which I dropped while wiping it clean for the asphaltum.

Finally I got one ready for the acid and had it completely etched in about three hours. At this point, I was able to get shading and highlights, if not readily, at least with some confidence that all would not work out too badly. I had learned how to manipulate the acid.

First, I would paint the edge of the glass with asphaltum. I also used it to paint thin lines to define the emerging petals. The asphaltum was allowed to dry thoroughly before the next step was taken. In effect, the asphaltum divided the piece into two separate sections for the front. I covered the back of the glass with

Contact paper. The glass was now entirely sealed to protect all but the working surface from the acid. Only in this way can you get the acid to do what you want it to do—rather than let it wander at random on the glass.

I used the acid in an open container rather than a tray. I used a plastic cup (no glass, please) for the acid and another one for water. A maximum of ten drops was transferred at one time from the commercial vessel to the working surface of the glass. A third cup was ready for diluting the acid (which I didn't have to do at this point, allowing that the commercial mix of 52-percent acid was about right for the job). I thus dropped straight 52-percent acid on the exposed surface of both sections of the rose petal piece, trying to get an even coverage over the surface. I watched the acid turn the red area a darker red. This meant the acid was lifting the top surface of glass away. After a minute or so, I rinsed the entire piece in running tap water and carefully dabbed dry the etched areas. This had to be done carefully because any rubbing of the asphaltum that was now dividing the glass might loosen it. This would necessitate reapplication of the asphaltum and then allowing it to dry (harden) once again. After about three of these baths, I could distinguish a substantial lightening of the red color, a gentle fading toward orange. This meant I was getting fairly close to the amber base color. At this point, I began to work the individual sections of the glass piece separately, so as to get different hues.

I found I could now control the acid in this way: If I just dampened a portion of the glass with a plastic paint brush and then dropped a very small quantity of acid on the damp area, the acid would not move from that spot. I used a plastic brush that was nicely pointed and could move the acid precisely where I wanted it to etch. To transfer acid from cup to glass surface, I used the small plastic fluid droppers that come with the oil-storage-handle glass cutters, the Supercutters. These work very well and allow very small amounts of acid to be transferred, or water, or a mix of acid and water.

After figuring out how to control the acid for the roses, it would seem that the purple flowers, the next items to be etched, would be simple enough. But a new problem came up. We had two colors of purple flashed on clear that we could use, but when we started to etch them, the glass pitted and pocked like a mini mine field. No matter how well I kept the acid in motion, a white crusty surface formed. I couldn't overcome the tendency of the glass surface to self-destruct. Out of desperation, we went so far as to send a sample of glass to the dealer (Bienenfeld) to send to the French manufacturer for some answers. None was forthcoming—nor have any come to date.

At last we decided to have Barbara paint the flowers. But first we tried one more thing, with a different glass—red flashed on blue. And this worked fine so far as lack of pitting went. It was only the color that was wrong. So we tried some back-side colors for lamination. After going through some different rose colors, we settled on the Fisher German Antique Gold Pink. However, this still was not exactly perfect, because the red on blue was so dark I couldn't see the flower design through the glass well enough to paint on the asphaltum. The solution: trace the flowers with heavy black marker, which, when illuminated with an intense light, I could see through the dark glass. At this point, my wife contributed the idea of making spokes radiating from the center of the flowers. So now I began working with very delicate lines within the petal areas. This was good practice for the etching on the red hats. Each petal on the purple flowers was individually etched and shaded. Again, constant consultation with Barbara on just how much should be etched away and how much line area should be left was the rule. This was a complicated etching procedure because I had to use the backing glass to get the right depth of color, which meant the asphaltum had to be removed, the piece cleaned and inspected, and, if more etching was required, the asphaltum had to be reapplied and re-etched. This was all time consuming and frustrating.

The final etching process was on the red hats. Here, again, we learned several new processes. To begin with, I was now etching a much larger area than in the case of the roses or the flowers. I was also using a very thin red flash on a rose base glass. We had a selection of four different ruby-on-rose flashed glass. We started etching with the front of the hat and because Barbara wanted a lacy effect, we had to get some very fine lines in the etching. I tried freehand painting the asphaltum but was unable to get it as fine as was needed. I next tried a process of applying Contact paper on the red surface and cutting from it fine lines where I wanted the asphaltum to be. We then applied the asphaltum over the Contact paper, and before the asphaltum got very hard—in fact, almost immediately after application— we pulled off the Contact paper. We had to use tweezers to get off the very small piece without disturbing the asphaltum. This now left us with a very delicate design of asphaltum resist. I diluted the acid about 50 percent, thus making it a 25-percent acid solution. I did this in sections of ten-drop water amounts adding ten drops of 52-percent acid. I never had a very large amount of acid open and fuming, so I never got into difficulties with it. In doing the larger areas of the hat, I found it best to dampen an area again and etch only that area at a time. Again I watched the surface darken as the acid worked. Periodically, I water-bathed the entire surface, very carefully drying it to inspect the depth of etch.

The back of the hat presented more of a problem. The first piece of glass used had a very heavy flash in one area, which I didn't know about until I had gone through the whole asphaltum process. The result was blotchy but acceptable. And then, the more we looked at it, the worse it seemed—until we knew we were simply going to have to do it again. At this point, I couldn't remember exactly which ruby on rose we had used. I picked one that I thought was close, but it came out slightly darker when it was etched. Luck was with us here; it looked beautiful in the context of the entire composition, giving a nice feeling of depth to the whole.

I should note that these last etched pieces I have been talking about were cut backwards, because the flash had to be on the backside so that we would have a smooth surface for the painted ostrich feathers on the front.

The final piece of etching for the panel was a sandblasting process on the lower flowers. The red in that area is a brand-new triple-flashed German antique, opal on red on clear. As it was sandblasted in the test, we found that at a certain depth of blast the red went to orange. It was a beautiful answer to the red-orange roses at the top. The flowers under the veil were painted and fired and came fairly close to the sandblasted area.

A final word: I had absolutely no problems with the acid. I am sure that most of the difficulties people experience with hydrofluoric acid come about through carelessness or taking it for granted. The effects possible with this material render it an essential tool for working in glass. However, it is only fair to point out that the effects should be on the glass, not on the worker. This can be the case if you remember to treat the acid with a great deal of respect and caution.

Barbara's Final Word

We were hoping to have the panel completed in time to enter it in the 6th Annual Stained Glass Exposition held in Boulder, Colorado, each year. As a result, we had to work many long hours, but we all agreed that under no circumstances would we compromise the quality for the time schedule. In the end, we delivered the panel to the show five minutes early. It took two blue ribbons and has since won other prizes elsewhere. The biggest prize, however, was an intangible one. It was the reaffirmation in my own mind that one must always be true to one's ideal of workmanship. We all did the very best we could, with no compromising. It was a rewarding experience for that alone.

The field of glass seems almost limitless. There is so much to learn and discover, so many avenues to explore. And glass itself is its own best teacher. One learns by doing. Perhaps, in the long run, that is really the secret behind any craft—and any art.

Appendix

Some Stencil and Decal Techniques

Although stenciling and decaling are not, strictly speaking, glass-crafting processes, they are related and are worth pursuing.

Stenciling

One of the most interesting companies providing stencils is Quicksilver Designs. These Super Stencils come layered between two protective coverings, so the delicately cut stencil is never handled. Instead, it is applied to the glass while still attached to its low-tac adhesive covering. All you have to do is remove the nonadhesive layer, apply the stencil to clean glass, press firmly, and slowly pull away the top protective layer. The stencil must be placed on an absolutely clean surface. After you remove the top layer, remove the excess part of the stencil with a razor blade, an X-Acto knife, and tweezers. Press down on what remains of the stencil, or, better yet, use an inking roller. Do *not* rub because you may loosen a margin of the stencil or tear or wrinkle it. If the stencil is smaller than the glass, you can protect the exposed surfaces with Contact paper. The stenciled surface is now ready to etch, sandblast, engrave, or paint. When you are finished, the stencil can be removed by running it under hot water and peeling it off. Here are some tips from Quicksilver Designs:

Application. To clean the glass, try hot ammonia water, then rinse in hot water and dry well. The warm surface of the glass will hold the stencil better. Before removing the top protective layer, rub the stencil hard from the middle out to press out air bubbles. Some stencil pieces may adhere to the nonadhesive backing during removal. Usually these are pieces you would remove anyway, but be careful to replace any pieces that are part of the design.

Etching. We use etching cream with stencils, but you can get all sorts of effects with many different media. A cream etch is probably better than the more liquid types. Be sure to burnish all edges of the design so that the etching compound doesn't leak under. The warmer it is, the less time is necessary to leave on the etch. If it is left on too long, the edges of the design may be less sharp. If there are lumps in the etch, it can leave uneven frost. Straining the etch cream will eliminate this. Keep all etching creams away from your skin for safety's sake.

Spray Painting. Spray evenly and not too thick. Carefully remove the stencil while the paint is still wet by cutting it into sections with an X-Acto knife. Use the knife and tweezers to remove inside detail. If allowed to dry, the paint may seal to the stencil.

Reversibility. To achieve a different effect, leave the foreground space intact and remove the background and inside detail. The designs can then be framed as they are, or they can be incorporated into the design of a larger panel. Since they can be applied to any nonporous surface, such as metal, glass, and plastic, they can even personalize the body and windows of cars, vans, campers, planes, and boats. Any window or mirror in the house can have its own special accent. The possibilities are endless.

Other types of stencils can also be used in glass work, such as the doily we used in Fig. 6–12.

Decal Technique

For decaling, you must use decal paper, which is coated with a water-soluble glue. We get ours in sheet form from Brittain's Papers Ltd. in Stamford, Connecticut. Next you need a color or colors for painting. You can use any *powdered* colorant that you would use ordinarily in glass painting, but it must be mixed with a special decal medium, similar to a squeegee medium. Reusche supplies this. The proportions of the mix to make a paste consistency is a 1 to 4 mix of powder to medium. If you want a fairly heavy deposit of color, screen the mix through a silkscreen mesh of about 180; for a very heavy deposit, screen through 150- to 160-mesh; and for a very fine deposition, use a screen of 200- to 220-mesh.

Once you have your color to the proper consistency, print or paint with it on the paper. Because of the thickness of the paint, your brush can drag the paper. To make sure your paper doesn't move, tape the paper down or use a vacuum table to hold it. Be very careful about applying second and third colors. Make sure the first one is dry. You should allow each color to dry

Fig. 1. Mixing colorant and decal medium. The mix is to a pasty consistency.

overnight. This means doing each color on separate days, which makes it a long process, but it's best to do it this way. Some workers try to hurry the drying process by putting heat to the paper, but this makes the paper curl. You can use a fan to try to dry the paint more rapidly. We have found it best to just put on a color and go on to something else, forgetting about the decal until the next day.

When the decal is dry, cover it with Covercoat, a thick, quixotic, clear lacquer, also supplied by Reusche. It is *thixotropic*, meaning that it has a false viscosity. It will look heavy, but when you go to stir it, it is the reverse of what you would expect, stirring as easily as if it were a thin liquid. Paint the Covercoat over the decal so that it overlaps by ⅜ inch all around. Let this dry for a day. Then cut off as much of the decal as you want to use, soak it in water, and put it on the glass. It is important that once the decal has been floated off and reanchored on the glass that you squeeze, pat, or roll all the water out of it.

Firing should be a slow process so as to burn off the decal medium through the hard lacquer. If it is fired too fast, the decal medium will evaporate fast. If this happens, it forms a gas and bursts through the lacquer shell, leaving holes in the decal. A slow firing means going to 800 degrees F. in about three hours. Then you take your firing more rapidly to the maturing temperature of your color. If you were silkscreening directly onto the glass, you wouldn't have to take the kiln up so slowly, but in silkscreening you aren't dealing with decal medium.

A word about mixing: If you are going to do a lot of decal work, you will begin to find the mixing process a tedious one. It is also wearing. You could invest in a Kitchen-Aid mixer: We specify this make because, so far as we know, it is the only one that has a rotary motion of the bowl, which aids in mixing colorant and medium. Perhaps you can find a used one at a garage sale.

Fig. 2. Painting a decal design on decal paper.

Fig. 3. The decal design is completed.

Temperature Conversion Table

0 to 99

C.		F.	C.		F.
−17.8	0	32.0	10.0	50	122.0
−17.2	1	33.8	10.6	51	123.8
−16.7	2	35.6	11.1	52	125.6
−16.1	3	37.4	11.7	53	127.4
−15.6	4	39.2	12.2	54	129.2
−15.0	5	41.0	12.8	55	131.0
−14.4	6	42.8	13.3	56	132.8
−13.9	7	44.6	13.9	57	134.6
−13.3	8	46.4	14.4	58	136.4
−12.8	9	48.2	15.0	59	138.2
−12.2	10	50.0	15.6	60	140.0
−11.7	11	51.8	16.1	61	141.8
−11.1	12	53.6	16.7	62	143.6
−10.6	13	55.4	17.2	63	145.4
−10.0	14	57.2	17.8	64	147.2
− 9.44	15	59.0	18.3	65	149.0
− 8.89	16	60.8	18.9	66	150.8
− 8.33	17	62.6	19.4	67	152.6
− 7.78	18	64.4	20.0	68	154.4
− 7.22	19	66.2	20.6	69	156.2
− 6.67	20	68.0	21.1	70	158.0
− 6.11	21	69.8	21.7	71	159.8
− 5.56	22	71.6	22.2	72	161.6
− 5.00	23	73.4	22.8	73	163.4
− 4.44	24	75.2	23.3	74	165.2
− 3.89	25	77.0	23.9	75	167.0
− 3.33	26	78.8	24.4	76	168.8
− 2.78	27	80.6	25.0	77	170.6
− 2.22	28	82.4	25.6	78	172.4
− 1.67	29	84.2	26.1	79	174.2
− 1.11	30	86.0	26.7	80	176.0
− 0.56	31	87.8	27.2	81	177.8
0	32	89.6	27.8	82	179.6
0.56	33	91.4	28.3	83	181.4
1.11	34	93.2	28.9	84	183.2
1.67	35	95.0	29.4	85	185.0
2.22	36	96.8	30.0	86	186.8
2.78	37	98.6	30.6	87	188.6
3.33	38	100.4	31.1	88	190.4
3.89	39	102.2	31.7	89	192.2
4.44	40	104.0	32.2	90	194.0
5.00	41	105.8	32.8	91	195.8
5.56	42	107.6	33.3	92	197.6
6.11	43	109.4	33.9	93	199.4
6.67	44	111.2	34.4	94	201.2
7.22	45	113.0	35.0	95	203.0
7.78	46	114.8	35.6	96	204.8
8.33	47	116.6	36.1	97	206.6
8.89	48	118.4	36.7	98	208.4
9.44	49	120.2	37.2	99	210.2

100 to 1000

C.		F.	C.		F.
38	100	212	260	500	932
43	110	230	266	510	950
49	120	248	271	520	968
54	130	266	277	530	986
60	140	284	282	540	1004
66	150	302	288	550	1022
71	160	320	293	560	1040
77	170	338	299	570	1058
82	180	356	304	580	1076
88	190	374	310	590	1094
93	200	392	316	600	1112
99	210	410	321	610	1130
100	212	413	327	620	1148
104	220	428	332	630	1166
110	230	446	338	640	1184
116	240	464	343	650	1202
121	250	482	349	660	1220
127	260	500	354	670	1238
132	270	518	360	680	1256
138	280	536	366	690	1274
143	290	554	371	700	1292
149	300	572	377	710	1310
154	310	590	382	720	1328
160	320	608	388	730	1346
166	330	626	393	740	1364
171	340	644	399	750	1382
177	350	662	404	760	1400
182	360	680	410	770	1418
188	370	698	416	780	1436
193	380	716	421	790	1454
199	390	734	427	800	1472
204	400	752	432	810	1490
210	410	770	438	820	1508
216	420	788	443	830	1526
221	430	806	449	840	1544
227	440	824	454	850	1562
232	450	842	460	860	1580
238	460	860	466	870	1598
243	470	878	471	880	1616
249	480	896	477	890	1634
254	490	914	482	900	1652
			488	910	1670
			493	920	1688
			499	930	1706
			504	940	1724
			510	950	1742
			516	960	1760
			521	970	1778
			527	980	1796
			532	990	1814
			538	1000	1832

Interpolation Factors

C.		F.
0.56	1	1.8
1.11	2	3.6
1.67	3	5.4
2.22	4	7.2
2.78	5	9.0
3.33	6	10.8
3.89	7	12.6
4.44	8	14.4
5.00	9	16.2
5.56	10	18.0

1000 to 2000

C.	F.	C.	C.	F.
538	1000	1832	816	1500	2732
543	1010	1850	821	1510	2750
549	1020	1868	827	1520	2768
554	1030	1886	832	1530	2786
560	1040	1904	838	1540	2804
566	1050	1922	843	1550	2822
571	1060	1940	849	1560	2840
577	1070	1958	854	1570	2858
582	1080	1976	860	1580	2876
588	1090	1994	866	1590	2894
593	1100	2012	871	1600	2912
599	1110	2030	877	1610	2930
604	1120	2018	882	1620	2948
610	1130	2066	888	1630	2966
616	1140	2084	893	1640	2984
621	1150	2102	899	1650	3002
627	1160	2120	904	1660	3020
632	1170	2138	910	1670	3038
638	1180	2156	916	1680	3056
643	1190	2174	921	1690	3074
649	1200	2192	927	1700	3092
654	1210	2210	932	1710	3110
660	1220	2228	938	1720	3128
666	1230	2246	943	1730	3146
671	1240	2264	949	1740	3164
677	1250	2282	954	1750	3182
682	1260	2300	960	1760	3200
688	1270	2318	966	1770	3218
693	1280	2336	971	1780	3236
699	1290	2354	977	1790	3254
704	1300	2372	982	1800	3272
710	1310	2390	988	1810	3290
716	1320	2408	993	1820	3308
721	1330	2426	999	1830	3326
727	1340	2444	1004	1840	3344
732	1350	2462	1010	1850	3362
738	1360	2480	1016	1860	3380
743	1370	2498	1021	1870	3398
749	1380	2516	1027	1880	3416
754	1390	3534	1032	1890	3434
760	1400	2552	1038	1900	3452
766	1410	2570	1043	1910	3470
771	1420	2588	1049	1920	3488
777	1430	2606	1054	1930	3506
782	1440	2624	1060	1940	3524
788	1450	2642	1066	1950	3542
793	1460	2660	1071	1960	3560
799	1470	2678	1077	1970	3578
804	1480	2696	1082	1980	3596
810	1490	2714	1088	1990	3614
			1093	2000	3632

2000 to 3000

C.	F.	C.	C.	F.
1093	2000	3632	1371	2500	4532
1099	2010	3650	1377	2510	4550
1104	2020	3668	1382	2520	4568
1110	2030	3686	1388	2530	4586
1116	2040	3704	1393	2540	4604
1121	2050	3722	1399	2550	4622
1127	2060	3740	1404	2560	4640
1132	2070	3758	1410	2570	4658
1138	2080	3776	1416	2580	4676
1143	2090	3794	1421	2590	4694
1149	2100	3812	1427	2600	4712
1154	2110	3830	1432	2610	4730
1160	2120	3848	1438	2620	4748
1166	2130	3866	1443	2630	4766
1171	2140	3884	1449	2640	4784
1177	2150	3902	1454	2650	4802
1182	2160	3920	1460	2660	4820
1188	2170	3938	1466	2670	4838
1193	2180	3956	1471	2680	4856
1199	2190	3974	1477	2690	4874
1204	2200	3992	1482	2700	4892
1210	2210	4010	1488	2710	4910
1216	2220	4028	1493	2720	4928
1221	2230	4046	1499	2730	4946
1227	2240	4064	1504	2740	4964
1232	2250	4082	1510	2750	4982
1238	2260	4100	1516	2760	5000
1243	2270	4118	1521	2770	5018
1249	2280	4136	1527	2780	5036
1254	2290	4154	1532	2790	5054
1260	2300	4172	1538	2800	5072
1266	2310	4190	1543	2810	5090
1271	2320	4208	1549	2820	5108
1277	2330	4226	1554	2830	5126
1282	2340	4244	1560	2840	5144
1288	2350	4262	1566	2850	5162
1293	2360	4280	1571	2860	5180
1299	2370	4298	1577	2870	5198
1304	2380	4316	1582	2880	5216
1310	2390	4334	1588	2890	5234
1316	2400	4352	1593	2900	5252
1321	2410	4370	1599	2910	5270
1327	2420	4388	1604	2920	5288
1332	2430	4406	1610	2930	5306
1338	2440	4424	1616	2940	5324
1343	2450	4442	1621	2950	5342
1349	2460	4460	1627	2960	5360
1354	2470	4478	1632	2970	5378
1360	2480	4496	1638	2980	5396
1366	2490	4514	1643	2990	5414
			1649	3000	5432

Temperature Equivalents of Cone and Pyrometer

Cone	Pyrometer	Cone	Pyrometer
020	1175	02	2048
019	1261	01	2079
018	1323	1	2109
016	1458	2	2124
014	1540	3	2134
012	1623	4	2167
010	1641	5	2185
08	1751	6	2232
07	1803	7	2264
06	1830	8	2305
05	1915	9	2336
04	1940	10	2381
03	2014		

These are the Orton Cone Temperature Equivalents for a firing with a 270-degree temperature increase per hour.

Glossary

Although this book doesn't use all these terms, you will at one time or another encounter them. To gain a better understanding of glass crafting, you should know the "language" of the craft. This list is fairly complete. Some of our definitions are arbitrary; not everyone will agree with them all. However, these terms have worked well for us.

Types of Glass

Alabaster glass: A type of "milk" glass, which traps light like an opalescent but has a warm, soft sheen.

Bent glass: Flat glass that has been sagged over a mold.

Blown glass: Not a specific type of glass as much as a technical process.

Carrara glass: Flat glass containing crystals, similar to marblized glass, which it is also called.

Cased glass (or flashed glass): Either plain glass, or more likely a sheet of colored glass with another color laid on top. The top color can be acided off with hydrofluoric acid, leaving a two-color effect.

Chipped glass: More of a technique than an actual type of glass: A special glue is applied over the glass surface to give a unique impressed design.

Crown glass: Rather like a roundel. The circle of glass is formed by rapidly rotating molten glass at the end of a pontil or blowpipe. It's tricky and not to be done at home or in your workshop.

Crystal glass: Applies to glassware, rather than to sheet glass. Crystal is famous for its reflection and refraction of light because of its high percentage of lead oxide.

The lead oxide is added before the glass powder is made molten.

Cut glass: Applies to glassware, although not exclusively. Slab glass can be cut glass. The glass is decorated by grinding figures or patterns on its surface, usually with a grinding wheel. The glass is then polished. Brilliant effects can be obtained, as in Steubenglass.

Enameled glass: Glass decorated with opaque enamel paints. The paints are low fire and come in many colors. They are not as lasting as glass-stainer's paints, which fire at higher temperatures but are more difficult to use to effect.

Mold-blown glass: The glass is blown into a mold (often made of apple wood), which can give it specific texture as impressed into the glass from the wood.

Opalescent glass: Often used in lamps (and many windows of the 1920s). It is opaque and traps the light inside it so that the glass seems to glow rather than transmitting it.

Tiffany glass: Also known as "favrile" glass, this is a specific product of the Tiffany studios. The glass appears to luminesce, to have a velvet sheen of its own apart from the quantity of light playing upon it. No one seems to know how this was done precisely, although many of the newer glasses today come close to achieving the same effect.

Translucent glass: Another term for opalescent glass.

Transparent glass: A glass that is "see through," whether colored or plain window glass.

White glass: A confusing term but usually applied to a white opalescent. Many writers use the term for clear window glass.

Window glass: As used in this book, a clear glass, either single or double strength. It is transparent and usually of a soda-lime nature.

Types of Stained Glass

Antique glass: Indicates not age but technique. It is also called *handblown* glass, since it is produced by blowing the glass into cylindrical form. The blowing adds bubbles, seeds, and other irregularities to the glass (depending, legend has it, on what the glassblower had to eat shortly before blowing) and thus makes for a more interesting transmission of light. It is usually irregular in thickness and somewhat difficult to cut. France, England, and Germany have long been the major exporters of antique glasses, some sheets of which are complete patterns in themselves and can be framed just as they are for lightboxes or windows.

Rolled glass: Glass that is not blown but pressed out by machine from a large "blob" of molten glass spread by a roller. Opalescent glass, in particular, is made this way, although any glass can be. Rolled glass tends to be uniform throughout in thickness and in texture.

Semi-antique glass: Usually a rolled transparent glass, thin, uniform, and fairly easy to cut.

Streakies and Reamies: Antique glass with swirls and movements of delicate colors within the material.

General Terminology

Bead: An enlarged rounded edge of a piece of glass, whether a tumbler or the edge of a piece of flat glass that has been rounded

off by the heat of a kiln. The term is also applied to any raised section extending around an article or a piece of glass. Solder forms a bead because it is purposely raised over a solder line in copper foil work.

Beveling: The art of grinding and polishing glass edges to give a central raised section. This allows light to be reflected in several directions at once from the same linear statement.

Blank: A piece of glass cut to specific measurements for a specific use; for instance, for sagging or painting.

Blister: A bubble, or series of imperfections that lie within the glass and refract the light passing through. Particularly found in antique glass.

Blowpipe: A long, hollow metal tube, on the end of which the glassblower gathers a gob of molten glass from the furnace. He then blows to expand or to shape the glass.

Bond: To adhere glass to glass either by gluing or firing.

Came: A strip or "string" of flexible lead, channeled either on one side or both, used to lead up pieces of glass arranged in a pattern.

Casting: Shaping an object by pouring [molten substance] into a mold.

Cleavage: The score line as a result of glass cutting. This allows the glass to be separated into two or more pieces.

Cutting: Glass is not cut; rather, it is scored by specific instruments that disrupt the surface. When pressure is applied, the score line "breaks out."

Etching: Also known as *aciding* or *acid-etching.* Hydrofluoric acid attacks the silica in the glass, thereby marking the surface with an imposed design.

Fiber: An individual filament made by drawing molten glass into extremely fine threads.

Filigree: Transparent glass that carries within it colored threads.

Flux: A chemical agent that allows soldering to take place. Also a prepared low-melting glass, usually colorless, that will carry pigments onto a glass surface.

Marvering: Act of rolling molten glass against stone or other surface to shape it.

Pontil: A pipe used by glassblowers to hold and manipulate molten glass.

Sandblasting: The technique of blowing a fine quality sand onto a glass surface to achieve an "engraved" effect.

Slab Glass: Thick, fairly heavy squares of glass used with epoxy or cement to form broad, emphatic design statements. Slab glass is cut with a special chisel, not with a regular glass cutter.

Sources of Supply

Colorants

Englehard Industries Division
    1 West Central Ave.
    East Newark, NJ   07029
        (Hanovia Lusters, etc.)

Onita's Colours for Glass
    PO Box 85
    Moss, MS   39460

Decal Papers

Brittain's Papers Ltd.
    Strawberry Hill Rd.
    Stamford, CT   06901

Duplicating Machines

Stanford Engineering
    513 Manitou Ave.
    Manitou Springs, CO   80829

Epoxy Materials

Biwax Corp.
    45 E. Bradrock Drive
    Des Plaines, IL   60016

**Foilers and Foiling Machines
(for Copper)**

Diegel Engineering
    1524 East Culver
    Phoenix, AZ   85006
        (Foil-O-Matic)

Lamps Ltd.
    PO Box 218
    Lake Hiawatha, NJ   07034

Stained Glass Design, Inc.
    309 Blvd.
    Hasbrouck Heights, NJ   07604
        ("The Elite 1")

Sunshine Glass Works Inc.
    132 S. LaBrea Ave.
    Los Angeles, CA   90036

Glasscutters

Creative Stained Glass Studio Ltd.
    2533 Kipling
    Lakewood, CO   80215

The Fletcher-Terry Co.
    Spring Lane
    Farmington, CT   06032

Pro Glass Cutter Co.
    PO Box 2292
    Dearborn, MI   48123
        (The Cutter)

Glass Cutting Machines

The Great Cut-Up
    807 Baronridge Drive
    Seabrook, TX   77586

Glass Jewels

Mayer Import Co. Inc.
    25 West 37th Street
    New York, NY   10018

Stanford Art Glass
    513 Manitou
    Manitou Springs, CO   80829

Glass Paints and Stains

L. Reusche and Co.
2–6 Lister Ave.
Newark, NJ   07105

Titan Corp.
5629 208th Street S.W.
Lynnwood, WA   98036
(Non-fire paints and stains)

Glass Rods and Glass Tubing

Fisher Scientific Co.
Springfield, NJ   07081

Pope Scientific Co.
N90 W14337 Commerce Drive
Menomonee Falls, WI   53051

Glue Chips

Boulder Art Glass Co.
1920 Arapahoe
Boulder, CO   80302

H and N Specialty Products
844 East 11th St.
Oakland, CA   94606

Kilns

Paragon Industries
PO Box 10133
Dallas, TX   75207

Stewart Clay Co. Inc.
400 Jersey Ave.
New Brunswick, NJ   08902

Kits

Stanford Art Glass
513 Manitou Ave.
Manitou Springs, CO   80829
(Precut glass only)

Kwik-Krimp

Diegel Engineering
1524 E. Culver St.
Phoenix, AZ   85006

Lead Choppers

Anderson's Stained Glass Studio
21243 Pacific Coast Highway
Malibu, CA   90265

Molds

Chez Marquis
PO Box 392
Leonia, NJ   07605

Mold Supplies

Flore Glass Evercoat Co.
6600 Cornell Rd.
Cincinnati, OH   45242
(Crystal Cast Mold)

Healthco Dental Supply
382 Main St.
Hackensack, NJ   07601

Patterns

C.M.W. Publications
PO Box 385
Bethlehem, PA   18016

D and L Stained Glass
4919 N. Broadway
Boulder, CO   80302
(Patterns and supplies)

Glass Works Press
PO Box 81782
San Diego, CA   92138

Paul de Bruin and Associates
PO Box 294
La Mesa, CA   92041

Portable "Glass Workshop"

Morton Glass Works
Box 465
170 E. Washington
Morton, IL   61550

Routers

Glastar Corp.
19515 Business Ctr. Dr.
Northridge, CA   91324

Inland Craft Products Co.
1470 Temple City Drive
Troy, MI   48084
(The "Wizard")

Kindig Enterprises
1904 Serge Ave.
San Jose, CA   95130
(Glasscrafter)

Sandblasting

Pro-Tec Products
Transcoast Industrial
3333 Midway Drive, Suite 207
San Diego, CA   92110

Soldering Equipment

Hexacon Electric Co.
  161 West Clay Ave.
  Roselle Park, NJ   07204

Plato Products Inc.
  PO Box 5508
  4357 North Rowland Ave.
  El Monte, CA   91734

Soldering Supplies

Gardiner Solder Co.
Div. Gardiner Metal Co.
  4820 S. Campbell Ave.
  Chicago, IL   60632

Kester Solder
Div. of Litton Systems, Inc.
  4201 Wrightwood Ave.
  Chicago, IL   60639
    (Solder-Off)

Lake Chemical Co.
  250 N. Washtenaw Ave.
  Chicago, IL   60612
    (Non-acid solder flux)

Saylescraft Inc.
  171 Main Street
  Nyack, NY   10960

Soder-Wick
Solder Removal Co.
  Covina, CA   91724

Stained Glass Suppliers

Bienenfeld Industries, Inc.
  1539 Covert Street
  Brooklyn, NY   11227

Blenko Glass Co. Inc.
  Milton, WV   25541

Bullseye Glass Co.
  3722 SE 21st Ave.
  Portland, OR   97202

Chicago Art Glass, Inc.
  2382 United Lane
  Elk Grove Village, IL   60007

Heritage Glass Inc.
  1081 East 2200
  North Logan, UT   84321

Kokomo Opalescent Glass
  PO Box 2265
  1310 S. Market St.
  Kokomo, IN   46901

Merry Go Round Glass
  8010 Ball Road
  Fort Smith, AR   72916

Oceana Sheet Glass Co.
  2720 Rodeo Gulch Road
  Soquel, CA   95073

Optimum Art Glass
  PO Box 924
  Greeley, CO   80632

Uroboros Glass Studios
  1313 SE 3rd Avenue
  Portland, OR   97214

Stencil Designs

Quicksilver Super Stencil Designs
Transcoast Tapes
  PO Box A80847
  San Diego, CA   92138

Suction Cups

Glass House Studio, Inc.
  125 State Street
  St. Paul, MN   55107

Supercutters and Glass Duplicator

Glass Accessories International
  10112 Beverly Drive
  Huntington Beach, CA   92645

Tinning Blocks and
Soldering Supplies

Kester Solder
  4201 Wrightwood Ave.
  Chicago, IL   60639

Tools

Allnova Co.
  4069 Rainier Ave. So.
  Seattle, WA   98118
    (Copper patinas)

Diamond Tool and Horseshoe Co.
  4702 Grand Ave.
  Duluth, MN   55807

The Window Works
  PO Box 1643
  Weaverville, CA   96093
    (Saws for zinc and lead came)

Wire Bending Jig

Archer Wire Bending Jig
Tandy Corp.
  Fort Worth, TX   76107

Suppliers of Assorted Materials for Glass Crafting

Art Glass of Illinois
  105 Oakwood Park
  East Peoria, IL 61611

Cline Glass Co., Inc.
  1135 SE Grand Ave.
  Portland, OR 97214

Endeavor Products, Ltd.
  443 East First Ave.
  Roselle, NJ 07203

Franklin Glass Art Studio
  222 East Sycamore St.
  Columbus, OH 43206

Glass Haus Studio
  1819 South Alameda
  Corpus Christi, TX 78404

Glass House Studio, Inc.
  125 State St.
  St. Paul, MN 55107

Glass Masters, Inc.
  154 West 18th St.
  New York, NY 10010

Nervo Distributors
  650 University Ave.
  Berkeley, CA 94710

New Renaissance Glass Works
  5151 Broadway
  Oakland, CA 94611

Pendleton Studios
  3895 North Tulsa Ave.
  Oklahoma City, OK 73112

Northwest Art Glass
  904 Elliott Ave. West
  Seattle, WA 98117

The Stained Glass Club
  PO Box 244
  Norwood, NJ 07648

Stained Glass Forest
  2312 K St.
  Sacramento, CA 95816

Ed Hoy's Stained Glass
  999 East Chicago Ave.
  Naperville, IL 60540

Tiffany Stained Glass Ltd.
  549 N. Wells St.
  Chicago, IL 60610

The Stained Glass Shoppe
  2315 North 45th St.
  Seattle, WA 98103

Stained Glass & Supplies, Inc.
  2104 Colorado Blvd.
  Los Angeles, CA 90041

Tiffany Touch
  337 West 21st St.
  Norfolk, VA 23517

Yesterday's Glass
  110 West Colonial Drive
  Orlando, FL 32801

Village Hobby Mart
  2414 Bolsover
  Houston, TX 77005

Glassart Studio of America, Inc.
  510 S. 52nd St., Suite 104
  Tempe, AZ 85281

Dianne's Crafts
  18021 Chatsworth
  Granada Hills, CA 91344

Franciscan Glass Co.
  100 San Antonio Rd.
  Mountain View, CA 94040

Mad Dog
  18615 Topham St.
  Reseda, CA 91335

Scarab Glass Works
  729 Divisadero
  Fresno, CA 93721

The Stained Pane
  3160 E. La Palma Ave., Unit M
  Anaheim, CA 92806

Stephens Stained Glass Studio
  9637 Magnolia Ave.
  Riverside, CA 92503

D & L Stained Glass Supply
  4919 N. Broadway
  Boulder, CO 80302

Rocky Mountain Arts & Crafts
  5660 S. Syracuse Cir.
  Englewood, CO 80110

Stanford Art Glass
  513 Manitou Ave.
  Manitou Springs, CO 80829

Stained Glass Gallery
  5423 North Federal Highway
  Fort Lauderdale, FL 33308

Jennifer's Glassworks
2410 Piedmont Rd., N.E.
Atlanta, GA   30324

Landin's Lamps
2329 13th St.
Moline, IL   61265

The Macrame Man
127 N. Main St.
Decatur, IL   62521

Stained Glass of Barrington
712 S. Northwest Hwy.
Barrington, IL   60010

Delphi Craft Supply Center
2224 E. Michigan
Lansing, MI   48912

Rainbow Resources
1503 Lake Drive, S.E.
Grand Rapids, MI   49506

Houston Stained Glass Supply
1829 Arlington
Houston, TX   77008

Aladdin Stained Glass
1131 East Yandell Drive
El Paso, TX   79902

Occidental Associates
410 Occidental South
Seattle, WA   98104

Arts & Crafts Studio
7120 Little River Turnpike
Annandale, VA   22003

J. Ring Studio Company
2125 East Hennepin
Minneapolis, MN   55413

Classical Glass, Inc.
175 Church St.
Burlington, VT   05401

Buffalo Plate & Window Glass Corp.
1245 E. Ferry St.
Buffalo, NY   14211

Saylescraft, Inc.
171 Main St.
Nyack, NY   10960

Cookson and Thode
2960 GW S. Monroe St.
Denver, CO 80210

E. H. Watkeys, Jr.
463 Easton Rd.
Horsham, PA   19004

S. A. Bendheim Co.
122 Hudson St.
New York, NY   10013

C. and R. Loo
1550 62nd St.
Emeryville, CA   94662

Dorothy's Stained Glass Studio
903 N. Orchard
Boise, ID   83704

Sunrise Art Glass Studios
1113 Chicago Ave.
Oak Park, IL   60302

Stained Glass Caboose
6102 Springwood Court
Baltimore, MD   21206

Vortex Stained Glass Studio
Main Street
West Stockbridge, MA   01266

Gaytee Stained Glass
2744 Lyndale Ave. S.
Minneapolis, MN   55408

Glass House Studio, Inc.
125 State St.
St. Paul, MN   55107

Boesen's Glasscraft, Inc.
2203 North 91st Plaza
Omaha, NE   68134

Cline Glass Co., Inc.
1135 SE Grand Ave.
Portland, OR   97214

Black's Art Glass
3225 N. Flores
San Antonio, TX   78212

Stained Glass Studio
1232 East Brady St.
Milwaukee, WI   53202

Hudson Glass Co., Inc.
219 N. Division St.
Peekskill, NY 10566

Index

Date Due

JA 4 '82		
OCT 2 8 1982		
DEC 6 1982		
JA 2 '84		
AG 0 8 '85		
MAR 2 9 1989		
MAY 9 1989		
SEP 5 1989		
JAN 1 0 1990		
MAR 1 5 1990		
MAR 2 6 REC'D		